People on the Way

People on the Way

Asian North Americans Discovering Christ, Culture, and Community

Edited by David Ng

Judson Press ® Valley Forge

People on the Way: Asian North Americans Discovering
Christ, Culture, and Community
© 1996 Judson Press, Valley Forge, PA 19482-0851

Unless otherwise indicated, Scripture quotations in this volume are from the New Revised Standard Version of the Bible, copyright 1989 by the Division of Christian Education of the National Council of the Churches of Christ in the USA. Used by permission. All rights reserved. (NRSV)

Other quotations are from *The Holy Bible*, King James Version. (KJV)

Library of Congress Cataloging-in-Publication Data
People on the way : Asian North Americans discovering Christ, culture, and community / edited by David Ng.
    p. cm.
Includes bibliographical references.
ISBN 0-8170-1242-7 (pbk. : alk. paper)
1. Asians—North America—Religion. 2. Christianity and other religions—Asian. 3. Christianity and culture. 4. North America—Religion—20th century. 5. Asia—Religion—20th century. I. Ng, David.
BR510.P46 1996
277'.0829'08995—dc20   96-10668

Printed in the U.S.A.
05 04 03 02 01 00 99 98 97 96
10 9 8 7 6 5 4 3 2 1

Table of Contents

Preface

Receiving and Utilizing the Gift of Community in Asian North American Congregations

What This Book Is About

This book shares *stories* about experiences of how Asian North American Christians identify themselves and are shaped by their rich Asian religious and cultural heritage. Community life and ministry in Asian North American congregations reflect this Asian cultural diversity. The insights from Asian religious and cultural heritages need to be in dialogue with Christian theologies and ministries, to form congregations that are faithful to God and fulfilling to the people. The Project Team that shared in creating this book is composed of North Americans whose national heritages are East Asian—Chinese, Japanese, and Korean. The team members are inheritors of religious and cultural perspectives reflecting shamanism, native spiritual practices, Confucianism, Taoism, Buddhism, Shintoism, and other spiritualities. These religious perspectives are brought into dialogue with the Christian faith each Project Team member professes. The Project Team firmly believes that the church today, including its Asian North American congregations, can benefit from a dialogue between culture and faith. Thus people are met in the real places of life and are helped to live with faith and understanding. Congregations are helped to preach, teach, and minister with relevance and meaning.

This book is neither a theological treatise nor a handbook for ministry. It attempts to integrate theology and practice, to be "praxis." Such a combination of history, theory, and practical application is an ambitious undertaking! The main method for conveying ideas in this book is through *story*. Telling a bit of the story of the Christ, Culture, and Community Project Team's process illustrates what this book is about and how it can be used.

Over a period of three years, beginning in 1992, twelve persons met on three weekends to consider how Asian North American congregations understand and practice community and to prepare a book recounting their findings. These findings were shared at a conference for one hundred church leaders from Canada and the United States. The team was quite Asian North American—it was diverse! National heritage, gender, age, place of birth, native language, and numerous other diversities made the team's meetings interesting to say the least. The team enjoyed a common sense of urgency for working on Asian North American Christian issues and a camaraderie of personal friendliness and commitment to being a Christian community. But there always was the sense that there cannot be a single, simple expression of what it means to be Asian North American Christian congregations or to concoct a single, simple theology.

Every issue, topic, and strategy had to be discussed around and around so that individual views were heard. The team had to acknowledge that statements about Asian North American persons and congregations are interim statements, shared stories told *along the way*.

A difficult discussion took place during the second meeting. There was scant sense of how they were to write the book. At times it was as much a debate as a discussion. At the end of the first day, confusion reigned. Several team members continued the discussion when they adjourned to their housing unit. Overnight they came up with a plan for writing each chapter in a form that would be consistent with who Asian North Americans are and how they understand theology and ministry. Basically, it was to use a format that comes from their cultural tradition: a story format.

The team members spontaneously affirmed the use of story as the way to express their experiences and perceptions of identity, community, and ministry as Asian North American Christians. The following format was adopted for the chapters of this book:

 a. Tell a story about the topic.
 b. Raise questions.
 c. Offer an analysis.
 d. Invite the readers to "be on the way" with us.

For example, in dealing with the topic of pastoral care for Asian North Americans, a story is told of pastoral care or counseling of an Asian North American person. From that story, questions about Asian North American cultural values and traditions are raised and some examples of an analysis of the situation are shared. Throughout the chapter and at the end, the readers are invited to think of similar stories and situations from their own experiences. How do gospel and culture interact? Ultimately the readers are asked how they would deal with the issue. As you read, you, too, are "on the way" regarding the issues. How have you and your congregation experienced culture, and how would you express your Asian North American Christian faith at this point on the way?

 As you read this book of stories, you can bring along your stories and share the journey with us.

Four Clusters of Topics

 This book addresses concerns that Asian North American Christian congregations face in their community life, worship, teaching, pastoral care, programs, and organization. Present within these areas are the issues of identity, cultural values, tradition, change, theological integrity, and strategies. Four clusters of topics are offered to the reader. Each cluster can be read entirely, in sequence. Or individual clusters or chapters can be read in a fashion that suits you, the reader. You can choose your own "program" in a way similar to the way you can select discs and tracks to play on a compact disc player; it is not required that you read from the first page sequentially to the last page. Or think of the chapter titles as spokes in a wheel—each chapter is equally useful and no chapter is number one or number five or whatever. This book is a yin-yang circle of chapters, each contributing something to the whole.

The four clusters are these:

- The Asian North American Experience of Community
- Power, Authority, and Relationships in Community
- Culture, Identity, and Community
- On the Road to Community.

A Continuing Process

The Project Team discovered that this book is "in process." To be faithful to our understanding of ourselves as people on the way and people of the Way, the book should be "on the way." Being on the way means knowing that we have not yet arrived; there is much to experience and to learn along the way. The journey goes on. When this book was presented to a continental conference of one hundred Asian North American and other church leaders, they provided feedback that helped develop the book further. Each chapter is written so that the reader is invited to interact and to take the ideas and suggestions further. The Project Team hopes that this book evokes imagination and provokes Asian North Americans and others to share their own stories and theologies so that the church can be a community walking in faith. Let us journey together.

Acknowledgments

This book is "in process." It represents the experiences and reflections of a team of Christians attempting to practice ministry and do theology in an Asian North American way. Indeed, this team found that their Asian roots and Christian faith both present faith and life as being "on the way." As members of the household and family of God this team journeyed together, sharing questions, life stories, and responses. They discovered themselves to be people on the way, and to be people of the Way. Their findings are offered as signs for others along the way. They hope fellow sojourners who read this book will contribute their experiences and insights so that all of us along the way will be helped to reach the faith destination, the realm of God. Sharing by sojourners is an ongoing process within God's world.

The sojourners on the way who shared in creating this book are the **Christ, Culture, and Community Project Team**. They are **Richard C. Choe**, a pastor in Mississauga, Ontario; **Virstan B. Y. Choy**, a seminary field education director in San Anselmo, California; **Young Lee Hertig**, a seminary professor in Pasadena, California; **Sunny Kang**, a pastor in Minneapolis, Minnesota; **Grace Sangok Kim**, a teacher in Davis, California; **Heup Young Kim**, a university professor in Seoul, Korea; **Stephen S. Kim**, a seminary professor and associate dean in Claremont, California; **Greer Anne Wenh-In Ng**, a seminary professor in Toronto, Ontario; **Edward G. Tanng**, a university professor in Taipei, Taiwan; **Ellen Tanouye**, a pastor in El Cerrito, California; and **Michael Yoshii**, a pastor in Alameda, California. The project director and editor of this book is **David Ng**, a seminary professor in San Anselmo, California, and the project administrators are **Lonna Chang-Ren Lee**, a pastor in

San Francisco, California, and **Irene Young Ng**, a church office administrator in San Anselmo, California. **Franklin J. Woo**, formerly with the National Council of Churches, New York, and **Fumitaka Matsuoka**, a seminary dean in Berkeley, California, were consultants to the team, and **Penny Schoyer**, a graduate student in Berkeley, California, assisted the team.

When the Project Team met at San Francisco Theological Seminary in 1992 to begin its study, it was informed by the stories and perspectives of Asian North American congregations in the area. Representatives of the following Californian congregations told their stories to the team:

• Buena Vista United Methodist Church, Alameda
• Chinese Congregational Church, San Francisco
• Chinese Presbyterian Church, Oakland
• First Chinese Baptist Church, San Francisco
• First Korean Presbyterian Church, San Francisco
• Korean Presbyterian Church of Contra Costa, Concord
• Korean Presbyterian Church, San Rafael
• Presbyterian Church in Chinatown, San Francisco
• Sturge Presbyterian Church, San Mateo

The Christ, Culture, and Community Project was generously supported by the Louisville Institute for the Study of Protestantism and American Culture, through its parent body, The Lilly Endowment. The Marin Community Foundation gave support for the continental conference that introduced this book to one hundred church leaders. These foundations perceived the value of the project, not just for Asian North American congregations, but also for all churches and for all of North American society. Their vision of a multicultural society and their financial support made the project possible.

An advisory committee helped shape the project proposal and provided helpful critiques and evaluations. This advisory group was appointed by the organization that gave birth to the project and nurtured it: Pacific Asian American and Canadian Christian Education Ministries (PAACCE). The committee included Ella K. Campbell of Marysville, California; Victoria Lee Moy of Madison, New Jersey; and Donald Ng of Valley Forge, Pennsylvania. Also providing help and administrative support were the Ministries in Christian Education Unit of the National Council of Churches and its director, Dorothy L. Savage.

The Christ, Culture, and Community Project was a partnership effort, especially for all the persons and organizations listed. This sense of teamwork is entirely fitting; this project is about community—people on the way together, sharing the journey and offering each other the gifts of insight, encouragement, and discovery as we travel on the way. This book shares these discoveries.

Introduction

David Ng

Asian North American Congregations on the Way

"Jesus said to him, 'I am the way, and the truth, and the life. No one comes to the Father except through me. If you know me, you will know my Father also. From now on you do know him and have seen him' " (John 14:6,7).

Once you were not a people,
    but now you are God's people;
once you had not received mercy,
    but now you have received mercy.
    —1 Peter 2:10

The Strength of Asian North American Congregations

The church in North America marches toward a new century. One band of marchers is in the front ranks, with colorful banners unfurled and joyful music sounding forth. Asian North American congregations proclaim a vital gospel and a growing mission and outreach. While many churches struggle with decreases in attendance, participation, mission, and giving, Asian North American churches face the challenges of the need for more space, leadership development, expanded programming, and the desire for new expressions of faith and community.

You can observe spiritual fervor and enthusiasm in many

of the newer churches serving immigrant and second-generation Asian North Americans. Christians from Korea, Taiwan, Hong Kong, and Southeast Asia—many of them very recent immigrants to Canada and the United States—manifest a "young faith" that is seen in how they pray, worship, and care for one another and heard in how they sing unto the Lord. Christians of Japanese and Chinese background—some of them into the fourth and fifth generations in North America—manifest a faith informed by a recovery of ethnic and cultural identity, heritage, and values. They find treasures in their native Asian stories, festivals, family relationships, and world outlooks. These values enrich their understanding of the Christian faith and bring new life to congregational worship and programs.

Visit a new Korean or Taiwanese North American congregation. You will encounter members who take faith seriously and happily at the same time. Corporate worship is lively with attention paid to the Word read and preached. Enthusiasm pours out in music and singing. Sincere, serious prayer is offered expectantly (and at times almost unceasingly!). Church officers consider their election a calling to high responsibility. Youth workers understand themselves to be pastors to their young flocks. Women find various avenues of service in the church (while poised to assume roles of leadership and decision making as opportunities for change arise or are created). Pastors work overtime; they preach, teach, call on homes, minister in the community, and join in early morning prayer meetings.

Observe any Asian North American congregation and you will sense that being Christian oftentimes changes family relationships. Old hierarchies and traditional expectations for how children and parents relate to each other are illumined by the example of Christ's self-giving love. The reasons for and rewards of work in everyday life are transformed and workers find God's presence in the sewing factory, the social service agency, the grocery store, the computer laboratory, and the classroom. Churches and church members feel called to reach out to those of similar national, ethnic, cultural, and linguistic backgrounds. The call to mission is responded to through social services, tutoring, and personal support and outreach; non-Christians see the Christian church as a place of social support and even of advocacy regarding economic, educational, political, and health issues.

Sojourners and Pioneers

Asian North American Christians identify strongly with the biblical image of sojourners. Abraham and Sarah, Hagar, Rebekah and Isaac, Jacob and Rachel, generation upon generation were called by God and followed God's guidance, going to new lands and establishing new homes and new lives. Asian immigrants came to the new land of North America seeking wealth, knowledge, freedom, or other possibilities. Whatever the motivation, Asian North Americans identify with the biblical people of God in their sense of loss of home and tribe, sense of wandering in an inhospitable desert, and great sense of dependence on God's grace and guidance. Through God's calling, those who were not a people are now God's people. Asian North Americans left old worlds steeped in ancient wisdom, art, and history. They set forth in new lands with strange languages, modern and seemingly superficial customs, and peopled by strangers who can at the same time be friendly, kind, prejudiced, and hateful.

Asian North American sojourners are people on the move, simultaneously hopeful and vulnerable. Even those whose forebears came to North America a hundred or more years ago find life among the dominant peoples unsettling at times. They, too, are on the move, backward and forward, recovering ethnic and cultural identity and creating new mixes of personhood, families, and neighborhoods. By choice or by force, Asian North Americans are sojourners. Those who know the Bible story are comforted by the biblical models of faithful journeying, seeking the home where God is Father and members of the household of God are children of God and brothers and sisters in Christ.

Sojourners are also pioneers. They go forth into new territories knowing that they are not alone but are surrounded by a cloud of witnesses. Ancestors endow the sojourners and pioneers with religious and moral wisdom and practiced and practical structures of human relationship and community organization. Asian North Americans brought with them to the new lands their centuries of religious and philosophical understandings. In some cases the understandings came from shamanist or Taoist perspectives or other ancient wisdom. The sense of the cosmos being whole, and all of human life and nature interlocked in harmonious balance, is instilled in the Asian North American sojourner. This sense of life unity, harmony, and balance is brought into the church by Asian North American pioneers as gifts for the whole church, to enrich the church's theological understanding of God's creation. Asian forms of family and social relationships, nurtured over the centuries by Confucian teachings and practices, influence Asian North American Christian ways of being in community and of being the church. In some respects, such as in static hierarchical patterns of relationship, demanding formalities of filial piety, and sexist valuations of personhood, Asian and Confucian practices cast a shadow on the path of the Asian North American sojourner. But in other significant respects, the ancient practices enlighten family interdependence and communal membership and responsibilities. Much can be gained by a critical appreciation of the ancient traditions and values. The ideas for church life and educational ministry that this book seeks to share are illumined by these ancient truths, which continue to be markers on the road.

But Asian North American Christians also look to Jesus Christ as their pioneer and perfecter of faith. Sojourners following the ancient truths encounter a surprising Servant Lord whose prophetic teaching and sacrificial ministry call forth a new creation. Sojourners and pioneers enter into a new realm of God far removed from the old realms of human life.

By harmonizing old and new, Asian North American congregations are creating new forms of the church and sharing with the whole church great gifts of understanding and practice. They are helping the church to be more culturally diverse, more universal, and more faithful. A major goal of this book is to share Asian North American understandings and experiences of community that can recall the whole church to its essential being as the community of Jesus Christ, the community of the Way. We hope the church can celebrate these contributions of the Asian North American congregations.

Special Needs of Asian North American Congregations

In 1992 the Project Team of twelve Asian North American educators, pastors, students, and professors gathered to examine the meaning of community for the church, particularly for Asian North American congregations. (The names of the Project Team members are listed in the acknowledgments.) This team engaged in a study of "Christ, Culture, and Community." They met at San Francisco Theological Seminary with the support of The Lilly Endowment. The team was broadly representative of the Asian North American population of Japanese, Chinese, and Korean backgrounds; women and men; immigrant and succeeding generations; and various ages, languages, and denominations. This very diverse team held in common a realization that persons who come from East Asia (Japan, China, Korea, and also Vietnam) share a Confucian perspective on life, ethics, and social relationships. These people of East Asian heritage understand their own personal identity to be bound with their families and other communities so that each is an interdependent "person in community." This is in contrast to the approach to life and experiences of many Western people whose life goal is self-fulfillment as a free individual essentially independent of others.

Congregational Stories

When the Project Team met to discuss the issue of community and to plan this book, they invited nine Asian North American congregations to meet with them. (The congregations are listed in the acknowledgments.) Japanese, Korean, and Chinese North American congregations told their stories and reported on their programs.

Diversity of Languages

One Chinese North American congregation in San Francisco told a richly woven story of starting 140 years ago with a ministry to Cantonese immigrants in Chinatown, establishing a rescue mission for young women, then offering an outstanding youth ministry program. The influx of persons from mainland China and Taiwan led this congregation to develop a program for Mandarin-speaking recent immigrants.

This congregation is a federation of language fellowships. It includes Cantonese-speaking immigrants or first-generation Chinese Americans, mostly from Hong Kong. The worship service is in Cantonese. A worship service in English reaches the second and subsequent generations of predominantly American-born persons. A service in Mandarin serves those immigrants from Taiwan, the People's Republic of China, and many other parts of Asia and the Pacific who speak the major dialect of Chinese. This Chinatown congregation is a rich complexity of church life: a diversity of languages, ages, places of birth, cultural roots, generations, education, and social and economic classes. There are many potential gaps in communication, relationship, and understanding. Indeed, this congregation can tell several stories of severe miscommunications and the splitting off of whole clusters of members. This diverse congregation has the constant urgency of working on unity. The members continue to struggle with questions of how to organize and administer a complex institution, how to be able to hear the ideas and concerns of the language groups, and how to nurture young leaders and integrate them into decision-making roles while respecting and utilizing older, more experienced leaders. These special needs are real for this congregation and are a part of the story of every Asian North American congregation.

Parent-Child Relationships

The story of one Korean American congregation in suburban San Rafael mirrors that of most: the poignant search for ways for parents and children to communicate with and understand each other and to share faith in their families and as fellow members of a congregation. In this congregation the parents politely but with insistence ask the pastor and educational leaders to "please do something to help our young people." What the parents fear is that their young people will lose their Korean cultural values, language, and identity—not to mention the fervent faith so evident among Korean Christians. The Korean American young people are characterized by the length of stay in North America and their place of birth, such as "transgenerational," "1.5 generation," or "second generation." But most of the youth rapidly assimilate into Western culture. As far as some parents are concerned, the young people take on the worst characteristics Western society has to offer. It seems the young people are becoming materialistic, self-centered, ahistorical, and disrespectful of elders. This is not what the parents wished for when they came to North America seeking a better life for their children and themselves.

The young people have their uneasiness with the other generation too. Adults and parents are, some adolescents say, too rigid, too strict, too old-fashioned, too pious, too everything else! The young people see the worst characteristics of Korean culture practiced by their elders at home and in the church—or so it seems.

Of course, such a description of Korean North American parent-child relationships reflects the exaggeration of people who are emotionally caught up in a very vexing situation. With the reality of the generation gap, Korean North American congregations, particularly because they include so many recent immigrants, would identify a common problem. They need help for parents and young people regarding cultural identity and understanding the processes of acculturation or assimilation and of mutual communication. Most Asian North American congregations would agree that "we need help in dealing with our young people." And the more thoughtful ones would add, "And with our parents."

Uncovering Painful Stories

A Japanese North American congregation in San Mateo and one in Alameda reported to the Project Team. These churches have long histories and their members have had memorable common experiences, including the infamous relocation of Japanese Americans in internment camps during World War II. In recent years and in various ways, the Japanese Americans, including those in Christian churches, have uncovered their once-hidden feelings and thoughts about that tragic period of their history. In some cases it has been the gentle prying of the subsequent generations that has enabled the stories to be told. In the Alameda congregation, the young people helped lift the lids nearly a half century after the internment camps were closed and the Japanese people were allowed to return to whatever they could find of their previous lives and livelihoods. With tape recorders and sympathetic ears, the young people listened while their elders told their stories of pain and loss, bewilderment and betrayal, and courage and fortitude. The tape-recording project emboldened the pastor and others to try other ways of hearing stories and sharing cultural symbols and artifacts. It was discovered that the current annual teriyaki chicken fund-raising dinner started as a Doll Festival, a genuine Japanese cultural activity! The Doll Festival is being restored. In the educational program, Japanese forms of art are used to portray the story of Jesus; foods and festivals proudly reflect Japanese flavors and folklore; the older generation are storytellers and teachers to the younger.

Similar uncoverings of personal stories and recoveries of cultural identity are a vital part of the San Mateo congregation. In their case, young adults and young parents—third-, fourth-, and fifth-generation Japanese North Americans— were encouraged to learn their Japanese stories and to tell them to their children.

Congregational Culture and Self-esteem

These two congregations exhibit a need and a potential that are characteristic of all Asian North American congregations. The church needs to support the search for and the recovery of ethnic and cultural identity and values. Certainly self-esteem is at stake, but the need goes deeper. Asian North American Christians believe that their identity, culture, language, religious heritage—their whole way of life—is good and is where God is present and at work. Indeed, the story of Jesus confirms God's love for people and God's presence in the lives of people. By coming into the world, God affirmed life and culture. For Asian North American Christians, Jesus' participation in human life and culture is very basic good news.

Indigenous Worship

Cultural affirmation in the congregations should lead to cultural expressions of faith through prayer, worship, and liturgies. But no Asian North American congregation that reported could claim any sense of accomplishment in this area of church life. One common problem is that congregations tend to be divided into native-language and English worship services. And both the English services and the native-language services tend to use Western forms of worship and liturgical materials. While there is a natural desire for worship to reflect the theology and tradition of a denomination, it is remarkable that Asian North American worship services seldom utilize the cultural patterns and rhythms of the native cultures. Hymns, when they are sung in the native language, usually are sung to Western hymn tunes. Some symbolic artifacts such as silk banners reflect Asian expressions, but more often traditional Western symbols, styles of art, and chancel furnishings prevail.

Much of this Western approach is a sincere attempt by Asian North American Christians to assimilate and to avoid the incorporation of non-Christian or un-Christian pictures, symbols, gestures, and other expressions. When Asian and Asian North American persons became Christian, they were taught to forsake "pagan ways" and to devote themselves solely to Christian life and worship. Now a few Asian North American congregations are asking if there is a validity to indigenous worship. Cannot Christians who happen to be Asian use Asian forms? Is this not a bringing of one's best to God's temple and God's Table? And is it not appropriate for Western people to use Western forms and others with other cultural traditions to be able, if they choose, to use their own cultural forms? African American music; Native American ecological spirituality; Latin American candles, crosses, and statues—these seem to help the respective ethnic and cultural groups to praise God with integrity and meaning. Asian North American congregations are only now beginning to search for Asian forms and patterns. Some art in the Chinese, Japanese, or Korean tradition is appearing. Korean North American choirs and congregations are creating a musical style and tradition. But much needs to be done to enable worship and liturgy to be meaningfully Asian North American in character.

Culturally Sensitive Pastoral Care

The Asian North American congregations who reported hesitatingly admitted problems in providing pastoral care. Members have had relationships broken. Families have been at war within their homes. Pastors and officers have not trusted each other. Like any congregation, Asian North American congregations have "people problems." But these problems involve people with Confucian, Taoist, shamanist, Shintoist, or Buddhist religious and philosophical backgrounds and ways of talking or not talking and ways of relating or not relating that are somehow distinctly Asian. One congregation reporter used the popular notion of "face" and "saving face" to relate the complexities and difficulties that that congregation had in making a request for aid from its presbytery and then being turned down in its request. That request was years ago; the officers and members of the congregation still feel the embarrassment of that experience today. In another story, a pastor told of how a couple seeking counseling were helped to see that before they could resolve their marital problems they had to "unpack" the cultural influences that caused them to behave as they did and to interpret each other's actions as they did. This couple had to realize that their perceptions of what men and women, and husbands and wives, were expected to do were profoundly influenced by their cultural upbringing.

Pastors in Asian North American congregations are keenly aware of the uniqueness of the pastoral care and pastoral counseling requirements in their parishes. In fact, the possibility of doing counseling at all is a basic question. Only a very few seminaries offer help for persons preparing for ministry in Asian North American congregations. So most pastors and others who provide pastoral care resort to personal knowledge and intuition, often successfully, but just as often disastrously. The need for approaches to pastoral care is great. The need is equally great for pastoral care techniques that are safe and therapeutic (or to use Eastern terms, ways that are respectful and healing).

Asian North Americans carry in their history a rich tradition of the art of healing. Asian spirituality and Asian notions of personal identity and communal membership need to be brought into the congregation's and the pastor's repertory of skills of pastoral care.

Diversity, Unity, and Solidarity

At one time in North America the ideal was for people of various diversities to be integrated into one united church. The last decade of growing cultural pluralism, often militantly announced, casts doubts on the possibility of a united church. The ideal of Christian unity should not be discarded. It is right and it must happen. But a new understanding of how diversity can be brought into a unity is emerging. Unity is not necessarily a structural unity. Unity can be relational. Diverse groups, each professing Jesus Christ as Lord, can be in solidarity with each other without being united into a single organization or structure, especially a melting-pot unity imposed by the majority upon the minorities. One congregation need not look like every other congregation or like any other congregation.

A broader sense of unity, or at least of solidarity, could allow Asian North American congregations to discover and form the shapes and sizes that best help them to be communities of faith. There may need to be, at this time, congregations focusing on a specific language group or immigrant group or cluster of interests and social locations. Some Asian North Americans need to join English-speaking congregations of whatever cultural or multicultural makeup exists in the neighborhood. Pan-Asian congregations could serve certain needs. Numerous possibilities exist and new forms need to be tried and evaluated.

Congregational Models

Regarding models and designs of congregations, the needs at this time are for serious consideration of the meaning and possibilities of church unity, the discovery of effective forms of mission, and the acceptance of a variety of forms of congregations to meet the various needs of Asian North American Christians. In a later chapter we will consider existing models and explore new possibilities.

Learning to Be People on the Way

The short (but heavy) list of concerns of Asian North American congregations becomes an urgent agenda for the whole church today. We need to help deal with language, age, and cultural differences. Cultural identity and values need to be accepted and ways of teaching and affirming these values must be developed. Resources are needed to support new forms of worship. Culturally appropriate ways of providing pastoral care must be put together. Also on the agenda is the establishment of ways to organize congregations and to relate them to each other and to the church as a whole. This multitude of needs points to the basic need for Asian North American theologies. How are Asian North American Christians to state their faith? The need is not necessarily for another comprehensive, propositional, systematic theology to stand alongside the many systems of theology that the church, especially in the West, has written. Theology is being written, not necessarily in a systematic way, but *in situ*—on location—addressing pertinent issues *along the way*.

Perhaps a major contribution Asian North Americans will make to the church is a recovery of the New Testament perspective of faith as being, among other things, "the Way." Asian North Americans call it "the Tao."

Asian North Americans have unique theological perspectives and understandings. From their distinct experiences of God's salvation and Christ's call into the church and into mission, they have much to say. They have much to say about the experience of sojourning, of being pilgrims, of entering a strange new land, of being a community, of suffering, and of rejoicing. Asian North Americans can and need to tell their faith stories and to write theologies. For practical reasons, and for reasons of being and becoming, these theologies will be stories of people on the way.

Theology through Story

Asian North American Christians are not inclined to construct a "systematic theology," at least not in the traditional

(Western) style. Asian North Americans, like their ancestors, are people who tell stories and learn from community stories. Truth often is offered in a roundabout way or metaphorically or elliptically so as to require the listener to enter into the search for meanings. This is not to say that Asian North American Christians do not have faith; that they have. But faith often is known as a way, a path that is traveled and is still being explored. There is a goal, but it is yet to be reached. It is hard to write an abstract exposition of a faith that is a journey or of believers who are sojourners. Asian theologian C. S. Song points to the reality and profundity of theology based on story:

> For most of us a lofty subject matter such as theology has nothing to do with "mere" stories. The task of Christian theology is to think "deep thoughts" of God and about God. Nothing less than abstruse language—words, and concepts worthy of the reality that transcends human apprehension, systems, and structures and capable of disclosing the inner structure of the divine mystery—was considered worthy of theology. Little wonder theology became strange and irrelevant to everyday life of the people. It has become an abstract discourse carried on among theological "professionals." The question seldom arises whether it reflects the sweat and labor, sighs and longings of the men, women, and children who struggle just to survive in a world of harsh realities. Theology ironically has become "disincarnated." Instead of "the Word become flesh," theology becomes "the flesh become words."
>
> . . . The discovery of this world of stories gives us the theological freedom to travel between the world of the Bible and the world of Asia, to enlarge our theological horizon, and to deepen our experience of God's saving activity outside the history of Christianity as well as inside it. In reclaiming stories of people, we reclaim our Asian humanity. As we immerse ourselves in them, we touch the roots of our Asian being. Doing theology with folktales in Asia teaches an important lesson: stories of people, not preconceived theological ideas and criteria, lead us to deeper truths about humanity and God.[1]

Notes

1. Choan-Seng Song, *Third-eye Theology,* rev. ed. (Maryknoll, N.Y.: Orbis Books, 1991), 10-11.

CHAPTER 1

Seeking Home in North America: Colonialism in Asia; Confrontation in North America

By Stephen S. Kim

Introduction

To understand and appreciate the situation of Asian North American Christians and congregations today, it is important to recall how Christianity was introduced to their forebears during the surge of Christian evangelism in Asia in the nineteenth century. The Christian faith was proclaimed with great sincerity and fervor. Some Asians, particularly those of lower educational and economic stations, were drawn into this religion that offered new life, membership in an egalitarian community, personal salvation, and reconciliation with the Supreme Being and with family, neighbors, and nations.

What was not recognized at the time, but is quite evident today, is that along with this new and vibrant faith came the format of Western culture, thought forms, and world-view. The wondrous gift of the Christian faith was presented in Western gift wrappings.

In strenuous terms Stephen S. Kim, a theologian and church historian, recounts the introduction of Western Christianity into East Asian lands. Kim connects the missionary movement to two other historical phenomena: merchants and the military. He shows the problems "the three Ms" caused for all East Asians, including those who chose to become Christian.

The attitudes of Westerners toward East Asians, sometimes benevolent but patronizing and very often malevolent and racist, infected the efforts to bring the Christian gospel to already highly civilized and religious societies in China, Japan, and Korea.

Kim sees in the problems that Asian immigrants have encountered in North America, notably in the violence unleashed on Korean Americans during the Los Angeles riots of 1992, correlations with the ethnocentric and racist attitudes that the peoples of East Asia encountered when the nations of the West entered Asia with merchants, the military, and missionaries.

Asian immigrants and their children seek a home in North America. To find and secure that home they will need to affirm their own cultural heritage and identity and establish a faith that is true to their own wisdom and integrity. This chapter raises the question: "What will it take for Asians to find 'home' in North America?"

Sorrow and Suffering Confront Asian North American Sojourners

In our search for home here in North America, what hurts us most and is most detrimental to our common goal of achieving community is bigotry and discrimination. We often have encountered irrational suspicion or hatred of the Asian race. That this is a racist society was exposed for the whole world to see on one April day in 1992 in Los Angeles, the city of angels, which was once so promising and fabled as America's dreamland but now is stupefied by racial tension, gang and drug wars, and cynicism. The story of one Korean merchant in Koreatown is a telling example.

Mr. Hwang lamented after a small building that housed his tiny grocery store had been burned down by the rioters, on that gruesome day, "What in the world am I doing here?

"And for what?" He had left his home in Korea and emigrated to California in the early 1970s with a dream of providing his three young children with a better education and a better life in this land of opportunity. The first three years, however, saw him working as a grocery store clerk, cleaner, and security guard—sometimes two jobs at the same time. Mr. Hwang's hope was to save enough money to purchase his own store and perhaps even a house for his family. The long hours at work with minimum wages kept him from paying much attention to his children.

He finally was able to buy his own business: a tiny grocery store. In the meantime, the children suffered. Quite often his youngsters had to feed themselves, do their own laundry, and even help their parents at the store. They were unhappy and their grades suffered. Now the dream has been shattered, and he is left with ashes, pain, and failing children.

Mr. Hwang's children for whom he had a great plan are disillusioned beyond his imagination. Wishing to be identified with mainstream youth, they shy away from the old, traditional Korean or Asian ways. They are even ashamed of their parents' looks, style of life, and accent. They try to hide their Korean identity. At times, in heated arguments, they blame their parents for their Asian features. They have become hateful of themselves.

"What am I doing here? And for what?"

As many reporters and observers reflected, the riots were but a symptom of a much more serious malady of North American society. The Asians, African Americans, and Hispanics in the riots were all victims of a society in which the poor and powerless class are caught in a racial cage. The Los Angeles riots were disastrous, with people of one minority race destroying the works of other racial minority people. More devastating was the nation's response to the riots. According to a *Time* magazine reporter:

> . . . L. A.'s wealthy classes quickly fobbed off the burden of reconstruction to small volunteer organizations and an overstretched investment drive; the lame-duck mayor

receded into city hall; the federal government turned its back; minority groups fumed about the patronizing attitude of their would-be helpers; police remained unrepentant about the Rodney King beating; and gangs declared a truce but kept on selling drugs and robbing people.[1]

There certainly were differences in these riots from others such as the one in Newark, New Jersey, and the Watts district in Los Angeles in the 1960s, but one thing was common: classism and racism, the extent of which was underestimated by many observers, including one Indian reporter who contributed a column to *The Los Angeles Times* in which he wrote:

> Los Angeles could have been any Third World city caught in the chasm of tribal warfare. Ancient rage of one ethnic group boiled over after years of frustration with politicians who have shown an amazing ability to deny the obvious: that racism exists in America and that it thrives beyond the managed news conferences and the sound bites from cynical officials. The dirty little secret was out for the whole world to see. Only the most innocent would have asked the looters—as some television reporters did—why they were destroying their own community. Mob anger erupts only in ways it knows how—against the perceived prosperity of another group, another class.[2]

Poor Mr. Hwang, like many Asian merchants, was in triple jeopardy; he was neither white and rich nor black or Hispanic and poor nor politically powerful. He was lost in the dreamland.

This story of one Korean American merchant has been repeated many times over in the history of the Asian North American immigration. When we look back at the history of how the East came to meet the West, some of the reasons for our racial marginalization and victimization emerge.

Questions for Reflection and Discussion

1. Can you share a story of how an Asian immigrant experienced settling in North America?

2. Why did our Asian ancestors come to North America?

3. How were they treated?

4. How did they deal with the harsh realities in North America?

The Colonial Spirit Operated in Asia

The history of the colonial conquest of Asia by the Western powers reflects their attitude: most Westerners held the Asian race and its culture in low esteem. Today's bigots find it hard to improve on these impressions of the "Orientals." In such bigotry and prejudice, a culture lag,[3] the remnant of the colonial habit of mind, is evident. United Methodist Bishop Roy I. Sano, formerly a professor at the Pacific School of Religion, traced such a culture lag in contemporary classism and racism to what he called "internal colonialism," a residue of Western colonial history. Professor Sano urged the "humanizing of the emerging reality," the liberation of the Asian race from racism, sexism, and classism.[4] Despite a monumental advance in race relations and human rights spurred by the life, death, and spirit of the late Dr. Martin Luther King Jr. in the 1960s, internal colonialism is still rampant today in our society, particularly on an institutional level. Institutional racism is reflected then on personal levels. There are numerous instances of hate crimes against the minorities, and it gets worse in rough economic times.[5]

It may be simplistic, but not groundless, to connect classism and racism with colonialism. This colonial spirit was operative in the West's expansion in Asia during the past three centuries. The history of the Asian peoples' struggle with the West's expansion in Asia is the history of the struggle for identity and dignity. Simply stated, the West's expansion in Asia has affected the formation, or the deformation, of the Asian North Americans' identity, and our feelings about ourselves. The history of the West's encroachment affects our ways of being in, and our wish to become integral and contributing members of, our newly adopted home. Many

authors have attempted to put the best face on this encroachment by putting the most unprejudiced views to it,[6] but it is
intended here to show that the history of the West's encroachment indeed has affected our sense of identity and dignity
and how we act as Asian North American communities. If we
aspire to an authentic community of all peoples in North
America, we must first reflect on the meaning and effects of
the West's expansion in Asia.

I. Looking Back at the History of the West's Expansion in Asia

The Three Ms

Like relentless waves came merchants, the military, and
missionaries (the three Ms) from European and North
American countries to Asia. The West's expansion in Asia
is characterized by colonial ambitions, which include material and territorial greed, moral and cultural arrogance,
and an intellectual and spiritual superiority complex. We
may consider militarism and mercantilism as aspects of
the past, and, as did some historians, we may attempt to
justify them. But it is one of the poignant ironies of the
history of the Christian mission that the missionary movement was associated with colonial expansion, even when
we consider that the missionaries were taken advantage of
by the dishonorable colonialists. Most missionaries were
women and men of high ideals, devotion, and commitment
and are admired and honored by most of the people in Asia
even to this day. The association can be traced to inciden-
tals, such as the necessity to protect the missionaries from
the disgraced Asian rulers and court officials who reacted
violently. Furthermore, the missionaries had a felt need
to challenge the traditional ways and wisdom as "pagan."
As one American leader of the mission movement in the
late nineteenth century put it, "Who can reconcile the
professed motives of the Mission movement with the
obvious purposes of European governments? We know

they are irreconcilable and do not try, but they are the double face of a single party to the Chinese."[7] The mishaps were few in number but consequential in terms of bringing about serious conflicts, including martyrdom and even wars.

To Asian eyes, well-meaning missionary activities notwithstanding, mercantilism, militarism, and missions were so closely related that it is difficult to discuss one of the three Ms without considering the other two. The three Ms, in fact, were the three legs of the West's imperialist expansion policy. Missionaries, when faced with the harsh realities of foreign and hostile countries, needed protection, as did merchants, and such was the excuse for military intervention on most occasions. However, military intervention to protect their citizens, the well-meaning merchants, and dedicated missionaries was viewed as nothing less than aggression and vainglory by the Asian rulers, who felt that their sovereignty and honor were infringed upon and their venerable tradition scandalized. Indeed, many of the Asian rulers would rather have remained isolated from the rest of the world. They simply wanted to be left alone. But the so-called civilized nations of the world felt a strong mission, expressed in terms of "bringing light to these dark countries of superstition and hideous pagan practices." The western nations intruded upon Asian ways, often with cannon. Even the well-intended missionaries dealt with the Asian peoples with an air of moral, cultural, and spiritual superiority, and they dared to undo and disgrace thousand-year-old venerated traditions such as ancestor worship, whose significance far surpassed the understanding of the self-righteous missionaries. These self-righteous ones were few in number but were enough to warrant the Asian feeling that they were intruders with moral, cultural, and spiritual arrogance imposing a legacy of imperialism and colonialism.

European colonialism from the fifteenth to the nineteenth centuries was usually associated with the imperialism of the new nation-states and governed by the economic policies of mercantilism.[8] The governments of such countries as Portugal, Spain, England, and Germany in the sixteenth, seventeenth, and eighteenth centuries practiced mercantilism: they encouraged domestic industry, regulated production, controlled trading companies, placed restrictions such as tariffs and quotas on the importation of merchandise from other countries, and sought out raw materials and markets.

The voyages of discovery in the fifteenth and sixteenth centuries and the expansion of European trade and colonization marked the beginning of a new surge of missionary activity beginning with the Franciscans, the Dominicans, the Carmelites, and the Jesuits led by Francis Xavier, Matteo Ricci, and Roberto de Nobili, followed by Protestant missionaries. The great missionary expansion, however, took place in the nineteenth century when missionary societies were established in both Europe and the United States and when European colonialism was at its peak. Both Protestants and Roman Catholics sent missionaries to almost every country in Asia, and medical missionaries began to provide medical and educational assistance in conjunction with spiritual help.

Actually the Christian mission in China began in the early seventh century and made a considerable advance for a while. To this day the Nestorian story is little recognized in the West. Marco Polo's report of his life in China changed, though slowly, the West's image of the "barbarous" Far East. More importantly, Polo's remarkable stories aroused western curiosity and ambitions, leading to the so-called "age of discovery."[10] Expansion of the Christian church in this period, however, was mostly the consequence of the Crusades, which helped forge the colonial spirit. The Christian nations of Europe undertook military expeditions between the eleventh and fourteenth century to recapture the Holy Land from the Muslims. These religious-military wars reflected the hopes of the papacy for the reunification of the East and West, the nobility's hunger for land at a time of crop failures, population pressure in the West, and an alternative to warfare at home. Many were lured by the fabulous riches of the East; a campaign abroad appealed as a means of escaping from the pressures of feudal society. On a larger scale, the major European powers saw the Crusades as a means of establishing and extending trade routes.

The First Crusade (1096–99) was launched by Pope Urban II in a speech at the Council of Clermont, France, on November 27, 1095. By 1270 there were seven more crusades conducted in the name of Christianity. The Crusades were really bloody wars of hatred and greed and power politics among the leaders. This use of church persons as mere tools of power politics continued into the fifteenth and even into the nineteenth century. The growing economy of western Europe was drained of funds in support of the expeditions. The Crusades furthered the rapid growth of a money economy, of banking, and of new methods of taxation. Ranging from 950 to 1350, the Crusades ushered in an important phase of world history: the expansion of Europe, not only religiously, but also culturally and militarily.

The crusading spirit was the backdrop of what was to become European colonialism. Church historian K. S. Latourette wrote:

> The crusading idea, of a holy war commanded and blessed by the Church, had become deeply implanted in the Western European mind. Crusades were not confined to expeditions to retake or protect the Holy Places in Palestine. They were waged against Moslems in the Iberian Peninsula, against the pagan Wends and Prussians, against the heretical Cathari, and against still others, some of them Christians, whom the Popes adjudged enemies of the faith.[11]

This crusading spirit, whose trait was evident in many of the zealous missionaries and evangelicals, did help the church's expansion in terms of worldly gains, but it certainly did not help accomplish the original purpose, that is, the securing of the Holy Land. More harm was done; it widened the gap between the eastern and western churches, and a bad habit of mind—the imperialistic pattern—had set in the minds of the Christian leaders.

Out of curiosity and missionary zeal at first, but soon lured by the reports of fabulous riches and exotic cultures of the East, followed the colonialists. Europeans, the British in particular, were reluctant at first (as suggested by many authors, including W. E. Soothill, J. A. Graham, Robert E. Speer, and Stephen Neill),[12] but they soon were attracted by the pepper, spices, and silks that Arab traders were importing from the Orient. By the sixteenth century, steady contacts eventually resulted in the subjugation of much of the Asian continent by European powers.[13]

Asia Falls Victim to European Colonialism

The first phases of European colonial encroachment took the form of demands for desired Asian products and for missionary opportunities. Latourette noted that their "expansion was partly by exploration, partly by conquest, partly by vast migrations, and partly by commerce."[14] European culture, along with Christian missionaries, spread to Africa, South and East Asia, India, Ceylon, the East Indies, the Philippine Islands, and eventually to the Far East. Thus came the substantial expansion of European control in Asia by the end of the eighteenth century. Where previously there had been only European commercial posts, the European nations now sent troops along with commercial agents, officials, and Christian missionaries. These areas were turned into markets for Europe's industrial products and suppliers of its raw materials. By mid-nineteenth century the British controlled virtually all of India; the Dutch asserted similar control over Indonesia; and the French controlled Indochina. After suppression of the Indian Mutiny of 1857, the British government assumed direct rule over India. Farther east, the British founded the settlement of Singapore in 1819. An Anglo-Dutch treaty in 1824 granted Britain a free hand in Malacca and assigned the Indonesian archipelago to Dutch control. The latter concluded their conquest of Java in 1830 and gradually extended control over the other islands.

In Southeast Asia, Siam alone managed to keep its independence, although it lost border territories. France focused its attention on Vietnam, where national unity had been achieved only in 1802 after thirty years of civil strife. The French took over the southern provinces in 1862 and assumed control over Annam and Tonkin between 1883 and 1885. They also took control of Cambodia (1863) and Laos (1893), which were then consolidated with Vietnam to form the colony of Indochina.

Japan's efforts to maintain its isolation from the outside world were finally overcome when an United States fleet under Commodore Matthew Perry forced Japanese acceptance of a commercial treaty in 1853–54. The ensuing political uproar in Japan led to the overthrow of the Tokugawa shogunate and the resumption of imperial authority in the Meiji Restoration of 1868. In the following decades, Japan pursued a program of industrial modernization and social reform. It also inaugurated an expansionist foreign policy, challenging Chinese hegemony over Korea. After defeating China in the first Sino-Japanese war (1894–95), Japan assumed a virtual protectorate over Korea and forced China to cede Taiwan. Extending their interests to Manchuria, the Japanese came into conflict with Russia, which they defeated in the Russo-Japanese War (1904–05).

Meanwhile, in 1898, the United States took possession of the Philippines after defeating Spain in the Spanish-American War. Russian gains in northern Asia included territories in the Amur and Ussuri regions, where they founded Vladivostok in 1860. At the outbreak of World War I in 1914, most of Asia was under European or United States domination both politically and economically.

Persecution of the Christians and the destruction of a United States merchant ship in 1866 by the intimidated Koreans helped provoke Western assaults by France in 1866 and by the United States in 1871. In 1876, with the acquiescence of the powers, including the United States and China, the Japanese took advantage of the governmental disruption within Korea to force a commercial treaty on the Yi Dynasty. Korea was forced to open its doors to the Western nations, beginning with a treaty with the United States in 1882. Rivalries developed among China, Japan, and Russia for predominance of influence over the weak Korean state, resulting in Japan's formal annexation of the country in 1910. After forty-five years of political suppression, economic exploitation, and social and educational discrimination by Japanese colonial rule (1905–45), Korea was liberated in 1945 at the end of World War II. But since the devastating Korean War (1950–53) the country has been divided along the thirty-eighth parallel of latitude. There is only an uneasy truce along the line even today.

II. Asian Struggle for Identity and Independence

Asia's Reaction to Colonial Invasions

China has exemplified Asia's reaction to the West's colonial invasions. It turned to violent action against the West's encroachment. This ended in humiliating and costly defeat, and the inscrutable door was opened by force.

Two Opium Wars (1839–42, 1856–60) ended the long Chinese isolation from other civilizations.[15] For China, defeat in both conflicts began a century of humiliation through the imposition of unequal treaties that extracted commercial privileges, territory, and other benefits from the Chinese government. The First Opium War stemmed from China's efforts to bar the illegal importation of opium by British merchants. Britain scored an easy military victory. As a result, the treaties of Nanking (1842) and the Bogue (1843) were signed, and China was forced to open the ports of Canton, Amoy, Foochow, Ning-po, and Shanghai to British trade and residence. Other Western powers soon received similar privileges. The Second Opium War led to the Treaty of Tientsin, signed in 1858. In 1860 China was forced to open eleven more ports, allow foreign envoys to reside in Peking, admit missionaries to China, permit foreigners to travel in the Chinese interior, and legalize the importation of opium. Britain seized Hong Kong to secure a base for the opium traders expelled from Canton.[16] The peninsula of Kowloon on the mainland was added to the colony, and in 1898 a large area beyond Kowloon along with the surrounding islands was leased to Great Britain for ninety-nine years.

The Boxer Uprising

The Boxer Uprising from 1898 to 1900 was another example of violent reaction by the Chinese people to rid their country of foreigners and foreign influences.[17] The Boxers—militia units in the north called *I-ho Ch'uan* ("righteous harmony fists")—rampaged throughout the land, killing foreigners as well as Chinese Christians and other Chinese with ties to foreigners. In retaliation, an international force of British, French, German, Japanese, Russian, and U.S. troops entered Peking in August 1900 and lifted the siege of the foreign legations there. The imperial court fled to Xi'an. Under the subsequent protocol of September 1901, China was forced to pay a punitive indemnity and to yield to several new foreign demands, including the right to station troops in Peking and along the route to the sea.

Neocolonialism, Nationalism, and Liberation

A change in colonialism in Asia came when the European imperial powers weakened. In India, nationalist movements began in moderate form with the meeting of the first Congress nationalist group in 1885; in Burma, Indonesia, and Vietnam, nationalism started to emerge around the turn of the century. The Filipino revolt against the Spanish broke out in 1896, and the U.S. takeover of 1898 was tolerated because it helped climax the anti-Spanish movement. In China, the Kuomintang (Nationalist Party), led by Sun Yat-sen, initiated the revolution of 1911 that brought the downfall of the Manchu dynasty. Japan attempted in 1915 to take advantage of China's confusion for political ends, but it was forced to abandon some of its demands under British and U.S. pressure. In 1919 the Koreans declared independence against the Japanese colonial rule. In 1928 the Nationalist general Chiang Kai-shek restored a semblance of Chinese unity.

World War II formally ended direct Western domination of Asia. Following Japan's conquest of Southeast Asia in 1942, the British, French, and Dutch found it impossible to recover control, despite Japan's eventual defeat in 1945. The Asian peoples sought to take their fate into their own hands. Wars of liberation led to a Dutch withdrawal from Indonesia in 1949 and the French from Indochina in 1954. In 1947 the British acceded to the demands of the Indian national movement, personified by Mahatma Gandhi. Korea was liberated by the allied force in 1945. The Philippines gained independence in 1946; Ceylon and Burma, in 1948; and Malaya, in 1957.

With the end of colonialism, Communist agitation began in a number of Asian countries. In Southeast Asian countries, Communist insurgents refused to be content with mere political independence. The Communist governments of Mongolia and North Korea soon were joined by a massive Communist regime in China. When North Korea invaded South Korea in 1950, the United States and China were drawn into the war, which ended three years later with a truce. After a Communist-led nationalist revolution drove the French from Indochina in 1954, civil war broke out in South Vietnam. The prolonged Vietnam War, in which the United States backed the South Vietnamese government, finally ended with a North Vietnamese victory in 1975. That same year, U.S.-supported governments in Laos and Cambodia also fell to Communist forces. Communist insurgencies elsewhere, including Burma, Indonesia, Malaysia, and the Philippines, met with less success than those in Indochina.

In a concerted effort to reconstruct Asia, industrialization was widely promoted as the solution to Asia's liberation from poverty and unemployment problems. Japan, assisted by massive U.S. aid programs after World War II, achieved an "economic miracle," and Taiwan, South Korea, and Singapore followed suit. Southwest Asia benefited from foreign aid to some extent. China experimented briefly with a peasant-based industrialization program during its Great Leap Forward of 1958-60, but this approach was later abandoned as inefficient. After the Cultural Revolution, China began to import advanced technology from the West. Industries were encouraged to become more autonomous and responsive to market demands, although the pace of reform slowed in the late 1980s and early 1990s. Lingering problems caused uncertainty in China and political conflicts in Burma, Kampuchea, Sri Lanka, Kashmir, North Korea, and the Philippines.

It was during the period of uncertainty and confusion in the early twentieth century that many Asians set out for North America in search of opportunities for a better life.

Questions for Reflection and Discussion

1. How did the colonial activities in Asia affect attitudes toward Asian immigrants in North America?

2. What connections do you make with the colonial movements in Asia, the treatment of Asian North Americans, and racism?

3. How significant is the experience of racism in the lives of Asian North Americans and in Asian North American congregations?

III. Asian Immigrant Communities in North America

Asian Migration to North America

Our Asian foremothers and forefathers came to North America seeking a haven where they could provide their

children with better opportunities and perhaps enjoy some
dignity and peace. But America and Canada turned out to be
far from a dreamed-of refuge for our Asian pioneers. As other
racial minorities in North America have experienced, Asian
North Americans have endured racial discrimination and
restricted opportunity for full participation in North American life. Despite the adversities, however, Asian immigrants
made a unique contribution to the North American experience through their distinctive cultural heritage, industry,
and resourcefulness.[19]

In the United States, the California Gold Rush of the 1850s
provided the impetus for the initial wave of immigrants from
China. The immigrants were eager to escape problems of
overpopulation, poverty, and political unrest in their homeland. The reality was harsh for the immigrants, however.
Many were victimized by employers who paid low wages
for long hours of backbreaking labor. Chinese men who
ventured to the California gold fields found precious little
gold and many excruciatingly harsh conditions. Most of
them were cheated, robbed, violently beaten, or even killed
by white gold miners. The Chinese soon gave up mining
and turned to the service trades, small businesses, or
unskilled labor. An estimated 10,000 Chinese laborers
helped build the transcontinental railroad across the Sier-
ras and the Rockies.

From the beginning, the Chinese were targets of racial
discrimination; they were prohibited from owning property
or securing licenses and were barred from many occupations.
In 1882 Congress passed the first of the Chinese Exclusion
Acts, halting further immigration.[20] As a result of their
encounter with racial hostility and of their own tradition of
mutual aid, the Chinese congregated in Chinatowns, insular
ethnic communities that met their housing, economic, social,
and psychological needs. With the liberalization of immigration laws in 1965 under the Johnson administration, a new
wave of Chinese immigrants arrived, mainly from Hong
Kong. In the period between 1960 and 1975, more than

200,000 Chinese were admitted, and by 1980 the Chinese American population was more than 800,000. More immigrants are arriving from Hong Kong in the tidal change of the end of the ninety-nine-year British lease in July of 1997. The influx of new immigrants has created problems of economic survival, overcrowding, family tensions, and youth in turmoil. However, the industry and energy of the new immigrants have also revitalized the Chinatowns across the continent.

The Japanese formed the second wave of immigrants from Asia, beginning in the late 1880s. When Chinese immigration was cut off, Western agriculturists turned to Japan for cheap labor. Most Japanese immigrants were impoverished farmers or young unmarried males wishing to make their fortunes in North America. Like the Chinese immigrants, the Japanese also worked in railroad construction, lumbering, and fishing. They later moved into service trades and small businesses. With their hard work, they presented serious competition, and their success angered many North Americans. Anti-Japanese legislation followed, such as exclusion from further immigration, denial of land ownership, and segregation of schoolchildren. In response to hostility and discrimination, the Japanese found protection and mutual support in "Little Tokyos," ethnic enclaves similar to Chinatowns. They formed their own unions and social organizations, such as the Japanese American Citizens League (founded in 1930), to combat anti-Japanese acts. Following the Japanese attack on Pearl Harbor, the war hysteria led to the forced removal and internment of about 110,000 Japanese (two-thirds of whom were U.S. or Canadian citizens) in concentration camps. After World War II, attitudes toward the Japanese changed. Today the 700,000 Japanese North Americans are among the most acculturated of all Asians in terms of North American values and lifestyles.

The first Koreans to reach the United States were students and political refugees in the 1880s. Large-scale immigration, mostly of poor farmers, began in 1903 to Hawaiian sugar plantations. In 1905 the Korean government ended further emigration upon learning of harsh working conditions in Hawaii. Thereafter, until 1965, a small number of picture brides, students, and political exiles were admitted. After the quota system was abolished in 1965, immigration from Korea again increased. In 1989 there were 500,000 Koreans living in the United States and Canada. Among them were some 5,000 Korean orphans adopted by American families and nearly 30,000 Korean wives of American servicemen.

Filipino immigration in many respects has paralleled the Chinese and Japanese immigration. Early Filipino immigrants were mostly young men needed to replenish the labor force after the Japanese were excluded in 1924. They worked in seasonal agriculture in California and in salmon canneries in the Northwest and Alaska. They, too, faced racial discrimination through laws forbidding land ownership, the banning of interracial marriages, and imposition of an immigration quota of only 50 per year after 1935. They were frequently refused service in restaurants and barbershops, barred from swimming pools and movies, and forced to live in slum areas. Since 1965, when quotas were lifted, the Philippines has led all other nations except Mexico in immigration. Between 1960 and 1970, the Filipino American population increased from 176,000 to 343,000. By 1980 there were 775,000, surpassing the Japanese, and following the Chinese, as the second-largest Asian American group.

Southeast Asians are the most recent group to arrive in North America. They consist mainly of Cambodian, Laotian, and Vietnamese refugees who fled from South Vietnam in 1975 when it finally fell to the Communists after a drawn-out war. About 150,000 refugees were admitted initially, and the exodus has continued. By 1980 an estimated 200,000 or more Southeast Asian refugees were settled throughout the United States, with concentrations in California, Texas, New York, and Pennsylvania. The refugees were mainly young, and many arrived in family groups. Since their arrival, the Southeast Asian refugees have formed more than one hundred ethnic organizations offering job placement, English-language training, recreation, and other forms of mutual aid and support. Like other Asian immigrants before them, Southeast Asian Americans, faced with the harsh reality of prejudice and discrimination, have relied heavily on ethnic-group solidarity and self-help for their survival.

Ethnocentrism and Racism in North America

Racism typically takes the form of a claim that some human races are superior to others, and it was a prevalent ideology in Europe and America in the late nineteenth and early twentieth centuries. Racist theories advanced by Arthur de Gobineau and Houston Stewart Chamberlain insisted that supreme among the races were members of the mythical Nordic, or Aryan, race. For example, Nazi Germany under Adolf Hitler based its extermination of millions of Jews and other "non-Aryans" on this theory of race supremacy and the corollary concept of racial purity. Racism, such as we all experience in a multiracial, multicultural society like ours, including "reverse discrimination" (minority discrimination against the majority), is perceived as being most detrimental to the dignity and integrity of personhood and community, and therefore the most imperative to overcome. It is this task to which education through the Christ, Culture, and Community Project is dedicated.

Most scientists and researchers reject any scientific basis for racist theories. According to sociologists, race is a socially defined term, and the definition differs from society to society. That is, the social significance of race is limited to what people make of it: a society is racist to the extent that its members draw unwarranted conclusions from the physical differences between peoples.[22] The Chinese Exclusion Acts are an example. The U.S. Congress passed these laws in 1882, 1892, and 1902 to prevent Chinese immigration after large numbers of Chinese persons came to the West Coast following the discovery of gold in California (1848) and during the construction of the Central Pacific Railroad (1864–69).[23] This was done in violation of the Burlingame Treaty (1868), which was supposed to formally protect the right of the Chinese to immigrate to the United States. But economic competition resulting from the influx of the Chinese laborers aroused anti-Chinese agitation, which intensified during the depression of the 1870s and culminated in anti-Chinese riots in San Francisco in 1877. In 1879, Congress passed a law severely restricting Chinese immigration, but the act was vetoed by President Rutherford B. Hayes. In 1892, Congress extended the exclusion for ten more years, and in 1902 the prohibition was passed again without a terminal date. These laws were repealed in 1943, when China was an ally to the United States in World War II. But a quota of 105 immigrants a year severely restricted Chinese immigration until the implementation of much-liberalized rules under a 1965 amendment to the Immigration and Nationalization Act.

As we have discussed briefly, historically, racism has accompanied colonialism, slavery, and other forms of exploitation and gross inequality. The Los Angeles riots showed a more complicated and mixed pattern of race and class conflict. The minority status was characterized not only by ethnicity or racial origin, but also by social and economic class. Gross social and economic inequality in society have led to conflict. Powerless classes that felt threatened by social and economic instability have blamed other powerless classes for their predicament. The insecure white working class and lower-middle-class people of industrial societies, for example, often have expressed racist attitudes toward ethnic and economic minorities such as poor and powerless blacks and Asians.

Racism and classism add to culture shock,[24] from which all Asian North Americans, including second and subsequent generations, suffer. These "diseases" can be traced to ethnocentrism and colonialism. Social scientists use the term culture shock to denote the feeling of depression, often expressed as homesickness, caused by living in a foreign and hostile environment.

Researchers say that when recognized as such, this homesickness passes. But how long before it passes for the Asian North Americans? And what will it take for Asian North American sojourners to find "home"?

Questions for Reflection and Discussion

How do Asian North Americans cope and survive in North America?

1. How can Asian North Americans form a sense of identity, dignity, and integrity?

2. Who are we as Asian North American Christians and Asian North American congregations?

3. What does it mean for us to be "on the Way" ("on the Tao")?

Notes

1. Jordan Bonfante and Sylvester Monroe, "Unhealed Wounds," *Time*, April, 1993, 28.

2. Seema Sirohi, "No More U.S. Lectures," *Los Angeles Times*, April 25, 1992.

3. In the process of culture change, certain prejudices that change more slowly than others tend to persist in a society even after more efficient or rational elements have been developed to replace them. See Edward T. Hall, *Beyond Culture* (Garden City, New York: Anchor Press, 1976).

4. Roy I. Sano, "The Emerging Pacific Basin and Its Implications: Reflection on Training and Action," *Occasional Papers*, 1, no. 18, March 26, 1978.

5. For violent acts against Asian Americans, see *Recent Activities Against Citizens and Residents of Asian Descent*, U.S. Commission on Civil Rights, Clearing House Publication, no. 88, 1986.

6. See, for example, Robert E. Speer, *Missions and Politics in Asia* (New York: Fleming H. Revell Co., 1898); Stephen Neill, *Colonialism and Christian Missions* (New York: McGraw-Hill Book Co., 1966); W. E. Soothill, *A Typical Mission in China* (New York: Fleming H. Revell Co., 1906); Marta Sordi, *The Christians and the*

Roman Empire, trans. Annabel Bedini (Norman, Okla: University of Oklahoma Press, 1986).

7. Speer, *Missions and Politics in Asia.*

8. An influential advocate of mercantilism was Jean Baptiste Colbert, who directed French economic policies under Louis XIV. Great Britain also followed mercantilist policies; they were embodied in the Navigation Acts of the seventeenth century, which were intended to expand British shipping and exports at the expense of Dutch preeminence in international trade. Mercantilist thinking was based on the assumption that the volume of trade was limited and that countries could expand their trade only at the expense of others. Eli F. Heckscher, *Mercantilism*, trans. Mendel Shapiro: Authorized Translation (London: Allen & Unwin, 1935, reprint 1955).

9. Samuel Hugh Moffett, *A History of Christianity in Asia*, vol. 1 (San Francisco: Harper, 1992), 288.

10. Moffett mentions that Columbus carried a "letter of credence" from Ferdinand and Isabella for presentation to "the Great Cam [Khan]." Ibid., 447.

11. Kenneth S. Latourette, *A History of Christianity*, vol. 1 (New York: Harper and Row, Publishers, 1975 [1953]), 413.

12. Speer, *Missions and Politics in Asia*, 121–70.

13. Charles Verlinden, *The Beginnings of Modern Colonization* (Ithaca, N.Y.: Cornell University Press, 1970).

14. Latourette, *A History of Christianity*, vol. 2, 924.

15. Peter Ward Fay, *The Opium War, 1840–1842: Barbarians in the Celestial Empire in the Early Part of the Nineteenth Century and the War by which They Forced Her Gates Ajar* (Chapel Hill: University of North Carolina Press, 1975).

16. K. Rafferty, *City on the Rocks: Hong Kong's Uncertain Future* (New York: Viking, 1990).

17. John K. Fairbank, *The Great Chinese Revolution* (New York: Harper and Row, Publishers, 1986).

18. F. C. Darling, *The Westernization of Asia: A Comparative Political Analysis* (Boston: G. K. Hall, 1979).

19. Francis L. K. Hsu, *The Challenge of the American Dream: The Chinese in the United States* (Belmont, Calif.: Wadsworth Publishing Co.,1971); Ronald Takaki, *Strangers from a Different Shore: A History of Asian Americans* (Boston: Little, Brown, 1989).

20. Betty Lee Sung, *Mountain of Gold: The Story of the Chinese in America* (New York: Macmillan, 1967).

21. Vernon Reynolds et al., eds., *The Sociobiology of Ethnocentrism:*

Evolutionary Dimensions of Xenophobia, Discrimination, Racism, and Nationalism (Athens, Ga.: University of Georgia Press, 1987).

22. Michael P. Banton, *Racial Theories* (New York: Cambridge University Press, 1987).

23. Sung, *Mountain of Gold*.

24. Philip K. Bock, comp., *Culture Shock: A Reader in Modern Cultural Anthropology* (New York: Knopf, 1970).

CHAPTER 2

The Central Issue of Community: An Example of Asian North American Theology on the Way

By Heup Young Kim and David Ng

Introduction

Asian North Americans define individual personal identity in relation to other persons, notably to those sharing family ties. Personal attitudes are formed and decisions are made with the community in mind. One does not live for self alone and one's actions are always gauged by their effect on the community. To be a person is to be in community.

This chapter is written by Heup Young Kim, a professor of theology at Kangnam University near Seoul, who is a Confucian scholar, and David Ng, a seminary professor of Christian education whose lifework has dealt with helping the Christian church achieve community. Together they claim that community is woven into the fabric of Asian North Americans; the threads are primarily Confucian but include the multiple strands of Taoist, Buddhist, and various native religions and spiritual inclinations.

Asian perceptions and practices of community brought into the Christian church can resonate harmoniously with the Christian New Testament concept of koinonia, the community formed by Jesus Christ. Asian North American congregations have insights into the profundity of community; they can call

*their Western brothers and sisters in the church to a renewal
of their sense of being the church, the koinonia of Christ.*

The Issue of Community

One of the writers of this chapter was doing research at
the Chinese University of Hong Kong. To obtain a library
pass, he had to get the signature of the head of the department in his subject area—in this case, Dr. Allan Chan, head
of the Religion Department. Dr. Chan readily signed the
library pass and in a friendly tone asked the writer the
purpose of his studies at the university. "I am looking at
Chinese and Confucian understandings of community, and I
hope to compare this with Christian understandings of community." Immediately and spontaneously, Dr. Chan stated,
"But there is no Chinese term for community."

What is community and how is it practiced? At stake is the
very nature of the church: is it a gathering of individuals, or
does community mean something more? A sketch of Asian
understandings of community may provide helpful clues for
understanding community in the church.

Asian Ways of Spiritual Pluralism

Asian understandings of community begin within a framework of the pluralism of Asian religions and philosophies. In
China, artifacts such as oracle bones, going back six and more
thousands of years, testify to the practice of religion in Asian
communities. The ancient religions may seem primitive by
comparison to religious practice today, but they do point to
Asians as people who long ago had a sense of the transcen-
dent and who sought to relate to the world and to the Spirit
or spirits beyond the human spirit. In Korea shaman practices testified to a concern for the spiritual in the religious
sensibilities of the Korean people. Shamans were those
thought to have the gift of human communication with the
spirits. The practice of Shinto reflected Japanese religious
and spiritual sensibilities, relating all Japanese to a single

origin. Five centuries before Jesus, the teachings of Confucius established an ethical-philosophical approach to social relationships. About the same time, Lao Tzu helped bring into order the people's sense of the cosmos as a unity, a world that is holistic, balanced, and harmonious. The most famous expressions of this sense of cosmic unity, *tai chi* and *yin-yang*, symbolize how most Chinese, Korean, Japanese, and many Vietnamese persons think the world operates.

To the mix of religious, philosophical, and ethical ideas and beliefs briefly mentioned can be added those of Buddhism, a religion from India that traversed Vietnam and China and found its way to Korea and Japan. The specific teachings of Buddhism are detailed and historically complex, but it can be said that Buddhist spirituality greatly influenced most Asians whether or not they became adherents of that religion. Many Asians accept the notions that life involves suffering and that suffering must be overcome by denying material cravings and becoming wholly spiritual. This general sense informs the way many Asians deal with life. Who can enable humans to overcome materialism, suffering, and evil? Are there spiritual beings or deities who can intercede for us imperfect human beings? In the realm of cultural life, the influence of Zen Buddhism can be seen in the aesthetic sense of Japanese people: the simplicity and emphasis on nature that are found in Japanese art, landscaping, architecture, and poetry.

The details of Asian religions are beyond the purpose of this chapter, but it can be said that Asian North Americans— particularly persons of Chinese, Korean, Japanese, and Vietnamese heritage—practice a pluralistic approach to life, religion, philosophy, and social ethics. They tend to accept a variety of spiritual ideas, religious teachings, and moral practices that "make sense." Rather than limiting oneself to the strict boundaries of a specific religion, many Asians are open to ideas that seem useful and can be incorporated into one's existing cluster of beliefs. Being religious does not necessarily imply membership in a particular religious insti-

tution or the profession of a certain system of theology. A great
number of Asian North American Christians can tell of their
parents who observe basic Buddhist religious practices but
also have a world-view that is Taoist and behave according
to Confucian social principles and rites. In the case of parents
who are Chinese, for example, the New Year celebrations are
a wondrous amalgam of native ancestral spirit worship,
Buddhist prayers, Confucian family relationships, and Taoist expressions of the harmony and rhythms of life. Perhaps
a way to describe such Asian religious pluralism is to consider
that it is practical and even prudent to "cover all the possibilities" by including any practices that might enrich life and
bring about release from suffering and salvation for one's
soul. To an Asian, syncretism, or the incorporating of new or
outside elements into one's beliefs, is both positive and creative. It is not heresy.

A simple explanation of the Asian way is to consider the
circular symbols of *tai chi* and *yin-yang*. These symbols depict
very well the Asian outlook of the wholeness and unity of life,
wherein all things coexist in harmony and balance. The basic
elements of life are vitalized by the cosmic life force and
function interdependently. Day and night together make up
a full day; male and female make up a social relationship;
good and bad, suffering and joy, and life and death exist in
balance in one's life. Even so, religion/life/ethics/spirituality
(how can these be considered separately and without relationship to each other?) combine to make up a full life. This is
Tao, "the Way." This is life.

So theology, or the systematic statement of one's faith or
beliefs, is not necessarily a natural activity for Asians. One's
"system" of beliefs is always open to change, as new sensible
ideas are encountered. Faith or beliefs are not static; they are
not established in final form so long as there is life and the
possibility of new experiences and new learnings. It can be
said again and again that for Asians, life is "the Way."

Before dealing with the East Asian, Confucian sense of
community, a bit more setting of the framework may be

helpful. The main basis of Chinese, Korean, and Japanese social relationships and ethical practice is Confucian. The same could be said for most Vietnamese persons. However, ask those whose heritage or place of birth is one of these countries and they may offer puzzled looks and say that they have never studied Confucius's writings and do not claim to be Confucian. It is true that few Asians today have studied the Confucian classics or can readily recite the Confucian Virtues, also known as the Four (or is it Five?) Human Relationships. (It is Five.) Yet, listening to Asians and watching what they do, one can detect a framework of Confucian teachings in the lives of most Chinese, Korean, Japanese, and Vietnamese Asians. Handed down from generation to generation, family to family, parent to child are attitudes, behaviors, and values that are essentially Confucian. The sense of loyalty to the family is universally taught in such Asian families whether or not credit is given to Confucius as the one who taught such a virtue. Filial piety is another such universal teaching. In many families filial piety is rigidly enforced and the oldest son has very clear obligations he must follow and rituals he must practice to honor, respect, and even worship his father in life and especially in death. Funeral practices are expressly detailed in terms of rituals done over definite periods of time. In other families the obligations are more broadly understood, but the clear expectation is for sons to revere their fathers. The Confucian principles continue to operate however the details are spelled out. Filial piety is much, much more than the rules of behavior of a son toward his father. Filial piety is a practical expression of the way every person is to relate to one's elders with appreciation and respect.

A common assumption is that for Asians and Asian North American immigrants, if they are not the basic life attitude, Confucian social ethics are at least a very, very strong influence on their lives and world-view. Yoon Yee-heum, Professor of Religion at Seoul National University, found through a survey of Korean Christians that 90 percent of them reported

that they hold Confucian moral norms and practice traditional Confucian social customs. That is, these Koreans understood their religious commitment to be to the Christian
religion, but their social and ethical practices reflected Confucian ways (which were not necessarily seen to be of an
institutional religious nature). The Koreans surveyed were
Christian and Confucian at the same time.[2]

The Confucian influence is strong and sometimes pervasive and prevailing regarding Asian and Asian North American first- and second-generation understandings of
community. For example, Confucian ethics or social relationships usually are presented initially in the form of the Five
Virtues:

仁 *(rén)* being humane or benevolent;

義 *(yì)* doing righteousness;

禮 *(lǐ)* acting with propriety or observing rites;

智 *(zhi)* exhibiting wisdom;

信 *(xìn)* being mutually faithful.

Each of these virtues, when practiced properly, requires
the individual to accomplish these in relation to other people,
that is, in community. To be humane or to reach self-fulfillment is to become a person who is benevolent—one whose
actions benefit others. Righteousness, doing the right thing,
is to act justly toward others. Propriety comes from properly
acting out one's principles. In other words, when one's principles are acted on, they become real. The original purpose of
rites was to provide structures and forms for proper actions.
Propriety or right rituals and actions are understood socially;
propriety is performed in public and for the sake of right
relationships. Similarly, wisdom and mutual faithfulness
suggest virtues that an individual accomplishes for the sake
of right relationships or the practice of community. The Five
Virtues are not abstract principles existing for their own
sake; they are done in community and they enhance relationship. To be a good person is to be a person in community
acting for the sake of the community.

Confucian Understandings of Community

Recall the story at the beginning of this section, in which the noted professor of religion, Dr. Chan, spoke to the researcher on Chinese and Confucian understandings of community. Dr. Chan said, "But there is no Chinese term for community." Such a declaration could have scuttled the researcher's project and sent him back to America empty-handed. Fortunately Dr. Chan's explanation and that of numerous other Confucian and Christian scholars in Hong Kong assured the researcher that while there is no specific word in Chinese that directly corresponds with the English word "community," it is possible to learn much from the various ways Chinese characters have been put together to connote community. A tracing of several terms for community is offered in a following section.

Asian thinking, particularly Confucian thinking, does not conceive community in the abstract. When asked to define community, an Asian rather points to concrete examples of community. The most common description is this: "If you want to know what community is, look at a family. Community is a family living and relating together." It might be more grammatically correct to say, "Community *is like* a family." Nevertheless, community is understood through practice, beginning with how roles and relationships are defined by their practice in families. Members of the community that is a family do not choose each other, yet they are bound to each other in loyalty. Each member has roles, and each person's relationship to the others in the family reflects the roles of each individual in that relationship. One who is a mother performs that role in relation to one who is a child, and vice versa. The father is father to each child and to all the children; a son is son to his father. At the same time, the son may be first or elder brother to his siblings. The roles are established and are respected. Relationships depend on the wise and proper fulfillment of each person's roles. Happy is the family in which each member knows his or her roles and relates to the others accordingly. Such a family provides an example of—a definition of—community.

There is family, 家 *(jia)*. What is a larger group of people called? 大家 *(dà jia)*—"big family." A way of expressing "community" is to call such a group "big family."

Asians think of community in terms of family—the embodiment of community, or the "concrete-universal way" of being community. Most Asians understand the family as the practical expression of the concept of community. In a consistent pattern, "community" is practiced or exemplified in larger and larger concentric circles of relationships. Starting as an individual, the person finds self-fulfillment or self-cultivation only in relationship or in community. That relationship first of all is with one's family. The communal relationship then expands to the neighborhood or local community. One belongs to, and is helped to fulfill one's being by participating in, the neighborhood. The next larger communal relationship is with the nation, and finally, with the cosmos. Each concentric circle is an embodiment of the ideal of community. Community is defined by actual practice and relationships.

In Confucian terms, community is created and defined by the actual embodiment of the 禮 *li* (propriety, right practice, right performance of rites) of human relationships (仁 *rén*, humaneness, benevolence). To be in community in the proper ways is to achieve true humanity. It could be said that what Asians know about community is learned by living in community. Community is more than what Asians know; it is what they do.

This practical way of defining community has its risks. The practice of community can become structured to the point of being institutionalized. A static formal structure can replace the dynamic practice of community. Instead of being a family with dynamic and creative relationships, the family members may find themselves caught in a structure in which their actions are codified—made into rules or legalisms. The roles and responsibilities that should make for harmonious communal relationships instead become hierarchies and eventually are oppressive. Many stories can be told of Asian North American families in which roles are set in stone and the father is enthroned as the all-powerful head of the family. In such families it is the women who end up in roles that are second-class. More than a few Asian North American women cannot say anything good about Confucianism because in their situations what should have been dynamic, creative principles of social relationships got legislated into hierarchial structures and oppressive rules.

Another danger arises when the concentric circles of relationships are practiced in self-serving, self-centered ways. Family relationships and family loyalty degenerate into nepotism whereby family members favor each other over people not in the family. Neighborhood relationships and loyalties degenerate into sectionalism or tribalism. At the national level there is self-centered nationalism. At the cosmic level there is an anthropocentrism—a human-centeredness that puts humans in the middle of the universe so that all of life and all natural resources are dominated by human beings and the world is manipulated to serve humans, even to the point of the destruction of the world.

Particularly in the Western world, the anthropogenic or human-nature relationship often is forgotten; human beings forget that they are to be "in community" with creation. Rather than being in partnership with the world and its resources, many modern people seek to dominate the world and exploit it. A person infused with Confucian principles of community would say, "One person goes to the mountain and learns its legends; another goes and only studies its geology."

> "Heaven is my father and earth is my mother, and even such a small creature as I finds an intimate place in their midst. . . . All people are my brothers and sisters, and all things are my companions."
>
> Chang Tsai
> *Western Inscription*[3]

Contemporary Terms for Community

Earlier the story was told about the lack of a term in Chinese for the English term "community." Actually there are today numerous terms that attempt to express in an Asian language what community is. Most of these words are fairly recent constructions that take several Asian characters, each with a traditional meaning, and put them together to form a new meaning.

What impresses is the obvious effort required to construct a term in order to have a way to say "community." Again, we must remember that Asians have always *practiced* community and they know it from experience. But community was so basic, and so much taken for granted, that there did not seem to be a need for such a term. In the *Tao Te Ching* a revealing statement is made: "If you can name Tao, it is already not the true Tao."[4] Similarly, Lao Tzu said, "The Dao that can be expressed is not the eternal Dao. The name that can be named is not the eternal name."[5] For an Asian to define community, he or she would have to "step out of community" to offer an objective definition, perhaps a definition that is possible because one is superior to or has control over what is defined. Such a definition belies reality. Asians tend to avoid "definitive definitions" because they are in a process of learning about life all the time and are reluctant to claim the lofty perspective that would make it possible to state an objective definition. To define something is to separate oneself from that thing. A Confucian Asian would claim that the only community one can know is what one can do, what one can experience. Such community is explained through stories rather than definitions. One can no more define community than one can define riding a bicycle. However, one can tell a story about riding a bicycle. And one can explain what community is by telling stories of one's family. What is community? There is the story of a father who immigrated to North America in order to provide for his family—that is community. Or one could tell of a firstborn son who enters a profession that pleases his parents because the good salary will provide for the rest of the family and for the parents—that, too, is community.

Putting Words Together to Connote Community

Since there is no common term for community, terms had to be made up to convey it, or at least words in Asian languages could be put together to approximate Western concepts of community.

One example is 共同體 (*gòng tóng tǐ*, or in Japanese, *kodata*). When these characters are put together in this combination, the meaning derived is "the embodiment of a common, close-knit togetherness or unity." The connotation is that a community consists of persons who share something in common and are bonded together by that commonality.

A similar term for community is 團結 (*túan jie*), which suggests that community is being together in fellowship.

In the Korean language there is an interesting combination of words that connotes a community bonded together and identified as a unified body: 우리 모임 (*woori moim*, the group of fellowship in a common identification). Two words form this composite noun: (우리 *woori* and 모임 *moim*). 우리, *woori*, is the plural form of the first-person pronoun, equivalent to "we" in English. It is derived from 우리 (*woor-yi*), which means "of the same boundary." 모임 (*Moim*) denotes a gathering or meeting and is derived from 몸 (*mom*), which means body. When all this is combined into the composite noun 우리 모임 (*woori moim*), the meaning that is connoted is "a group of people within the same boundary who identify themselves as one body."

Koreans consider community to be created when a group of people develop mutual trust and a bond over a period of time; such a bond is established when the parties in the group can share certain traditions and can incorporate these traditions into a common world view. Such a group could say "we" and "us" with a great degree of certainty. Whether such a community is a family or an extended family or a group who come together because of shared values, it is evident that the community is not a quick and superficial gathering of people. Such a community has an identity established over a long period of time and after certain traditions are commonly valued. A church fellowship would fit such a description of community.

Two terms often are used to try to express the type of community described in the New Testament, the *koinonia*. To express the covenanting community, one term is 群體 (*qún tǐ*, a close-knit embodiment or close-knit group of people). Another term is a more suggestive statement of what a Christian community or *koinonia* can be: 團契 (*túan qì*, the fellowship characterized by solidarity and mutual responsibility). This term is consistent with Confucian ways of being in community. It provokes people into realizing what Christian community can be. The Christian community need not have a simple "lowest common denominator" approach to community. Instead, Christian community holds together in solidarity. People in the Christian community often disagree with each other, or they may even dislike each other. Whatever the case, the kind of fellowship or community is one in which the members are willing to stand together in solidarity no matter what. The other important aspect of such a community is provoked by the word 契 *(qì)*. 契 *(Qì)* invokes the picture of an Asian family that is totally committed to one another. Within such a faithful, loving community individuals are responsible to each other and also for each other. Community as defined by 團契 *(túan qì)* is one that shares solidarity and responsibility.

The idea that community involves solidarity is emphasized by the term 連帶 (*lían-dài*, mutual faithfulness). Advocated by Korean theologian Yong-Bok Kim, this term implies a priority for mutual faithfulness or solidarity rather than the usual priority for unity. This description of community implies a relational orientation of mutuality with certain persons irrespective of our feelings or ability to get along. Such a community is not based on sentiment, on liking each other, but on being responsible to each other. Such a fidelity can be seen in Asian families in which each member is prepared to stand with every other member and to work for the welfare and well-being of the others. 連帶 *(Lían-dài)* is similar to the Confucian virtue of 信 *(xìn)*, which can also be translated "devotion to each other" or "mutual faithfulness."

This collection of terms used by Japanese, Chinese, and Koreans to try to express "community" instructs in several ways. First, Asians and Asian North Americans so take for granted the concept of community that there is no one, simple, definitive word for it. Community *is*, so to speak! That is, community is present, always has been, and always will be. Furthermore, while certain Asian terms describe the structure of community, implying an association or organization, the terms that are used to speak of community or *koinonia* as it is described in the Bible and in Christian tradition are words that emphasize relationships more so than structures or institutions.

Perhaps the most telling term is 團契 *(túan qì)* , which characterizes community as solidarity and responsibility. This Asian perspective on community differs from other more sentimental versions of what community is. Some cultures and persons in North American society tend to view community with misty eyes, longing for that gathering of people who get along together, like each other, and share in common many character traits, tastes, and habits. A popular notion is that a community is a group of people who get along together happily without serious conflicts or differences. A major Asian perspective on community has a somewhat harder edge of reality to it. Whether or not the members of a community get along together, much less like each other, and whether or not the members are similar or different, they are all members. They may not have chosen to be in the community, but they are in it; they would not necessarily have chosen each other to share membership, but members together they are. The community is much like a family—bonded together for better or for worse and committed to each other forever. Such a community stands in solidarity with each other, is responsible for and to each other, and is mutually faithful to each other and to the community as a whole.

The Church as a Community

The community of solidarity and responsibility is an Asian perspective but also is one that can be found in biblical stories and descriptions of the church. An honest reading of the New Testament, for example, reveals a band of disciples who do not always get along, do not necessarily enjoy each other's company, and do not share common interests and values. What bonds them together is a common calling: they were called into the community of discipleship by Jesus Christ. Most of the letters of Paul to the young churches were occasioned by the need for discipline and correction for these churches, which had disputes, divisions, jealousy, and prejudices. It was all Paul could do to keep these congregations, these communities, alive and involved in the apostle's preaching and teaching, in fellowship and prayer, and in the breaking of bread together. It was not commonality that caused these congregations to be communities, it was something deeper, actually something beyond the group, that held them together. Paul wrote to these congregations to remind them that they were *en Christos*, "in Christ."

The Christian communities were not self-selected societies of like-minded persons; they were persons who were called out from society and called together by Christ and brought into a community different from any other in society. The church is the people of God, who at one time were not a people but through Christ's grace and Christ's call were made a people. The community or bonding relationship that the people experienced was not of their own doing but was a gift of Christ. Christ's grace, redemption, call, and sustaining Spirit are what make the church possible. The church was bonded together in Christ.

Having been called to be the church (that is what *ecclesia* means—the called-out assembly), the church became the church—by being the church! This bit of wordplay suggests that when the people did "churchly things," they became the church. When the church proclaimed Christ's grace and abiding presence by celebrating the sacraments, the church was the church. When it participated in preaching and teaching and in deeds of compassion and service to others, the church was the church. When these people took on the name of Christ, they were the church. At least in a practical, observable sense, the church could be known to be the church when it practiced what Christ called the church to do. It was in the realm of deeds more than in the realm of ideas that the church fulfilled its calling.

Asian North American Christians identify with the image of the church as "the household of God." Just as being in community is like being in a family or "house," being in community for the church is like being "in the household of God." The church is the family of God.

Asian North Americans can see themselves in such a practical church. In their own lives they know what community is because they have practiced being in community, particularly and practically, in families. They can appreciate what a church is when they can observe a church that practices community like a family does.

There are strong parallels between the Asian "way" and biblical "ways." Asians have become communal people by being in community, practicing community in their families, in their neighborhoods, in their nations, and as a part of the cosmos, in communion with all of creation. Biblical community is similar; it is meant to be practiced, to be done. Biblical community includes all sorts of people who might not have chosen each other had they that opportunity. However, because these people are in community, they are committed to one another and show solidarity with and responsibility for and to one another.

Not that Asian North American congregations have "arrived." They are as good and as imperfect as any other congregation. Nor do Asian North Americans hold a monopoly on the meaning and methods of community. African,

Latino, and Native American cultures and congregations are profoundly communal and offer significant examples of how to be in community. Asian North American congregations also have a sense of community and understand themselves to be "on the way" in their practice and perfecting of community. To be in community is to be "on the road," to be "on the *Tao*."

Asian North American congregations invite all the other partners in the church to journey with them. We call upon our sisters and brothers in Christ to join with Christ, who is the way, the truth, and the life.

Questions for Reflection

1. How have you come to know yourself as a "person in community"? Is any of this sense of community derived from Asian religious and cultural roots?

2. In what ways do Asian North American congregations understand and practice community?

3. How would you analyze and critique the Asian North American Christian sense of community?

4. Is the understanding of community as *teen c* (solidarity and responsibility) viable for you? How might this understanding be cultivated within and beyond Asian North American churches?

Notes

1. Choan-Seng Song, *Third-eye Theology,* rev. ed. (Maryknoll, N.Y.: Orbis Books, 1991), 10-11.

2. Yoon Yee-heun, "The Contemporary Situation in Korea," presented at the Conference on Religion and Contemporary Society in Korea; Berkeley, Calif., November 11-12, 1988. Reported in a dissertation by Heup Young Kim, *Sanctification and Self-Cultivation: A Study of Karl Barth and Neo-Confucianism (Wang Yang-Ming),* Graduate Theological Union, Berkeley, Calif., 1992, 7.

3. Chang Tsai, *Western Inscription,* quoted in *Sources of Chinese Tradition,* vol. 1, compiled by William Theodore de Bary, Wing-Sit Chan, and Burton Watson (New York: Columbia University Press, 1960), 49.

4. Lao Tzu, *Tao Te Ching,* poem 1, author's translation.

5. Ibid.

References

Ching, Julia. *Chinese Religions.* Maryknoll, N.Y.: Orbis Books, 1993. A comprehensive, concise introduction to Chinese religious thought and practice.

_____. *Confucianism and Christianity: A Comparative Study.* Tokyo, et al.: Kodansha International, 1978. A critical comparison of how some major themes are perceived.

Covell, Ralph R. *Confucius, the Buddha, and Christ: A History of the Gospel in Chinese.* Maryknoll, N.Y.: Orbis Books, 1986. An analysis of the history of interaction between major religions in China, including modern times.

Jochim, Christian. *Chinese Religions: A Cultural Perspective.* Englewood Cliffs, N.J.: Prentice-Hall, Inc., 1986. A concise, readable introduction.

Kraft, Charles H. *Christianity in Culture: A Study in Dynamic Biblical Theologizing in Cross-Cultural Perspective.* Maryknoll, N.Y.: Orbis Books, 1979. Using a process of "dynamic equivalence" to understand and communicate between various cultures.

Matsuoka, Fumitaka. *Out of Silence: Emerging Themes in Asian American Churches.* Cleveland: United Church Press, 1995. A strenuous lifting up of theological and social issues for Asian North American churches, including the issue of community.

Schreiter, Robert J. *Constructing Local Theologies.* Maryknoll, N.Y.: Orbis Books, 1985. Advocates and shows how local (regional) peoples can develop their own theologies. Deals with syncretism.

Tu, Wei-Ming. *Centrality and Commonality: An Essay on Confucian Religiousness.* Albany, N.Y.: State University of New York Press, 1989. An exposition on "the fiduciary community."

_____. *Confucian Thought: Selfhood as Creative Transformation.* Albany, N.Y.: State University of New York Press, 1985. This and numerous other works by Tu present a contemporary interpretation of Confucianism and its application to modern societies.

CHAPTER 3

The Buena Vista Church Bazaar: A Story within a Story

By Michael Yoshii

Introduction

Michael Yoshii, a Japanese American pastor, tells about an annual church bazaar featuring chicken teriyaki of renowned taste. Behind the story of a church bazaar, however, is the story of a congregation's down-to-earth expressions of its identity and theology. And behind this uncovering of identity and theology is another story of ethnic identity and cultural integrity that is being uncovered and possibly rediscovered and reclaimed.

Embedded in this story within a story is a cultural-theological process that enables Asian North American congregations to name themselves by claiming their heritage and living out their sense of community.

Prelude to the Story

On the third Sunday in May, were you to visit the Buena Vista United Methodist Church in Alameda, California, you would not experience worship in any tradition resembling John Wesley's liturgical sensibility. Instead you might notice the sweet scent of barbecued teriyaki chicken wafting through the air as you approached the church. You would notice children running around the grounds, as if they were in a park instead of at church. You would hear people bustling about in the social hall with the vinegary fragrance of sushi permeating the room. People would be chatting as they put their finishing touches on the culinary fare for the day. Outside the hall, behind the kitchen, a cadre of people would be working together in an assembly line. With laughter and frivolity, they would be scooping out rice and vegetables and packing the hot barbecued chicken into take-out boxes.

A few people acting as couriers would be transporting the chicken from the back of the lot where the scent of the barbecue originated. There, you would see concrete bricks lined up to create a fifty-foot-long barbecue pit. Young men and old would be standing and sitting, watching the charcoal and turning the chickens. Outside, children would be setting up booths for games. Bonsai plants would be spread out on a table, along with empty planters and tools laid out for demonstration. And in the back education room, there would be no Sunday church school for the day. Classrooms would be transformed into arts-and-crafts showrooms where church women would have set up their wares for sale.

The Annual Bazaar at the Buena Vista United Methodist Church is not unlike many church bazaars of other Japanese American Christian churches. Where have these traditions come from? And how do we understand how they function in the life of our communities? Much to my surprise, exploring the history behind our bazaar has been a rich experience. The island community of Alameda is a rich depository of stories of Japanese American life. Alameda is tucked away within the larger metropolitan Bay Area, but the story of our bazaar is connected to the stories of other church communities. Our story also raises important questions for reflection on the role of the bazaar in the life of the Japanese American church.

Roots of the Bazaar: A Doll Festival

In July of 1992 I was asked to participate in the Asian Theology Conference in the Philippines on behalf of the Pacific Asian Center for Theology and Strategies. The theme of the conference was "religious festivals." Each participant was asked to research a specific festival related to his or her religious community. In addition to sociological and historical research, theological reflection on the meaning and function of that event was to be prepared. Serving at the Buena Vista church, the immediate thought was to look at our bazaar tradition.

At a special meeting I asked some of our members about the origin of our bazaar. At first some could not seem to remember exactly when it started. They had been doing it for so long that it seemed like it had been a part of the church forever. Then Katherine Yamawaki recalled that it started in 1959. She based that date on her recollection of the age of her daughter. To my surprise, she said that the first bazaar was actually a Doll Festival, or *Hinamatsuri*. This was the day in Japan when people brought out their doll collections for display. It was associated with Girls Day, celebrated annually in Japan.

George Nakamoto vividly remembered the Doll Festival origins of the bazaar. The dolls were set up in the social hall of the church, along with other displays of Japanese culture, including *Ikenobo* (flower arrangements) and bonsai (dwarfed landscaped trees). Foods were sold as a small fund-raiser, and other activities were organized for children and families. After two years, however, a friend from the Watson-ville Buddhist Temple suggested to George that we try selling chicken teriyaki as a fund-raising item. He said that the Caucasian population particularly liked the chicken, and it was popular at their festival events.

Copying the recipe, and the formula for the barbecue setup, the church began to add chicken teriyaki to the menu the very next year. It soon became such a popular item that by popular demand it became the main food item for the bazaar. At some point in time the Doll Festival was discontinued. No one remembers exactly when or why. The chicken teriyaki was so well liked that other churches in the area also began to replicate the recipe for their own bazaars. To this day the selling of chicken teriyaki is the focus of the bazaar event. Bonsai demonstrations continue, as well as arts and crafts, but the Doll Festival had long faded away.

A Story within a Story

Then for the 1992 bazaar, members were invited to bring doll collections to be put on display. A number of collections were set up in a delightful presentation. Along with some of the dolls, a local newspaper article was brought in. It was about the revival of the Doll Festival in the Towata family in 1950. The article referred to the fact that the family was reviving this display after nine years of dormancy. Marking back from the 1950 date of the article, the last Doll Festival for the family would have been held in 1941, or the year that the United States entered the Pacific War with Japan.

In July, just a few days before I was to leave for the Philippines, Sadie Tajima, one of the Towata sisters, came by the office to show me pictures of the family doll collection. Her daughter had blown up some snapshots of it. She explained that they did not bring out their collection for the bazaar because it was in storage in her garage. Sadie shared with me an amazing story of the family doll collection, which dated back before the war.

The Towata parents spent a great deal of time in San Francisco in the late 1930s. They often attended the Shinto temple, located in the Japantown area. Over a period of time Mrs. Towata began to collect dolls. When her first grandchild, Carol, was born in the late 1930s, they celebrated her birth with the Doll Festival. The family had never celebrated the festival before because in growing up, they had not been able to afford such expensive dolls. The festival was usually celebrated with the birth of a granddaughter. Carol was the first *Sansei* girl born in the Towata family. She was the first granddaughter, giving them the opportunity to celebrate Girls Day and the Doll Festival.

Following the outbreak of the Pacific War came the order for the evacuation of Japanese Americans to internment camps on February 19, 1942. Mr. Towata was taken away by the Federal Bureau of Investigation because of his affiliation with the local Japanese Association, or *kenjinkai.*

The family members were in confusion as to what to do with some of their belongings. They destroyed some of their possessions that associated them with the Japanese. But they decided to keep the dolls. In the basement, they opened a space to store the dolls in hiding. They boarded it up for safekeeping before leaving for the converted horse stalls of Tanforan, California, which would become their temporary home. Friends were enlisted to look after the house. Upon their return from the camps four years later, the dolls were found intact under the house just as they had been stored.

Ironically, during the compilation of these stories, I found out that my sister-in-law's relatives destroyed their family doll collection during this same period of time. The only reminder of the dolls was in a snapshot of her older sister posing with the dolls before their destruction. Similar stories of burned dolls were told to me by others during this research.

A few years after they settled back into Alameda, the Towata family resumed the practice of observing Girls Day. The newspaper article and picture dated in 1950 showed the family displaying the dolls at their home. Children from the local elementary school were invited to come and see the dolls. And later in that decade, the church sponsored its first Doll Festival. According to Sadie, the Towata family dolls were central to that first festival display. The blown up photographs showed the display set up in the educational building much later.

The Newsletter Perspective

In addition to hearing the story of the bazaar's beginnings and the doll collection, there was also information in the church newsletters to review. The way the newsletters portrayed the event was intriguing. Newsletters dated from January to June of 1959 contained numerous announcements regarding the bazaar. But nowhere was there any mention of a Doll Festival or any reference to the Japanese cultural displays. The newsletter announced a bazaar whose intention was to raise money for the purchase of a church car. The bazaar was described as a "carnival" with hot dogs, snow cones, and carnival games for children. *Issei*, it announced, would make some Japanese food and would keep their proceeds for the purchase of their own refrigerator. It seemed the bazaar was many different events in one. Curiously, there was no mention of the Doll Festival.

Questions for Reflection

Several questions emerge from the process of recovering the history of the bazaar.

1. The history of the bazaar:
    a. How did the bazaar begin?
    b. What was the original intent of the bazaar?
    c. What changes evolved over the years?

2. The historical, social, and cultural circumstances:
    a. What were the historical circumstances at the beginning and over the years?
    b. What were the social situations?
    c. What were the cultural situations?

3. Spiritual and religious perspectives:
    a. What Japanese religious perspectives seem to have been included in the bazaar?
    b. How did Confucian perspectives influence the conduct of the bazaar?
    c. What Christian theological perspectives seem to have been expressed?

4. Functions of the bazaar today:
    a. What seems to be the function of the bazaar today?
    b. How does the bazaar affect community life in the congregation today?

5. Christian theological implications today:

    a. How does the bazaar reflect Christian perspectives on community?

    b. How does the bazaar reflect Christian perspectives on cultural values?

    c. How does the bazaar reflect Christian perspectives on the presence of God in the lives of people?

    d. How might festivals in the church teach Christian values?

The story of the bazaar raises these questions. What follows continues the report of the changing place of the bazaar in the life of this Japanese American congregation and reflections on what the bazaar can mean to the people.

The Original Intent of the Bazaar: A Cultural Celebration

Looking back at the origins of the bazaar from the stories of the church members, it appears that the original bazaar was primarily a cultural event. The first bazaar was a Doll Festival, or *Hinamatsuri,* which was celebrated by the church community. But as mentioned, the church newsletter seems to avoid any reference to Doll Festival or *Hinamatsuri.*

Ambivalence over a "cultural festival" at the church is not surprising. The Christian church has long struggled with the role of native cultural practices within its own activities. But, although the Doll Festival did have connections to the Shinto religion, it was not seen as a religious festival but more as a family-oriented custom.

Cultural Background of Hinamatsuri

The roots of *Hinamatsuri* date back to a mixture of traditions and rituals celebrated on the third day of the third lunar month in the Heian Era in Japan (794–1192). By 1770 *Hinamatsuri* had evolved into a national holiday in Japan associated with the imperial palace, where a day was designated for dolls to be displayed. Although the holiday status was removed in 1874, the custom gradually gained popularity not just among nobility but among the general population. It has continued as a cultural custom where families and daughters, schools and public offices display doll sets for the day.

Hinamatsuri and Girls Day also evolved from a cultural framework that both celebrates and designates the place of the girls within their family units. The way in which the custom evolved during the Meiji Era of Japan reflected a notion of social order and hierarchy inherent in Confucian values. In fact, these Confucian influences, combined with Shinto and Buddhist religious beliefs, formed the basis for much of Meiji Era Japanese culture.

The Meaning of Hinamatsuri *in America*

As mentioned earlier, many Japanese American families in the early times of their settlement in the United States did not have easy access to the dolls for both economic and logistical reasons. The possibility of celebrating *Hinamatsuri* took place in the Towata family as the grandmother began to collect dolls from Japantown. The celebration of *Hinamatsuri* could only be fulfilled when the first granddaughter was born. The Doll Festival was a way to be connected to the Old World of Japan that the grandmother had left. At the same time, it was a way to pass on some of that world to a new generation as they celebrated the birth of new life in America.

The Towata family began to celebrate the Doll Festival in a new world, away from the social reinforcement that Japan would provide. It must have been difficult to celebrate a cultural custom of a people who were seen to be the enemy by the majority of American society. But when others were destroying their Japanese articles, the Towata family saved their doll collection. It endured the bitter years of war and remains as a living witness to their history.

When families decided to have a Doll Festival at the church, it was a significant community statement, considering the ambivalence they must have had as Japanese Americans.

Particularly in Alameda, which had now been established as a military town with a naval base, it must have been difficult to wear one's cultural pride on one's sleeve. As a celebration sponsored by the Christian church, it also must have been a bold statement of cultural affirmation at a time when this was not yet a popular sentiment.

Perhaps the church newsletter reflects some of the ambiguity, as the description depicts a more Americanized event in the form of a "carnival" with snow cones and hot dogs rather than the cultural festival that it was based upon. After all, the newsletter went out to the mainstream community and to the denominational offices. It was not until the next decade of the 1960s that cultural identity and ethnic empowerment came to be embraced by some denominational leaders.

Whether affirmed by others or not, the development of the observance of *Hinamatsuri* by these members expressed a clear need to have some connection to the traditions of the motherland while establishing some basis for new life in America. The relationship between the festival and the understanding of faith is a question to explore next.

Cultural Festival and Spirituality

Those with whom I talked made no overt connection between the holding of a Doll Festival and their understanding of Christian faith and spirituality. That is, most people just saw it as a cultural event. It had nothing overtly to do with the Christian faith except for the fact that the congregation was Japanese and it was logical that its members would celebrate cultural customs that were part of their lives. Sadie remembers one person who objected to the practice of Japanese dancing at the church because it was associated with the Buddhist *Obon* tradition (a festival for the Day of the Dead). But with the Doll Festival, she could not recall any objection or question around its relevance or irrelevance to the Christian faith.

Theologian Paul Tillich popularized the notion that

"culture is the form of religion," and "religion is the substance of culture" (1963). If so, then any cultural practices reflect some kind of spiritual perspective. Cultural festivals are a form by which spiritual values are expressed. What values were expressed in the Doll Festival, and what values continue to be expressed in the continuing bazaar event?

Culture, Women's Roles, Family, Social Structure

One value expressed in the celebration of the Doll Festival has to do with family structure and social harmony. This festival specifically focuses on the girls in the family. It implies a relationship between the grandmother and granddaughter. There is a sense of the continuity of life between the generations of women. In the ritual of the festival, both the life of the old and the life of the new are honored.

The doll display also has other implications for family structure and social order. The display reflects the sense of social structure inherent in the Imperial Court and royal family. The doll display also reflects Japanese race mythology and social hierarchy, which developed in the Meiji Era. The desire for national unity led to the incorporation of Shinto belief systems and Confucian values into this new cultural myth.

The festival was a way of symbolizing the role of the girl in a larger social hierarchy. The practice served to ritually reinforce that social hierarchy and sense of social harmony. If culture is the form of religion, then this cultural tradition certainly reflected the spiritual ethos of Meiji Era Japan. It reflected an image of cosmic harmony, but one that also included a social hierarchy.

Feminist critiques would question the validity of that social order and the place of women in Japanese society. The subordinate role of women in Japanese society is questioned today in Japan and to some extent has been transformed in Japanese American life. A great number of

Japanese American women born and raised in the United States, with values of women's equality, have a much different view of their role within the family, community, and society.

They also continue to struggle with what it means to be a Japanese American woman. What traditional values do they seek to retain from Japanese cultural tradition? What values do they seek to relinquish in embracing a North American identity? How do they choose to express themselves as minority women in the dominant society? The dolls reflect a cultural tradition of an old Japan. How might their meaning be transformed for a community of Japanese Americans that has undergone changes in cultural identity? What are the spiritual values that would be reflective of Japanese American women today? How might they be expressed in the Doll Festival tradition? These questions are prompted as we seek to understand the relationship between cultural festival and faith as they relate to family, women's roles, and social structures. Social structures also involve the next question of community.

Culture, Community, and Spirituality

Although the emphasis for the Doll Festival is on the girls for this one day, we might observe that this festival reflects a common spiritual value of all festivals of Japan. That is the coming together of people for work and play as a community, in acknowledgment of a greater source of life than our own individuality.

The notion of community in Confucian-based cultures was presented in an earlier chapter in this book. Confucian notions of community are not abstract but understood through practice both in family and community. An event such as the Doll Festival gives the community an opportunity to emphasize family as well as to operate in practice as a community for the day. And even as the practice of living in a family is a reflection of the cosmic order of reality, so, too, living in community is a reflection of a larger spiritual reality. In the festival event, we find a collective expression of spirituality.

Developmental Changes in the Bazaar

It is interesting to note that within a matter of two years or so the Doll Festival disappeared from the bazaar festivity. The central focus today is upon the selling of chicken teriyaki. One of the reasons a member gave for the disappearance of the Doll Festival was that young children were not interested in that aspect of the culture. They were more interested in setting up game booths and having fun with the more carnival-like activities. The other pragmatic change in focus was that as the sales for chicken teriyaki began to increase, the work also began to increase. There was less time to prepare for a Doll Festival. Into the 1960s the bazaar was a well-established tradition for the church. The church was thriving with a new generation of *Sansei* children. The bazaar has continued for a number of years. It would be fascinating to find out how people understood the purpose behind the bazaar as time went on. It seems as if it began to take on the function of fund-raiser. But somehow the community-participation aspect of the bazaar seems to have continued through the years. In reflecting upon cultural and religious festivals, particularly in Asian North American congregations, a common issue to confront is the balance between the economic aspect of an event as compared to the value emphasis. Over the years, the bazaar has continued to provide the community with a special festivity that has also served as a primary fund-raiser for the church.

Twenty years after the beginning of the bazaar, many members had grown up, moved away, and were not actively a part of the church. The image of the bazaar was that of an annual fund-raiser that was needed to meet the budget of the church. The bazaar was still a time for the young people to come back and help out at the church. Many would come from miles away to assist on bazaar day. The planning and bulk of the work, though, continued to rest with the older *Nisei* members of the congregation. There was talk of discontinuing the bazaar because it was getting more difficult each year to carry on the work. A *Sansei*, Mark Koike, who returned to the church volunteered to take over as chairperson of the bazaar in 1990. Marshaling the energy of younger and new members while drawing upon the experience and tradition from the elders, he has been able to renew the spirit behind the annual bazaar. Through his leadership we are now beginning also to rethink the role of the bazaar in the life of the church.

Theological Reflections on the Role of the Bazaar

Syncretism and Interreligious Experience

Archie Lee, a professor of religion in Hong Kong, pointed out during the Seminar on Asian Theology that the Christian faith is syncretistic. Its own history of festival events was the result of political and social factors that shaped the understanding of faith. Jewish faith blended its ritual and festival from Canaanite origins, and later Christian ritual and festival did likewise, built upon Jewish traditions. We are familiar with how Christmas is a compilation of many diverse cultural traditions. Because culture and religion intersect one another, we can see such syncretism reflected in the tradition of our bazaar. The Doll Festival, which gave birth to the bazaar, had roots in Japanese culture shaped very much by Confucian, Shinto, and Buddhist belief systems. It would be difficult to be Japanese American and not have some Confucian, Shinto, and Buddhist influence in oneself.

On another level, Japanese Americans also have had the social necessity to embrace interfaith experience because of their sociopolitical history. Although some segments of the Japanese American Christian community may have been taught not to associate with Buddhists, the social reality of the internment camps of 1942 changed that. Buddhists and

Christians were forced to live together in camps and for better or worse to try to work together toward common goals. The relational bonds between Japanese Christians and Buddhists are unique stories in each particular community. In the case of the Alameda bazaar, it was a member of the Buddhist temple in Watsonville who gave the Methodist church the idea of the chicken teriyaki. Mutual support was common among the Buddhists and Christians striving for survival in a postwar anti-Japan society in North America.

Theologically what can we say about how God was working with the people of different faiths? The people's experience often was that God was there for them in the acts of kindness and mutual support that cut across the boundaries of religious institutions. The mutual support between Buddhist and Christian communities in such events as bazaars demonstrates the history of interfaith collaboration and activity. Do we have here a model for interfaith discussion today among new faith communities?

History, Theology, and Spirituality

Can we also say that God is present where life is being affirmed and cultivated? The revival of the Doll Festival was such a cultivation of community life in a time when the affirmation of cultural identity was very important. Its historical significance is equally important from a theological and spiritual perspective.

I recall when I testified for the congressional hearings studying the wartime evacuation of Japanese Americans in 1981. It was a significant spiritual experience. The regional hearings were held in San Francisco. That event was the first occasion for me to hear people talking in the context of community about the World War II camp experience. In their testimonies people expressed long-suppressed anger and bitterness. Many also wept tears of unhealed wounds. My own testimony was filled with anger and a sense that the past acts of the government had an impact on our community in adverse ways far beyond the legal violation of civil rights.

As I left the building that day, I felt a tremendous feeling of God being with us. A veil was being lifted and we were walking into a different corridor of human life. At the time, I had no formal connection with an institutional church. This was prior to my seminary education. An issue I was struggling with was my understanding of Christian spirituality in the context of my cultural and ethnic identity. As I walked out of the building feeling this sense of spiritual empowerment, I made a realization. It struck me that the Christian faith was a historical one. It was a faith that spoke of God's coming into the life of human history. It was a faith in which God was *incarnate* in the world. Jesus was God incarnate. And salvation was a process of liberation. But it was a communal process, not just an individual one. And it was bound by our historical being. Christianity was an incarnate and historical faith because Jesus was a historical person, fully enfleshed, fully incarnate. Not to discount other spiritual perspectives, the Christian perspective seemed to speak to me at that moment because at its core it was not a faith of otherworldliness but of this world and of our evolving history.

As I have ministered in the context of the local church, I have found the continual uncovering of stories of Japanese American community life to be a liberating experience. When Jesus said, "I am the way, the truth, and the life," he might also have been saying that when we are on the way, Jesus is our companion. We will find the truth, and also the fullness of life. Or, where the truth is found, so also will we find life, and our place on the way. When we meander both as individuals and as communities of people without the truth in front of us, we are often not living in the fullness of life. Our spiritual path has become crooked. How can Japanese Americans be fully empowered without knowledge of our history? As we continue to uncover stories of the past, we are freeing ourselves to the way, the life, and the truth.

Bazaar as a Japanese American Passover

The story of the Towata dolls is significant because in addition to being part of the origin of the bazaar, the dolls also symbolically contain the history of an important episode in the life of Japanese Americans in the Alameda community. They represent the beginning of the bazaar, but they are also a window into the past life of the evacuation and prewar times. They are witnesses to living history for this community.

In biblical tradition, festivals had a storytelling function. The Feast of Passover was a pilgrim event in which the diaspora gathered to recall the story of being spared by God. It was a time to remember the history of the Jews and the oppression that they encountered along the way. The Hebrew faith was bound to its history as a people. To be a person of faith was also to be part of that history. In the foods that were eaten, the story was symbolically told and retold to new generations of the faithful.

From a theological frame of reference, our bazaars can be a fund-raising event or a cultural time of festivity. They also can be teaching events that share the story of a community's past. They can be times when the lessons of human experience are passed on from one generation to another. Looking at the origins of our bazaar, we see a reservoir of living history. Like the Feast of Passover, it is a time of community renewal, a time of remembrance of the common story, a time to honor those who passed on in the faith, and a time for celebration.

From Passover to Eucharist: The "Chicken of God"

Lest we get ourselves stuck in self-serving preservation of "racial identity" and community history, it is good for us to remember that the Passover was transformed into the Eucharist. As Jesus shared the meal with the disciples for the last time, he was *in deed* evoking through the meal the shared history of the oppression of Jews. The words of institution (1 Corinthians 11:23-26) revealed later give us the meaning that in remembrance of Jesus, we would eat with him and in so doing also remember the history of struggle. The church was a community of "memory," or *anamnesis*, as opposed to a community of *amnesia*, or forgotten history.

Jesus was the "Lamb of God" who, like the ritual lamb, was slaughtered, shedding the blood that continued to be a marker for the story of the people.

Jesus, however, ate the holy meal with the outcasts of that society. He did not eat only with those who claimed the purity of the Jewish faith. He ate with those who were marginalized from the embrace of God. As Jesus' life and deeds pointed to a transformation of the exclusive religious piety of the time, his death upon the cross also transformed their particular sense of history into a shared history with all others who suffer, are oppressed, and seek to find communion within the domain of God's world. The resurrection appearances of Jesus often coincided with the sharing of a meal. It was these appearances that began to create a new people.

A theology that proposes a Japanese American Passover Festival searches for a place in which our memory and history are reclaimed. This theology must also proclaim the "anamnestic solidarity" with the memory and history of all others who have or still struggle today. In this way we are empowered to share our truth and life of spiritual liberation with others who also seek the Way.

As the reflection for this paper developed, I began to see with new eyes the activities leading up to the bazaar. On the day before the bazaar, men and women customarily come together and prepare the chickens. Waking before dawn on the morning of the bazaar, men gather to prepare the barbecue pits and then go through their annual ritual of cooking the chickens to be served later that day. The aroma of chicken teriyaki fills the air, and the time for celebration soon arrives. Families begin their annual pilgrimage to the church community, both from nearby neighborhoods and faraway stretches of highway. The sacrifice of the chickens and the ritual cooking is completed, and the feasting begins. People of various backgrounds gather in reaffirmation of who they are in community together. People gather at a place, the church, which also tells a continuing story of those who have come before them. The spirits of the survivors and the saints who have gone on are with us on this day of communion and retelling of the stories.

In the retelling of the stories of the people of this community, we hear the voice of Jesus, the Spirit of truth. He has been the companion of people on their sojourn across the Pacific Ocean. He has been with them in their struggles against racism and bleak economic conditions. He has been alongside them in their exodus and liberation experiences. In their faces he has lived and died with them.

Jesus witnesses to the meaning of their lives and the sacrifices of their lives. Because of their lives others may now live in the newness of life. In the gathering of the people, the Spirit of Christ will remind us that life is born of sacrifice. But in our story the sacrificial Spirit of Christ is not the "Lamb of God," but, of course, the "Chicken of God."

As people gather to eat their chicken teriyaki lunches, through the eating and the fellowship, in the festivity and the storytelling, the Spirit of the community of the faithful will be remembered as a new community is born.

References

Bausch, William J. *Storytelling: Imagination and Faith.* Mystic, Conn.: Twenty-Third Publications, 1984.

Cox, Harvey. *The Feast of Fools: A Theological Essay on Festivity and Fantasy.* Cambridge, Mass.: Harvard University Press, 1969.

Elizondo, Virgilio P. *Christianity and Culture: An Introduction to Pastoral Theology and Ministry for the Bicultural Community.* Huntington, Ind.:Our Sunday Visitor, Inc., 1975.

Nelson, Gertrud Mueller. *To Dance with God: Family Ritual and Community Celebration.* New York: Paulist Press, 1986.

Schreiter, Robert J. *Constructing Local Theologies.* Maryknoll, N.Y.: Orbis Books, 1985.

Takenaka, Masao. *God Is Rice: Asian Culture and Christian Faith.* Geneva: World Council of Churches, 1986.

Tilley, Terrence W. *Story Theology.* Wilmington, Del.: Michael Glazier, 1985.

Tillich, Paul. *Systematic Theology.* Vol. 3. Chicago: University of Chicago Press, 1963.

Westerhoff, John H., and Gwen Kennedy Neville. *Learning through Liturgy.* New York: Seabury Press, 1978.

CHAPTER 4

Asian Sociocultural Values: Oppressive and Liberating Aspects from a Woman's Perspective

By Greer Anne Wenh-In Ng

Introduction

Chapters 1, 2, and 3 conveyed dimensions of the Asian North American experiences of community. Chapters 4, 5, and 6 offer critiques and suggestions for three severe problems Asian North Americans encounter in their practice of community. Confucian and other Asian religious and social values are communal, but in practice, power, authority, and relationships often are structured into hierarchies. Men and elders dominate; women and children suffer the consequences.

Asian North Americans who bring with them into the Christian church their communal lifestyles will find that the gospel can be informed by Asian perspectives, but the gospel also informs Asian culture and heritage. The gospel often sharply criticizes culture. When culture and gospel interact, new life and new ways can emerge.

Greer Anne Wenh-In Ng, a professor of Christian education in Toronto, Ontario, describes the problems of Asian hierarchial social relationships and offers fresh, positive ways to bring Christian love and acceptance together with Asian respect and responsibility. Professor Ng sets us on the path toward liberating practice within the Christian community.

Contemporary Asian North American Christians live in a predominantly western Euro-Anglo culture in Canada and the United States. At the same time, they carry many elements of sociocultural values present in their "collective unconscious," embedded "in the blood" and passed on from generation to generation through socialization at home and in their ethnic communities. Often, especially in the case of recent immigrants, there are expectations of behaving in traditional ways within their families, churches, and ethnic communities, even if they are permitted or encouraged to behave in more acculturated, Western ways at work or in school so as to achieve and succeed. How do Asian North American Christians respond to the challenge posed by this double, bicultural existence? How do women and girls, in particular, survive and, perchance, thrive in this situation? This chapter attempts to engage this enquiry by:

a. tracing the philosophical and religious roots of these values that still pervade the life and conduct of Asians living in North America today, paying special attention to the place of women in each historical development;

b. looking at some contemporary expressions and embodiments of these values in concrete life situations and how they interact with gospel values and demands, wrestling with both the oppressive and liberating aspects of both sets of values; and

c. exploring ways our faith communities can address the issues in order to confront the oppressive elements and their manifestations as well as lift up the liberating elements for the greater "life-giving" quality of our life together.

Asian Sociocultural Values: An Historical Overview of Their Philosophical and Religious Roots

The East Asian civilizations of China, Korea, and Japan (and their diaspora presence in Southeast Asia and other parts of the globe) have been shaped by the interpenetration

of four main religio-philosophical streams: indigenous religions (ancient divination and shamanic practices in China,
shamanism in Korea, Shintoism in Japan), Confucianism (in
its various historical developments), Taoism (in two distinct
manifestations—as philosophy and as religious practice),
and Buddhism (introduced from India but soon "Sino-ized"
and in turn introduced to Korea and Japan).

Ancient Indigenous Religions

In her recent work *Chinese Religions*, Canadian Confucian
scholar Julia Ching describes the dawn of ancient religion in
China in the period between the eighteenth and twelfth
centuries B.C.E. as one characterized by "dragon bones and
oracle inscriptions," a time when the will and advice of the
dead, especially that of ancestors, was sought for human
affairs (such as war and marriage) through divination. One
way was through the burning of tortoise shells with lighted
incense sticks and reading the cracks for signs, giving rise
to the earliest extant record of writing in China, the "oracle
bone" script. It was a period when the shaman or *wu,*
originally a female, acted as spiritual broker to make
known to human devotees the pleasures or displeasures
of the spirits of the departed. As in many other parts of
the world (for example, ancient Rome, contemporary
Africa), an "ancestral cult" developed, giving rise to and
being fed by a sense of "filial piety" much as ancient
Israel enshrined a similar trend in its commandment to
"honor thy father and thy mother." Sacrificing animals
for food and offering prayers for ancestors became expected duties of families, leading to the gradual eleva-
tion of the importance and position of the oldest male
heir. The first records of the Chinese character for *xiao*
("filial") came from bronze inscriptions presumably of the
Chou [Juo] dynasty (1111–256 B.C.E.), depicting a hand
resting upon the head of another person, perhaps an older
upon a younger (the character for "son" or "child") as a sign
of affection or for support. Ancient kings in that same

dynasty gradually assumed shamanic powers, leading to the later practice of Chinese emperors, as "Sons of Heaven," making annual sacrifices to *Tian* (which means heaven), the great ancestral spirit.

Ching contends that as the term *wu* became extended to include male shamans and as the professional role of shamans in general declined, the role of women in society suffered a parallel fate. This happened in spite of the central role females had played in Chinese creation myths (Nu-wa making humans out of clay, Nu-wa mending the sky, etc.) and in spite of recorded shamanic queenships in ancient Japan (Ching 1993:47). Certainly, by the time of the *Book of Poetry*, gender roles were already being determined at birth, with the male child treated as future ruler ("clothes him in robes/Gives him a jade sceptre to play with"—hence the saying "Congratulations on your joy of playing with jade pendant" still in use among the Chinese today) and the female child destined for the workforce (hence the saying "Congratulations on your joy of playing with pot shard" on the birth of a daughter).

Vestiges of ancient Chinese religions have survived in the form of popular religion and cultural-religious festivals for the nation's deified or sainted heroes. Pictures and statues of the latter are placed alongside those of the Buddha and boddhisattvas for veneration in temples. That female deity figures, such as Ma-zu, are venerated especially among the southern coastal people even today, which supports Ching's conclusion that women's place seems to have fared better in popular religion than in institutional ideologies.

In Korea, shamanic practices remained largely in the hands of women shamans (*mudungs*). It was one of the few ways in which women could exercise religious leadership since, as in China, the ancestral cult could only be performed by a male—a practice that is at the root of the quest for at least one son in all families. Shamanistic rituals were performed for healing purposes, especially for healing from mental illness, and for improving one's fortunes or to appease the perceived anger of the family's spirits. It provided the occasion and space for females of the household or community to gather in solidarity.

Confucianism

By the time Master Kung (or Kong, Confucius being the Western Latinized name for him) came on the scene (551–479 B.C.E.), the cult of ancestral veneration and the practice of filial piety was already alive and well. What Confucius did was to give philosophical and moral support to their continuance and strengthening. Like Jesus did later in Palestine, Confucius himself declared time and again that he, to borrow Jesus' words from Matthew 5:17, came "not to abolish but to fulfill" the laws and customs of the ancients. Confucius was committed to bringing order out of chaos at a time of social and political disorder—the period of the Spring and Autumn Annals and the Warring States. He exercised his genius in working at a humanistic and moral way of achieving harmony and peace in the land, a quest that was continued by later philosophers (S. Liu, 1988:321–24).

Confucius began with the ideal of the self-actualization of the individual ("the superior one," or *juinzi*) through *jen (ren)*, "humanity love" (see chapter 2 in this volume for fuller exploration), but it was quite different from the Faustian quest of an individual in isolation. In Confucian thought, the individual functions most authentically in a web of familial and social relationships, namely, the *wu-luen*, or Five Human Relationships, mutual and reciprocal—that between ruler and minister or subject, father and son, husband and wife, older brother or sibling and younger brother or sibling, and [older] friend and [younger] friend. These are the social virtues that govern not only relationships within the family, but also outside it. The elder or superior of each pair was to exercise caring and protection toward the younger or junior partner while the latter was to accord respect and loyalty.

However, the hierarchy incipient in these relationships was later exacerbated by certain developments:

a. the establishment of Confucianism as state philosophy and governing ideology in the Han dynasty (206
B.C.E.—220 C.E.) for the sake of promoting political stability
in a great empire (Man, 1992);

b. the incorporation of *yin-yang* cosmology and meta-
physics from ancient schools, especially as augmented by
the commentaries to *The Book of Changes (I-Ching)*, into
human relationships; and

c. the adoption of legalist theories of the rule of law and
power, resulting in rigid notions of authority and obedience. Since the state was viewed as an extension of the
family, this "orthodoxy" was in turn applied strictly to the
home.

It was the Han thinker Tung Chung-shu (179–104 B.C.E.)
who in reinterpreting these relationships gave the superior
partners ("master" was the term used) more rights over their
inferior partners, who ended up with more duties and obediences. He came up with the idea of the "three bonds," according to which "the ruler, the father, and the husband are to be
the standards of the ruled, the son, and the wife" (Chan
1963:272). This is how Chung-shu synthesized the inter-
wovenness of the three developments above, to the detriment
of the treatment of women thereafter:

> The meaning of sovereign and subject, father and son, and
> husband and wife is expressed by the way of *yin-yang*. The
> sovereign is *yang* and the subject is *yin*: father is *yang* and
> son is *yin*: husband is *yang* and wife is *yin*. The way of *yin*
> cannot go independently. . . . This means that *yin* relies on
> *yang*. . . . Wife's achievement relies on husband . . . and the
> earth's achievement relies on heaven (quoted in Fung
> 1948:196).

Hence followed the "three obediences" for women (obeying
father when unmarried, husband when married, and son
when widowed), which became the ideal behavior pattern
down the ages until probably the May Fourth Student Movement (1911) in China. At any rate, by the time of the formu-
lation of the philosophical school *Li-xueh* (named by Western

scholars "neo-Confucianism") in the Sung dynasty (960–1276 C.E.) as a response to Buddhism and Taoism, the subordination of female to male was taken as "natural."

Confucianism in Korea and Japan

Confucianism was introduced into Korea and adopted as state ideology by the Yi dynasty (1392–1910 C.E.), partly to suppress the influence and power of Buddhist monasteries. Buddhist land holdings were confiscated and given to Confucian aristocrats, the *yangban*, who comprised about 3 percent of the population. Strict social-class distinctions were observed, and women's movements became extremely restricted. Gone were the matriarchal structures of earlier times (for example, in the Silla period, 668–935 C.E.) when women could act as heads of households, or even the Koryo period (918–1392 C.E.), when women could still interact with men in public. This Confucian legacy seems to have lasted with even more force in Korea than in China.

The influence of Confucianism in Japan, coming via Korea, is best seen in the adoption of family rituals around the ancestral shrine, especially as promoted by the neo-Confucian thinker Chu Hsi (1130–1200 C.E.). These rituals have been melded with Buddhist rituals and have survived to this day in Japan. As in China and Korea, the position of males is again reinforced by this cult.

Taoism

The supposed founder of Taoist philosophy, Lao-tzu, could have been a contemporary of Confucius (sixth to fourth century B.C.E.). A "way of life" as well as "the Way," its characteristics, especially as formulated in the writings of Chuang-tzu (c. 399–295 B.C.E.), were freedom and nature. This attitude of "nonbeing" or *wu-wei*, like water filling and taking the shape of whatever cavities it finds itself in, stands in stark contrast to the earnest assertiveness of the Confucian school. Its influence on Chinese aesthetics and spirituality speaks for itself. It helped to shape the submissive and noncombative "go with the flow" tendency of the Chinese and indeed the East Asian personality (S. Ho 1963). The ideas in its short, cryptic founding text, the *Tao-Te-Ching*, exerted a decisive influence in the development of the Ch'an (Zen) school of Buddhism in China. Taoist philosophy, and the art and spirituality it fosters, is the heritage of every East Asian even to this day, including those of us who have embraced Christianity and who live in North America.

Taoism as a religion, with its priests, rituals, exorcisms, funeral rites, and the search for physical immortality via a "pill of immortality," actually rivals Christianity in a number of ways. Both believe in a Supreme Being; there is a priesthood; and, as in Roman Catholicism and Anglicanism, there is a pantheon of saints—women as well as men. Its famous emblem, the *yin-yang* within a circle, represents the cosmic force which, as shown in *The Book of Changes*, posits a dynamic, not static, universe. Taoist religion is often looked upon as being superstitious because of its magical and ecstatic character. At the same time, in typical integrative style, the "common person" would combine similar rituals from another religious tradition, such as Buddhism or Shintoism, as well. It seems the People's Republic of China has good reason to include Taoism as one of the five official religions of the land.

Women's place in Taoism

It has been pointed out that Taoism, in both its expressions, tends to accord a higher place to women than does Confucianism. With the Tao being referred to as "the mother of the ten thousand things" and its preponderance of softer and more receptive images (water, valley, emptiness), one can see why this is so. To make up the whole of reality, the *yin* force is every bit as important as the *yang* force. Philosophically, this requires more equality between the two. Taoist religious practice would also mean that both female and male sexuality is indispensable. One wonders, however, whether the tendency to be acted upon instead of acting, of receiving and, by analogy, suffering, has not aggravated women's suffering in all of East Asia.

Buddhism

Like the monotheistic Middle Eastern faiths Judaism, Christianity, and Islam, Buddhism is a proselytizing or missionary religion. Its founder was roughly contemporaneous with Confucius and possibly Lao-tzu. It espouses a philosophy or theology of the inevitability of human suffering and its solution (or salvation) of escaping the endless cycle of birth-suffering-rebirth through reaching *nirvana* by becoming freed from all sensuous desire. Devoted followers were to practice the eightfold path of holiness, to adhere to Buddha's teachings (the *dharma*), and to join the Buddhist community or monastic (the *samgha* or *sangha*) life. These disciplines, with their implicit abandonment of the human family and the duty of procreation, caused resistance at Buddhism's initial introduction into China (first century C.E.) However, within a few centuries Buddhist Scriptures were being translated and much missionary activity took place not only in China, but also in Korea and Japan, where it was adopted as state religion in 594 C.E. It reached its zenith of influence during China's Tang dynasty (618–917 C.E.). The various schools (Mahayana, Pure Land, Therravada, Tantric) were supplemented (or rounded out, completed) by the development of a Chinese form, Ch'an (Zen in Japan) Buddhism, which took into itself many of the elements of Taoism (hence the importance of *Chuang-tzu* and the *Tao-Te-Ching* in Zen).

Another result of the spread of Buddhism in China was to stimulate the development of metaphysical dimensions in Confucianism into a school known as "metaphysical thought" (*Li-xueh*, neo-Confucianism). These philosophers, under the leadership of Chu Hsi (1130–1200 C.E.), reorganized the classics, making a new orthodox corpus or canon of the Four Books (the *Great Learning*, the *Book of Mencius,* the *Book of Rites*, and the *Doctrine of the Mean*). The emphasis moved from moral teaching to metaphysical and spiritual questions. Chu Hsi, in fact, consciously combined the naturalist legacy of the Taoists (for example, taking the *Tai-chi* or Great Ultimate into account) and the anthropology of the Buddhists.

What of women's place in Buddhism? As expounded by its followers, Buddhism by its world-view and philosophy should be emancipating and liberating, since all living things are seen as having the Buddha nature. Buddhism founder Siddhartha Gautama himself, after strong persuasion by his aunt/foster mother, admitted women to the monastic community, though in a separate section and always with nuns being obedient to monks. Some contemporary Buddhist women thinkers point out that in our time, younger women who want to "seek a multidimensional personality, a totally centered and integrated life, and the ability to fulfill their role not only as wife and mother, but also as their own person" are turning to Buddhism (Leo 1992:29).

Women's Place

We have traced in the previous subsections how women fared historically under each of the main philosophical and religious systems of the East. We have seen how these systems either reinforced or gave rise to values that made an impact on women's lives. Historically, women's place seemed to be higher in Taoism and in the popular religion it helped to shape and lower in either Confucianism or Buddhism (Ching 1993). We will turn to our time to see whether this is still true and how Asian women in the Christian communities of North America fare when they bring the values and ideals of the Christian tradition into their social, familial, and church community lives.

Contemporary Expressions

Story 1: Mr. Stone Enters a Home for the Aged

It was dinnertime at the Yans's. Sharon, the youngest,

most talkative one, was unusually quiet. Finally, Mr. Yan could stand it no longer. "Is anything the matter, Sharon?" he asked.

Sharon stopped fiddling with her fork. "After school today I took some cookies over to Mr. Stone next door—you know, the ones I decorated with special icing," she began. "He wasn't there. Instead, someone was cleaning up the place. She said that Mr. Stone has gone away, to one of those homes for senior citizens who can't manage on their own any longer."

"That's too bad," Alan, the oldest, commented. "He loves his place so much. I'm going to miss him. He knows more about baseball than anyone else around here. No offense, Dad," he added hastily.

Mrs. Yan chimed in. "I gather it's a case of his children and grandchildren not being able to take care of him, now that he needs more care and they live so far away. I suppose the day will come, too, for Dad and me to do the same thing."

A chorus of protest erupted. "No fear, Mom!" "We'll never let that happen!" And then, more tentatively from Sharon and Carol, "How come Alan gets to have you with him, just because he's the oldest?" "I hope you can come and stay with me and my family sometimes too—can you, with daughters?" "Yeah, me too. Only, I may not get married. You'll have to be content with plain old me."

Over the babble, Mr. and Mrs. Yan caught each other's eye and smiled. So their efforts had paid off, after all. So it did make some impression on them, all those stories about how Guan Ning used to warm up blankets for his father by lying in the bed ahead of time in winter, and how Kong Yong chose the smallest pear for himself because he was the youngest, even though he was given first choice. When their time came, they said to each other later, they might actually elect to do exactly as Mr. Stone had done. Still, it was gratifying to know that all three of their children had learned the lessons of filial piety so well.

"Your parents would have been proud," Mrs. Yan said wistfully.

"They probably are," Mr. Yan gently replied.

Story 2: We've Got to Think of the Family

"Must we go?" Lisa pleaded, half hopefully. "You know how much May's recital means to me. Not to say that you don't also know how much I detest big family gatherings."

"I wish I could go hear May too," Don replied. "But you know Mother; she would have a fit if we didn't show up. 'Siblings are like limbs to one another,' she used to drum it in to us. Family solidarity and all that."

"Even though I know, and she knows, that you and Charles can't stand each other. Not since you were kids," Lisa said.

"Likes and dislikes have nothing to do with it," Don reminded her, trying to sound neutral. "Mother always expects everyone to show up on occasions like this. Especially as this is the 'full moon' banquet for her first male grandchild, from one of her sons. We've got to think of the family. Let's make sure we catch May at her next recital in town."

"You mean, as long as it doesn't clash with some family celebration or other," Lisa retorted, resigned. "Sometimes I almost wish I had married an only child!"

Story 3: Of Curfews and Such

It was the beginning of a workshop on gender awareness, and participants were sharing their first memories. "For me," said one woman, "it was when my parents imposed different curfews for my twin brother and me when we were teens. I had to ask, 'How come we are being treated differently in this one case, when we've always been treated equally before?'"

"For me," said another, "it was my parents' reluctance to send me, their daughter, to the Ivy League school that had accepted me. They pretty much made me go to the state university instead. It wasn't until years later that I found out why: they were saving up money to send my younger brother out east."

"With me, it was easy. We three older girls got hit with it the day our younger brother arrived—the first male child in the family. All the rules about seniority simply got thrown out, in his favor. There it is, in a nutshell: my rude, crude catapulting into feminist consciousness at the tender age of six."

Story 4: What's in a Name?

It was introduction time at the special congregational meeting. The chair was doing the honors. "Here are our guests from presbytery: Rev. Downing, Rev. Mak, Mrs. Chung . . ."

I almost jumped out of my seat. Mrs. Chung, indeed! Why wasn't she introduced with at least the same title as her fellow pastors, if indeed not with her earned doctorate as well? She was the only guest there with one! This is definitely a case where a rose by any other name does not smell as sweet.

Before I could rise up to my feet to protest, however, the secretary had risen to *his* feet. "And most of us will recall the great jubilation of our church when Dr. Chung was ordained last year, thereby increasing the percentage of Asian women ministers of our denomination by 100 percent . . ."

Thank God for this show of solidarity. Then I could give the meeting the attention it deserved.

Identifying Issues

Story 1 shows the success of a Chinese family in socializing the younger generation into the important cornerstone cultural value of filial piety. As young women living in late-twentieth-century North America, however, the daughters have some questions about the basis of their oldest brother's special privilege and responsibility. Is it strictly seniority in age, or is it also because he is male? They suspect it is both, and they are not far wrong.

Story 2 sees an individual's wishes pitted against that of

her extended family. Not only that; in this case it is also the wishes of a daughter-in-law pitted against those of a mother-in-law. Entwined with the high value of the group over the individual, therefore, is that of the hierarchy not only of age, but also the particular, often oppressive, pecking order of females within a family. The son/spouse is caught in his struggle to maintain a conjugal relationship and the demands of the larger community, plus those of filial piety. Overall looms the ideal of striving for harmony within the family and the community.

In story 3 the age-old discrimination against females, *nam jo nu bi* in Korean, is manifested in all three instances. It is interesting to note that although the Confucian values of education and achievement apply to both sons and daughters, the latter still lose out. As Christian leaders poised on the edge of the third millennium, we need to ask ourselves if we still tend to shortchange girls and women in terms of personal freedom, educational opportunity, and self-worth at home and in church.

At issue in story 4 is not simply a lack of courtesy but also in fact a lack of justice in the persistent identification of women by one of the "three bonds" rather than "in her own right." This could also be the expression of a latent disapproval of women leaders who dare to assume untraditional roles, roles thought to be the prerogative of males alone.

All these stories are contemporary expressions of major East Asian sociocultural values and the impact of those values on younger, female members of the community. Because they live not in first-century China or fourteenth-century Korea or sixteenth-century Japan but on the eve of the twenty-first century in North America, these members are beginning to ask questions about those values and the way they are being interpreted. At the same time, because we are also members of Christian faith communities, we need to raise another set of questions: "What does the gospel, the Good News of Jesus Christ, have to say about these values? How do Christian values confirm, challenge, or at times even replace the cultural values we have grown up with?" We will explore this tension together, analyzing Scripture and Western Christian tradition in the context of renewed understandings of both made possible by the work of women theologians and biblical scholars of the last two decades. Our quest is for a genuine life abundant together in today's Asian-origin Christian communities for all its members rather than for some at the expense of others.

Analysis

"Honor Your Father and Your Mother" (Exodus 20:12)

It is comparatively easy for East Asians, like their native American or Canadian sisters and brothers, to heed the fifth commandment: "Honor your father and your mother, so that your days may be long . . ." Both in ancient Israel and the ancient Far East, the extended command to respecting and honoring elders, and thus caring for them, was a matter of course. The continuation of this practice in present-day North America is the envy of members of the dominant culture. Jesus himself, in a confrontation with the religiously righteous of his day, criticizes the latter for letting some people "off the hook" in the support of their parents by declaring their support money *"Corban,"* that is, given over to the temple (Mark 7:9-13).

Filial piety requires supporting and caring for parents, mourning for them in death, and keeping up the practice of ancestral remembrance. Filial piety also demands the continuation of the ancestral line and, of course, reverence and obedience from children, even married sons with their own families (S. Ho 1963; Chi-Ping Yu 1990). The dire consequences of failing to produce a son could mean wives being put away or, at the least, having to tolerate the presence of concubines. Expectations of total obedience from the younger generation have given rise not only to moral sanctions and authoritarian control, but also even to physical punishment.

And yet, when we examine Jesus' own behavior, we find
more than one occasion on which he seems to ignore or to
question parental authority. First, there was that famous
incident at age twelve (the onset of adulthood for boys in his
time) when he stayed behind to discuss theology with the
rabbis in the temple without first letting his parents know—
the equivalent of not phoning home to ask for an extension
of curfew. Second, when his mother and siblings showed
natural concern over his overzealous dedication to his ministry (". . . so that they could not even eat . . ." Mark 3:20-21)
and over his supposed mental imbalance (". . .'He has gone
out of his mind'" v. 21), he did not thank them, but gave them
the cold shoulder. He even went on to indicate that those who
do "the will of God" are his true family (vv. 33-35)! Third, he
never married, even when well past the usual age, thus never
fulfilling the obligation to perpetuate a new generation,
surely an antifamilial and ultimately antisocial behavior in
Israel as in ancient China or Korea or Japan, especially in
the case of the oldest male offspring. Fourth, by putting his
life in danger and suffering an early death, he was not able
to discharge his natural obligation of caring for his aging
parent himself (John 19:26-27).

In our preaching and educating, how often have we wres-
tled with the implications of Jesus' behavior for ourselves?
When we as elders or more mature church members expect
unquestioning obedience from our younger people, maybe
we are putting our cultural values above the alternative
stance Jesus offers. When we ignore the different needs of
younger, "1.5," or subsequent generations, we are not remembering the faith quests of children and teens that
Jesus demonstrated. And when we insist on our offspring's
following family expectations in either marriage and parenthood or career even when they feel called differently, do
we not ignore Jesus' own example? This becomes especially
unacceptable when that different call happens to be to a
less-lucrative or -secure career, such as to be an artist or
to enter "accountable paid ministry." Maybe rather than

ruling out such choices arbitrarily, or dismissing them as simply selfish or modern, Asian faith communities and families need to pay more attention to gospel demands as they deal with these tensions. (See the resource *Generations Trying to Live Together* for some suggestions of how to go about this.)

Primogeniture Issues

The primacy of the firstborn son is still observed in varying degrees among Chinese, Japanese, and Korean Americans or Canadians. Giving special privileges to oldest sons, however, also places a heavier burden on them—and on their wives, who even today remain providers of filial care for their husband's parents (Gleb and Palley 1994). Is greater acculturation into dominant customs and values having any effect on this value—for example, by expecting younger sons to share in the care?

It is interesting to recall the many instances in Israel's history when the older sibling, the natural inheritor, got ousted by a younger sibling. Just think of Cain being passed over in favor of Abel, Ishmael in favor of Isaac, Esau in favor of Jacob, Judah and all the older brothers of Joseph in favor of the dreamer with the many-colored coat. It sometimes makes one wonder whether the biblical storytellers and recorders were overcompensating! Maybe even in those ancient days there was a feeling of injustice and inequality on behalf of younger sons. Incidentally, notice how daughters were never very much in the picture unless the story involved their physical violation (sanctioned by their fathers, no less—as when Lot offered his virgin daughter as a means of discharging hospitality obligations [Genesis 19:8], or when Jephthah sacrificed his daughter in fulfillment of a vow for victory in battle [Judges 11:30-39]). The one case where they won something for themselves was when the five daughters of Zelophehad who ably and successfully contested with Moses their right to inherit their father's property (Numbers 27: 1-11).

Who Are My Mother and My Brothers? (Mark 3:33)

One of the easily recognized characteristics of Asian families in North America is their family cohesiveness. On public occasions such as festivals and banquets this is demonstrated by their high visibility as *families*. Even adult children, if unmarried and living at home, are expected to be present in all clan and extended-family gatherings. Once married, the network simply gets wider. More than one highly successful screen production featuring Asians in North America has opened with a scene of a family or clan gathered at a meal (for example, *The Joy Luck Club, Double Happiness*). While there is no doubt that family togetherness makes for clan solidarity and mutual help, its expectations on individual members sometimes can become too demanding or even oppressive. The ideal of harmony in the home, regulated by social pressures, is all too often won at the expense of personal choice and freedom of movement.

In the life of Christians such expectations are carried over to church behavior. This is seen as an asset, as it certainly boosts church attendance and brings many younger people into the church. On the other hand, if the same hierarchal arrangements are simply mirrored in the life of the church as a family, it does not bring Good News to those on the lower end of the scale. Their movements would continue to be restricted and their contributions not sought or valued.

In the case of new converts whose family members remain non-Christian, there is the psychological burden of acting differently or even of deserting the family. Evangelists and pastors need to take this reality into account as they welcome newly converted individuals into their church and learn to refrain from requiring inappropriate commitment until they have checked out the situation. New converts have chosen to align themselves with a new family, that of the church; their natural families may not fully understand the reason and at any rate may feel emotionally abandoned, as Jesus' family must have felt at one time.

To add fuel to the fire, Jesus is recorded as declaring (probably as early church members were recognizing the cost of joining the Christian community from their existing Jewish or Gentile families) that he had " 'not come to bring peace, but a sword,' " with divisive effects on natural family life and harmony:

"For I have come to set a man against his father,
    and a daughter against her mother,
    and a daughter-in-law against her mother-in-law; . . .
Whoever loves father or mother more than me is not worthy of me, and whoever loves son or daughter more than me is not worthy of me; . . ."
    —Matthew 1:34-37

Because of its conflictual stance, this is not a passage often referred to. Yet it is there in our Scriptures, and we need to recognize some of the anticultural dimensions of our gospel by recalling its existence and warning from time to time. For the individual who feels stifled by family demands, it might give a ray of brightness and act as Good News indeed.

Mother-in-Law/Daughter-in-Law Relationships

One of the most destructive effects of traditional family life in East Asia is the generation-to-generation oppressive rule from mother-in-law to daughter-in-law. Socialized from young girlhood to serve father, husband, and son and regarded as virtual nonpersons until the birth of their first son (daughters do not count), women in such a system have no other role models and can become virtual tyrants when their turns come (see the instructions in the classical training manuals for girls and women, such as *Nu Erjing*, quoted in Ng 1995). Although modern-day mothers-in-law may be much more enlightened (as some among our readers very well are), there is still an attitude of deference accorded them.

A dynamic that can become problematic, even in the most courteous of relationships, is the latent competition for the son's affection and loyalty, which a mother considers rightfully hers even after her son's marriage. The circumstances of modern-day couples may be a far cry from the tragedy of the devoted young couple in the ancient tale "The Peacock Flies Southeast," where the son is forced by his mother to put away his wife. Yet there have been cases where sons have felt they could not openly celebrate their wedding anniversaries for fear of offending their widowed mothers. Thus, the dilemma of the husband in story 2 is by no means a rare case.

The most famous mother-in-law/daughter-in-law relationship from our Judeo-Christian heritage surely must be that between Naomi and Ruth. While Ruth's loyalty to her mother-in-law is seen as natural by most Asian daughters-in-law, the bond of affection between the two poses a real challenge. What is even more unthinkable is the fact that Naomi actually schemes to get Ruth remarried, since traditionally remarriage has been unacceptable if not prohibited outright. The great emphasis on the traditional biblical interpretation of the book of Ruth, and the holding up of Ruth as the ideal daughter-in-law who abandons her own people and her own gods to follow her husband's, often has been oppressive to Asian married women. We can try an alternative interpretation by turning to the silenced voice of Ruth's sister-in-law, Orpah, who went back to her mother's house and her own people and culture.

There Is No Longer Male and Female (Galatians 3:28)

One would think that in the closing years of the twentieth century, with the advances made by the women's movement of the seventies and eighties, equality between males and females would be a matter of course. Much has been gained: women breaking ground in nontraditional professions such as engineering and law, women's experience and voice being taken more seriously in research, women's studies becoming established as a legitimate branch of study at universities, feminist theology and feminist interpretation of Scripture gaining a foothold in theological education, and so forth. But this is not to say that patriarchal structures have been transformed significantly. We only have to call to mind the recent backlash against affirmative action in employment practices in the United States and the continued devaluation of work done by women the world over. There is still a big gap between the "espoused ideal" of gender equality and the actual practice of it in society.

In the struggle to preserve their ethno-cultural identity in a transplanted context, Asian communities in North America have sometimes condemned wholesale anything Western or modern. Or, conversely, they have embraced indiscriminately all and anything coming from the dominant culture as a way of becoming more American or Canadian. In clinging to values and attitudes from their cultures of origin, people in the first group may not realize that things actually may not have remained the way they were when they left, since cultures are not static but dynamic. In adopting the customs and values of the host country wholesale, on the other hand, unhealthy values may have been taken over as well. A third attitude is to select from the host country only those values that fit one's traditional ones.

All three options seem to be operative within the Christian communities of Asian immigrants and their families and descendants. The complicating factor here, of course, is that the Judeo-Christian tradition has not developed in a cultural vacuum. In adopting values "from the Bible," therefore, it is important to try to identify the historical, social, and cultural elements that accompanied the development of the gospel at certain historical periods, testing them against their validity or "health-givingness" for today, before either taking them over or rejecting them outright.

In consideration of women-men relationships, several scriptural cases come easily to mind: the heritage of the curse of Eve and the injunctions to wifely obedience in Ephesians 5:22. As has been made clear in recent biblical scholarship, the "Eve as curse" tradition in Genesis 3 needs to be balanced by the other Creation story in Genesis 1:26-29 (W. Ho 1988). Through better exegesis

(explanations of the meanings of biblical words and constructions based on their original Hebrew or Greek—for
example, moving from subordinate ideas of "helpmate" into
equal "partner," from "dominion" over the earth to "stewardship" and care of the earth), we now realize that some
of the traditionally accepted interpretations have been mis-
taken or misleading. In the Ephesians passage, the emphasis
on mutual submission traditionally has been ignored or
neglected ("Husbands, love your wives, . . . He who loves his
wife loves himself. For no one ever hates his own body, but
he nourishes and tenderly cares for it, just as Christ does for
the church, because we are members of his body" [vv. 25-30]).
It is all too tempting, but scarcely faithful, for the more
androcentric verses to be appropriated by cultures that have
inherited largely patriarchal social values in men-women
relationships.

Christ came that all "may have life, and have it abun-
dantly" (John 10:10). In his earthly ministry he accomplished
this partly by including the socially unacceptable in his
healing and teaching actions. Among these were women with
whom no respectable Jewish male was to hold discourse in
public—respectable householders like Martha, social outcasts such as the woman suffering from a hemorrhage for
twelve years, ethnically ostracized women such as the Syro-
phoenician woman and the Samaritan woman at the well.
Women were among his followers and disciples (Luke 8:2-3;
Mark 15:40-41) and were entrusted with the first news of his
resurrection. These actions made it natural for the early
church to be a community of both women and men engaged
in ministry as well as fellowship. Paul articulated this elimination of social discriminations eloquently in Galatians 3:28:
"There is no longer Jew or Greek, there is no longer slave or
free, there is no longer male and female; for all of you are one
in Christ Jesus."

Such scriptural traditions are indeed Good News to those
who have for thousands of years been told they did not exist
in their own right but are simply appendages of their fathers,

husbands, or sons. This, according to theologian Kwok Pui Lan, is exactly how women converts felt in China in the second half of the nineteenth and the first quarter of the twentieth centuries (1992). Having embraced this Good News joyfully and gratefully, these women in turn joined their sisters in the struggle for women's emancipation from age-old feudal fetters on several fronts, fighting for access to education for women and girls, to abolish footbinding, and so forth. They were instrumental in "the feminization of Christian symbols" (Kwok 1992), thus contributing to the theological enterprise as well.

To what extent have the Christian faith communities of our time and space followed Jesus' invitation to life abundant for its female members? In our Christian nurture and education programs, what efforts have we made to recover some of these life-giving scriptural traditions for our girls and women (Ng 1995)? In our church life and denominational life, have we made special efforts to nurture and lift up women's leadership potential (Matsui-Estrella and Ng 1995)? To be truly "people on the Way" in this area of gender equality poses some of the hardest challenges facing our faith communities as we move toward the third millennium.

To reiterate, we need to ask ourselves, "What kind of communities do we perpetuate, knowingly or unknowingly? Communities that oppress more than half our congregations, or communities that value their experience, decision making, and potential, to the good of the whole?" Section 3 of this chapter offers concrete suggestions on how to begin to address this question seriously.

In Remembrance of Her
(Mark 14:3-9, Matthew 26:6-13)

The woman in the anointing episodes in Mark and Matthew remains nameless to this day, though her story is indeed told and retold. Married women in Asia, regarded as having become members of their spouses' families, were not identified by their own (family of origin) names on ancestral tablets. The

actual practice in the twentieth century, however, has been
to continue going by one's maiden family name in formal
records (school, university) and in the exercise of one's profession. The Chinese practice is to add the spouse's family
name to one's own. When a couple is engaged in the same
profession, the woman simply cannot be addressed by the
husband's name, as it would cause too much confusion. Thus
one quite often finds a medical clinic, for instance, with a pair
of physicians' names in parallel belonging to a married couple. In the case of story 4, if the Reverend Dr. Chung's
husband happened also to be an ordained minister, the title
"Rev. Chung" would refer to him, not to her.

By ignoring, downplaying, or making invisible the roles
women assume in their work sphere, we perpetuate the
feudal stereotype of women as appendages of their fathers,
spouses, or sons, plus the stereotype of the domestic sphere
being the only legitimate area for the exercise of their gifts.
We devalue the contribution they make toward society,
church, and the world. Whereas, in ensuring visibility by
their proper titles, we not only accord them their rightful
recognition, but also help their particular profession or occu-
pation be seen as gender inclusive. In the case of Asian
women, we also render it ethnically inclusive, and thus
support affirmative action twice over.

Furthermore, failing to name Asian women by their proper
titles, especially when males are properly addressed on the
same public occasion, deprives the community of much-
needed but rare role models for its young and its female
members (Ng 1995). This is of particular importance in the
case of the ordained ministry, the typical practitioner of
which still remains male in the Asian churches of North
America. The adults of both sexes, too, need their consciousness raised. It is a sad comment on our churches that
most members these days have no hesitation making use
of the services of lawyers, realtors, or physicians who
happen to be women, but they can hardly conceive of pastors
or bishops who are women. The unenviable situation of

women in traditionally male-dominated roles or positions inside and outside the church is studied in chapter 5 of this volume.

Being on the Way:
Suggestions for Ministry Action

To move from reflection and discussion to actual ministerial action, more than one step is needed, developing strategies for both raising awareness and engaging in liberating practice. We will consider these in turn.

Raising Awareness

Raising awareness around the issues we have been discussing in this chapter could bring discomfort to our faith communities, our families, and ourselves. It might be risky just to initiate any conversation at all. Most of us East Asians in North America have been socialized into these values in one way or another; we all feel very strongly about them. Anyone daring to suggest that things could or should be changed is apt to be seen as a troublemaker if not a rebel or public danger, sometimes even by those for whom our action will bring relief, so deeply has their oppression been internalized. On the other hand, not to do anything is to vote for the status quo with its oppressive structures and consequences not only for more than half the congregation, but also for the community as a whole. In order to go about this risky task in a faithful yet caring way, we suggest some guidelines to govern any strategizing:

a. Never work alone; always work with one or more others who share your vision.

b. Know your target group so you can enter into their space and not overwhelm them, nor underchallenge them.

c. Strengthen your own awareness and skills by consulting with others, reading, attending workshops, and so on.

d. Pay extra attention to your prayer and spiritual lives while concentrating on this work. Much patience, courage, discernment, and wisdom are called for since misunderstandings and even attacks by others may arise from time to time.

Raising Awareness Step 1:
Examine Existing Practice Individually

Ask yourself, "How have I, intentionally or unintentionally, been contributing to the perpetuation of the oppressive aspects of the pervasive sociocultural values we have inherited both from our culture and from Christianity?" Concrete cases to examine could include these:

• *In my interpretation of Scripture* in preaching and leading Bible study, how have I been reinforcing dominance-submission paradigms and sex-role stereotypical expectations? How have I been intentional in lifting up the stories and perspectives of women and younger people and other marginalized persons or groups in the Bible?

• *In my interaction with others* within the congregation or in my ethnic community, have I gone overboard in expecting younger folk to listen and obey their elders, even when the demands of the latter were excessive and unreasonable?

• *In classroom, study group, and committee situations,* have I tended to listen to or expect more from boys and men than girls and women or devalued the contributions of the latter even when they had a chance to speak?

• *In my worship and prayer leadership,* have I assumed I am speaking for everyone, even the weak and silenced, without consulting with them or taking their situations into account?

• *What else?*

After individual reflection, it is helpful to discuss these matters, and how you feel about them, with peers you trust. You may want to arrange for this to happen at a local ministerial meeting or over dessert in someone's home.

Raising Awareness Step 2:
Examine Existing Practice Communally

Do the same awareness-raising step with your faith community. This could take place in a committee, session, or council meeting or at the beginning of a retreat or study session on the topic of this chapter. Divide your committee or total group into smaller groups of three or four if necessary. Where men and women members are present together, try placing them in small same-sex groups when examining issues pertaining to women's roles so the women can feel safe and speak more freely. Do the same subdivision for different generations when examining age-power issues. Where some members may not have the same degree of facility with one of the languages spoken (for instance, younger people with original-heritage language or more recent immigrants with English), subdivide into small same-language groups to achieve the same goal. Here are a few areas to focus on:

a. *Leadership in committee membership*: conduct an audit of the present membership of your congregation's *decision-making bodies* (the session or parish council, the finance or property committee, trustees, pastoral relations or search committee, etc.). Be specific. Count up the numbers and calculate the proportion of women to men, younger folk to older adults who have been recruited to engage in these central and valued ministries. What did you find?

• In the subgroups, ask people to reflect individually on, then talk about, whether they feel they have been encouraged by their church to *use their gifts to their potential*. Ask for concrete instances. In the total group, compare the findings from the all-men with the all-women subgroups and those from the older-generation with the younger-generation subgroups. Do you see any similarities? any differences? any startling contrasts? Talk about them and the implications for life together as a Christian community.

• Examine the *topics (the curriculum) of your Bible study or other study groups, Sunday school, or of conferences and workshops* you attended within the last two years. How many instances can you recall of sessions that dealt with the oppressive or liberating aspects of family or church and community life together? Recall the occasion, the content, the process, and whether anything changed after that, either for you or for the community, church, and family. If no one can identify any such instances, record "zero." This reflects a "null curriculum," which, by its absence of certain topics, teaches that these topics are not important or should not be addressed, that the status quo should remain as it is.

• Examine the *worship life* of your faith community. Who gets to participate in the leadership and who does not? Are the worship acts, symbols, music and hymns, language, and concepts user-friendly to children and younger people as well as to grown-ups? to girls and women as well as to boys and men? Was the worship space conducive to participation? Ask subgroup members to cite concrete instances, both when they felt welcomed and included and when they felt not welcome or excluded because of any of the items listed, plus others. Have people brainstorm on how they would change things to make worship in their church more life-giving.

• Examine the *social life* of your faith community. Who gets to set the agenda most of the time? Whose needs predominate, or is there a rotation of different needs and preferences? Whose styles predominate? Is there sufficient consultation with the groups who are not on the planning team? Ask members for examples of how they have participated or not participated or have not been invited to take leadership and how they would like to change things.

• Go through copies of your *congregational newsletter, annual reports, and such* to check whether the same criteria are used in referring to females and males, using proper titles for both, using first names for people of the same rank, serving similar offices, etc. Go back go the story "What's in a Name?" and its reflections to discuss why equality here is important.

Raising Awareness Step 3:
Examine Existing Practice in Families

The church could facilitate this step by holding sessions for parents and grandparents, for women (as daughters-in-law, mothers-in-law, young singles living at home, etc.), for men (as fathers, brothers, boyfriends, etc.), for teens and young adults, for children, as well as for intergenerational and mixed groups. Often it is difficult for members of a family to raise or discuss these issues without getting into arguments. The church can provide a more neutral space and also the critical mass of one age group or sex in sufficient numbers to feel that they are not alone, to share experiences, and to get their voice heard. Once again, provide opportunities for original-heritage language groups and discussion whenever needed, especially in talking about generational dynamics.

Depending on your own church's makeup and situation, and when which time is ripe for what, you need to make careful selection from among the following list of gender and generational issues:

a. Gender issues:

• What are the present guidelines regarding the distribution of *home chores* in your family? For instance, do you expect only girls and women to help in the kitchen and only boys and men to take out the garbage and do (or learn to do) repairs, or do you expect both sexes to engage in both types of chores, taking turns?

• Does your family set different rules such as curfews or types of *leisure activities* (for example, ballet, needlecraft, and pottery permitted for females but not males, and rock climbing, winter camping, hockey, and soccer permitted for males but not for females), *range of career choice* (encouraging males but discouraging females toward occupations such as engineer, businessperson, ordained minister, commercial pilot or vehicle operator, and public official), and *commitment to profession and career*? Go back to the story "Of Curfews and Such" for ideas.

• Do you detect any tolerance toward "keeping women in their place" in your extended family circles and thus a hidden, unspoken approval of or at least "turning a blind eye" toward possible cases of domestic violence and wife battering? Remind the group(s) that physical violence against another, whether a child, a spouse, or an older parent, is a crime in Canada and the United States.

• *Are there any other matters you want to bring up?*

b. Generational issues:

Plan an intergenerational evening at church to watch the film *Double Happiness* (rent the video version). Make sure there are several original-language parents and grandparents or recent immigrants as well as English-speaking "1.5" and subsequent generations in the group. Prepare snacks that would satisfy both types of tastes: prawn crackers and Japanese rice cookies as well as popcorn. The debriefing of the film is the main learning activity. Enlist the help of bilingual facilitators with good "people skills."

Watch the film together, but divide by generation for the first round of discussion. In the second round, mix the generations in small groups. In the third and final round, meet together in plenary.

Focus questions
for the first round can include:

• What is your reaction to this film? What had the greatest impact on you?

• List on newsprint the themes that jumped out at you. Which issues are alive for your relationship with the other generation(s) in your family? What are some issues operative in your home not touched on in the film?

• How have you and your family dealt with these issues? Is there much similarity, or a lot of difference?

For the second round (mixing up family members from one family with those of another to allow for more candid participation), let the generations compare notes from their first round of discussion and go further. Remind the bilingual facilitators to arbitrate in a reconciliatory manner, ensuring that everyone's voice is heard. The notes from this round may also turn out to be bilingual.

For the third round, meet in plenary to hear reports from round-two groups. Ask if they see patterns of how issues are dealt with. The focus for this round is: "What can we, as a church, do to help generations live together more creatively?"

If you elect not to begin by watching *Double Happiness*, use some of the following questions to focus discussion at youth group, women's group, or adult group meetings:

- Who in your family has the final word in most things? On *major decisions* (moving to a new house, buying a new car, where to go for vacation this year) do just the parents decide, or do they involve the children in the decision? Give examples one way or another. Compare the ways different families in your group work. What are the advantages and disadvantages, and how would you like to improve the situation? If there is a grandparent in the family, to what extent does she or he have a say?

- How does your family handle the matter of *discipline* of its younger members? What approach or method is used? Compare the way discipline is exercised in the original culture (such as in the use or nonuse of physical force) and in North America. Do you remember ever being physically punished or physically punishing your children? As in the case of wife assault, this is a case where what is *legally* allowed or not allowed may come into conflict with centuries-old practice and where "culture" should not be used as a stalking-horse. This is a case where quoting Scripture (for example, Proverbs 13:24; 22:15; and 29:15, from whence we get the saying "Spare the rod and spoil the child") without acknowledging changed social mores and legal standards does more harm than good.

- Do a brief *Bible study on Ephesians 6:1-4,* stressing the injunction to parents not to anger their children (v. 4) in

order to counteract the well-known and often-quoted injunctions to children to "obey your parents" (v. 1).

- Invite *mothers-in-law* to share their experiences and feelings of living in present-day North American culture. What
anxieties, fears, senses of loss of status and power (for
recent immigrants) do they experience? Make a list on
newsprint (translated into English if necessary). Ask the
daughters-in-law gathered to do the same. Have the two
groups come together to share the two lists and talk about
them. In a brief Bible study, discuss: "How has the traditional interpretation of the story of Ruth tended to oppress
daughters-in-law?"

Engage in Liberating Practice

Engage in liberating Bible study and interpretation. We
have had a taste of this with the "brief Bible study on
Ephesians 6:1-4" in the foregoing section. To begin this practice, try the following steps:

a. Identify oppressive passages and interpretations: the story
   about Eve and the fall, about Delilah and Jezebel, about
   the pitting of Mary against Martha, and so on.

b. Employ a "hermeneutics of suspicion" (that is, not taking
   traditional interpretations as inevitably correct or the only
   way to approach a passage) by looking at things from the
   perspective of the silenced and marginalized, asking questions and raising issues from their experience. A useful
   resource for beginning to do this is *The Liberating Pulpit*
   by Catherine and Justo González. (See References.)

c. Access contemporary and up-to-date feminist scholarship,
   consulting commentaries embodying the fruits of feminist
   research, such as *The Women's Bible Commentary*, and
   volumes 1 and 2 of Elizabeth Schussler Fiorenza's *Searching the Scriptures.* (See References.)

d. Pay attention to stories and characters generally neglected
   by mainstream (Eurocentric, Western, male, academic)

interpreters, especially unnamed children, girls and women who were vital to certain stories and must have been there, but whose presence was never acknowledged or valued. An interesting resource in this area is *Miriam, Mary, and Me* by Lois M. Wilson (see references); a challenging, in-depth resource is *Voices from the Margin*, edited by R. S. Sugirtharajah (see References).

For a sample Bible study using this approach (based on the principles of liberatory pedagogy and educative practice) and the kind of resources used, please see the design used with the women of the Chinese Presbyterian Church, Oakland, for studying Vashti and Esther, found in the appendix to this chapter.

• Existing Bible study groups, lectionary groups, or Sunday school divisions could be invited to try this approach. Or band together several congregations to do some sessions, both to introduce the idea and to train a core group of concerned people and leaders.

In addressing the "null curriculum" in the church's educational programs and resources, *make use of existing resources,* adapting their emphases to reflect the issues raised in this chapter where necessary. In particular cases, for instance on intergenerational life together, mainstream Anglo-American resources generally concentrate on the inclusion of children at worship and do not deal with issues specific to East Asian Christian communities, such as the tension between immigrant and subsequent generations; the inability to communicate ideas and feelings, owing to a lack of proficiency in a common language for those same generations; the way that historically Asian North American cohorts differ from their Anglo-American, African American, Latino/Latina American or native American and Canadian counterparts, etc. A recent resource that looks at some of these issues from a racial ethnic minority perspective and experience is *Generations Trying to Live Together* (see suggested references.)

Provide training for church school and youth group leaders,

parents, and grandparents that pays special attention to
the socialization of children and young people, especially
of girls and women, using some of the insights and questions raised in this chapter as well in chapter 5 on "Asian
North American Women in the Workplace and the Church"
and chapter 6 on "Asian North American Immigrant Parents and Youth." A resource focusing on the socialization
and education of Asian North American women and girls
is the article "Toward Wholesome Nurture: Challenges in
the Religious Education of Asian North American Female
Christians" in the journal *Religious Education* (see suggested references.)

*Provide alternative images of God in worship and theologi-
cal reflection.* Our ideas of who and what God is are potently
shaped by the way God is addressed in corporate and private
prayers, the way God is represented in the hymns we sing,
and the way we think of God in our theological reflection. If
we remain locked in male-only God language and aggressive-
omnipotent divine attributes, we and those with whom we
minister and educate will not be able to break out of the bonds
of such a God, thus perpetuating patriarchal and hierarchal
values to reinforce already oppressive Asian ones. Try beginning by using alternative images of God from Scripture
(Mother Eagle from Deuteronomy 32:11 [KJV], Rock from
Psalms, etc). In prayers, use the second-person address more
for God. In hymns, print out inclusive versions that do not
violate the integrity of the original's style. A helpful resource
is hymn writer Brian Wren's *What Language Shall I Borrow?*
(see suggested references.)

Form support communities and allies for struggling
through issues yourself and for acting as resources and
supports for one another, both within and outside your congregation and denomination or institution. Share strategies
and compare notes of what worked and what did not work.
Inform one another of important reading materials and useful resources. Plan to attend workshops, continuing-educa-
tion courses and events, and conferences together. From time

to time, invite a guest resource person to bring a fresh voice
and viewpoint and to offer you some friendly support!

References

Carter, Aiko. "Women in Church and Society: A Japanese Perspective." In *In God's Image*, December 1985/February 1986, 34-36.

Chan, Wing-Tsit. *A Source Book in Chinese Philosophy*. Princeton, N.J.: Princeton University Press, 1963.

Ching, Julia. *Chinese Religions*. Maryknoll, N.Y.: Orbis Books, 1993.

_____. *Confucianism and Christianity: A Comparative Study*. Tokyo et al.: Kodansha International, 1977.

Chung, Hyun Kyung. *Struggle to Be the Sun Again: Introducing Asian Women's Theology*. Maryknoll, N.Y.: Orbis Books, 1990.

de Bary, W. T., W. T. Chan, and B. Watson. *Sources of Chinese Tradition*. New York: Columbia University Press, 1960.

Fung, Yu-Lan. *A Short History of Chinese Philosophy: A Systematic Account of Chinese Thought from Its Origins to the Present Day*. Edited by Derek Bodde. New York and London: Macmillan, The Free Press, 1948.

Gleb, Joyce, and Marian Lief Palley, eds. *Women of Japan and Korea: Continuity and Change*. Philadelphia: Temple University Press, 1994.

Gilmartin, Christina K. et al., eds. *Engendering China: Women, Culture, and the State*. Cambridge, Mass.: Harvard University Press, 1994.

Ho, Simon Sai-ming. *Christianity and Filial Piety* (in Chinese). Hong Kong: Christian Cultural Society Editorial and Translation Department, 1963, 1986.

Ho, Winnie, comp. *Toward a Chinese Feminist Theology*. Hong Kong: Lutheran Theological Seminary, 1988.

Jue, Jennifer. *Chinese American Women's Development of Voice and Cultural Identity: A Participatory Research Study via Feminist Oral History*. Dissertation, Doctor of Education, University of San Francisco, 1993.

Kung, Hans, and Julia Ching. *Christianity and Chinese Religions*. New York, et al.: Doubleday, 1989.

Kwok, Pui Lan. "Mothers and Daughters, Writers and Fighters." In *Inheriting Our Mothers' Gardens: Feminist Theology in Third*

World Perspective. Edited by Letty Russell et al. Louisville, Ky.: Westminster Press, 1988, 21-34.

Kwok, Pui Lan. *Chinese Women and Christianity, 1860-1927*. Atlanta: Scholars Press, 1992.

Lee, Peter K. H. "Contextualization and Inculturation of Christianity and Confucianism in the Contemporary World." In *Ching Feng*. Vol. 34 no. 2, June 1991, pp.84-93.

Lee, Peter K. H., and Hyun Kyung Chung. "A Cross-cultural Dialogue on the Yin-Yang Symbol." In *Ching Feng*. Vol. 33, no. 3, September 1990, 136-157.

Lee Park, Sun Ai. "Confucianism and Women." In *Ching Feng*. Vol. 32, no. 2, June 1989, 27-29.

Leo, L.S. "Chinese Women and Family from the Buddhist Perspective." *Interreligio*. Vol. 21, Summer 1992, 29.

Liu, Lianbuo, Yangfeng Chen, and Sianjuan Siung. *Zhongguo Nuzi Jaoyushi* (in Chinese) (History of Women's Education in China). Wuhan, Hubei, China: Wuhan Publishing Co., 1993.

Liu, Shu-hsien, and Robert E. Allinson. *Harmony and Strife: Contemporary Perspectives, East and West*. Hong Kong: The Chinese University Press, 1988.

Man, Eva K. W. "Chinese Women and the Family from the Confucian Perspective." In *Interreligio*. Vol. 21, summer 1992, 28.

Mattielli, Sandra, ed. *Virtues in Conflict: Tradition and the Korean Woman Today*. Seoul: Royal Asiatic Society, Korean Branch, 1977.

Nakano, Mei T. *Japanese American Women: Three Generations 1890-1990*. Berkeley, Calif.: Mina Press Publishing, 1990.

Ng, Greer Anne. "Family and Education from an Asian-North American Perspective: Implications for the Church's Educational Ministry." In *Religious Education*, vol. 87, no. 1, Winter 1992, 52-61.

Pao, Chiu-Lin. "Yin-Yang Thought and the Status of Women." In *Confucian-Christian Encounter in Historical and Contemporary Perspective*. Edited by Peter K. H. Lee. London: Edwin Mellen Press, 1991, 314-338.

Parrinder, Geoffrey. *Asian Religions*. London: Sheldon Press, 1957.

Pieris, Aloyius, ed. *Woman and Man in Buddhism and Christianity*. Dialogue Vols. 19-20, 1992-1993.

Suwanbubba, Parichart. "The Position of Women in Buddhism." In *In God's Image*, June 1989, 37-42.

Yoon, Jin-Sun. *Second Generation Korean Canadian Women: The Historical Context of Their Ethnic Identity.* Research paper, Master of Education, University of British Columbia, 1995.

Yu, Chai-Shin, ed. *Korean and Asian Religious Traditions.* Toronto: Korean and Related Studies Press, University of Toronto Press, 1977.

Yu, Chi-Ping. "Filial Piety and Chinese Pastoral Care." In *Asian Journal of Theology.* Vol. 4, no. 1, 1990, 316-328.

Yu, Diana. *Winds of Change: Korean Women in America.* Silver Spring, Md.: The Women's Institute Press, 1991.

Suggested Resources for Action Strategies

Fiorenza, Elisabeth Schussler, ed. *Searching the Scriptures. Volume One: An Introduction to Feminist Interpretation.* New York: Crossroad, 1993.

_____. *Searching the Scriptures. Volume Two: A Feminist Commentary.* New York: Crossroad, 1994.

González, Justo L. and Catherine G. González, *The Liberating Pulpit.* Nashville: Abingdon Press, 1994.

Matsui-Estrella, Julia and Greer Anne Wenh-In Ng. "Culture, Theology and Leadership." In *Women of Power.* Issue 24, 1995, 68-70.

Newsom, Carol A., and Sharon H. Ringe, eds. *The Women's Bible Commentary.* Louisville, Ky.: Westminster/John Knox Press, 1989.

Ng, Greer Anne Wenh-In, ed. *Generations Trying to Live Together.* Toronto: United Church of Canada, 1995.

Ng, Greer Anne Wenh-In. "Toward Wholesome Nurture: Challenges in the Religious Education of Asian North American Female Christians." In *Religious Education.* Vol.91, no. 2, Spring 1996.

Russell, Letty M., ed. *Feminist Interpretation of the Bible.* Philadelphia: Westminster Press, 1985.

Shum, Mina, director. *Double Happiness* (film). 1994.

Sugirtharajah, R. S., editor. *Voices from the Margin: Interpreting the Bible in the Third World.* Maryknoll, N.Y.: Orbis Books, 1991.

Wahlberg, Rachel Conrad. *Jesus According to a Woman.* New York: Paulist Press, 1975.

Wilson, Lois M. *Miriam, Mary, and Me.* Winfield, British Columbia: Wood Lake Books, 1992.

Wren, Brian. *What Language Shall I Borrow? God-Talk in*

Worship: A Male Response to Feminist Theology. New York: Cross-road, 1989, 1993.

Appendix to Chapter 4
Design of a Bible Study on Vashti and Esther

Target participants: members of the women's group at the Chinese Presbyterian Church, Oakland, California.

Objectives:

1. to introduce participants to a feminist interpretation of the Book of Esther and to highlight the theme of ethnic survival;

2. to demonstrate an alternative way of doing Bible study—that is, from a feminist and Asian North American perspective; and

3. to provide an empowering experience of searching the Scriptures using participants' own experiences, thus exposing some myths attached to traditional male-dominant and Judeo-Christian-centric approaches.

Time available: two hours.

Resources consulted:

Standard, traditional commentaries and references:

• Anderson, Bernhard W., *Esther*, in The Interpreter's Bible. Vol. 3, ed. George A. Buttrick, et. al. (Nashville: Abingdon Press, 1954).

• Moore, Carey A. *Esther*, in the Anchor Bible. Vol. 7b (New York: Doubleday, 1971).

• Paton, Lewis Bayles, *Esther*, in The International Critical Commentary on the Holy Scriptures of the Old and New Testaments. Vol. 13 (Edinburgh:T. & T. Clark, 1908, 1951).

Contemporary and nontraditional commentaries and references:

• Berg, Sandra Beth, *The Book of Esther: Motive, Themes and Structure*, SBL Dissertation Series 44 (Missoula, Mont.: Scholars Press, 1979).

• Fox, Michael V., *Character and Ideology in the Book of Esther*, Studies in Biblical Personalities (South Carolina:University of South Carolina Press, 1991).

- Laocque, Andre, *The Feminine Unconventional: Four Subversive Figures in Israel's Tradition.* Overtures to Biblical Theology (Philadelphia: Fortress Press, 1990).
- Newsom, Carol A. and Sharon H. Ringe, *The Women's Bible Commentary* (Louisville: Westminster/John Knox Press, 1992).
- White, Sidney Ann, "Esther: A Feminine Model for Jewish Diaspora," in *Gender and Difference in Ancient Israel*, ed. Peggy L. Day (Philadelphia: Fortress Press, 1989).

Process:
1. Get acquainted, discussing expectations and assumptions.
   a. Begin group building—welcome and introduce newcomers, old-timers; check-in.
   b. Discuss expectations—"What do you hope to take away from this session?"
   c. Discuss assumptions and agenda:
      i. As leader, share your stance of doing the Bible study (adult education, popular education, and feminist pedagogical principles, plus six convictions from the United Church of Canada's *Authority and Interpretation of Scripture* report).
      ii. Present the objectives of today's session, comparing them with the expectations voiced by participants; agree on which to keep, which to leave out.
      iii. Outline the process on newsprint or chalkboard.
2. Explore traditional understandings of the text.
   a. "What do you remember of Esther's story?" (Get a story outline only from participants' knowledge.)
   b. Give input on the historical background to the book, using a time line.
3. Raise "hermeneutics of suspicion."
   a. Divide participants into three groups; have each read among themselves chapter 1 of the Book of Esther.
   b. Ask each group to experience the Vashti incident

from the experience and point of view, respectively, of:

    i. a woman-in-waiting at the queen's court, or

    ii. commoners at the banquet, or

    iii. Vashti herself.

  c. Allow each group to present the story from that group's perspective.

  d. Use the following questions/directions in debriefing:

- "What do you notice that is similar, different, missing?"
- "Compare your group's perspective with the viewpoint of the biblical text (androcentric or male perspective)."
- "Why do you think Vashti's story is there?"

4. Look at Esther together.

  a. "What are some words you would use to describe Esther and how you feel about her?" (Have someone put these on the board or newsprint.)

- "Did any of these surprise you, or were they predictable?"

  b. "What is Esther usually held up for? Have you ever felt the pressure to be like her—as, for example, to be like Ruth or Mary? Do you feel any tension within yourself?"

  c. "What would you say is the theme or main point of the book for Jews in the Diaspora? Explain."

- "What is the main point for contemporary Asian Christians in North America?"
- "What difference does it make to remember that we are 'Asians in diaspora'?"

  d. "What insights does Esther's story provide about how Asians survive and thrive in a "diaspora" situation here in North America? Give examples from your personal or community life."

5. Move into action.

  a. "What one thing would you do differently because of what you've learned about Vashti—about how you

act as a woman, how you treat other women and
girls, how you respond to men's demands, etc.?"

b. "What suggestions do you have for retaining or re-
claiming your ethnic and cultural identity in a Christian and church setting?"

6. *Reflect on and evaluate today's learning experience.*

a. "On the whole, did you get what you came for? Why
or why not?"

b. "What are some of your learnings (content, process,
personal)?"

c. "Were there any surprises?"

d. "What would have made it an even better learning
experience for you?"

CHAPTER 5

Asian North American Women in the Workplace and the Church

By Young Lee Hertig

Introduction

The ideal for a community is the mutual acceptance of all persons as valued members. In a nurturing and productive community, persons of diverse character and talent contribute to the welfare of the whole. Diversity is accepted as a reality of life and differences are fitted in harmoniously. The yin-and-yang explanation of life implies the wisdom of such a pattern of living.

However, in many Asian North American congregations, the ideal of a community of diverse elements in harmonious relationship is not fully realized. Asian practices have been influenced by thousands of years of interpretation of Confucian and other social systems of relationships. What originally were benevolent principles of mutuality, reciprocity, respect, and good will demonstrated by the practice of rites and proprieties have evolved into codes and regulations directing young people to obey their elders and women to submit to men.

The previous chapter sought to address the problems of relationships within families, between parents and children (expressed through filial piety), and between women and men. Asian North American professional women face special problems regarding roles and relationships. Working outside the home, these women's efforts are resisted or rejected by those who hold power and authority in churches and professional organizations.

Young Lee Hertig, an ordained minister who teaches at Fuller Theological Seminary, has seen and experienced the use of power and authority to "keep women in their place." This chapter offers a series of vignettes—little stories—that show that in regard to women, the Asian North American church has a long, long path to travel toward the ideal community of mutual respect and acceptance.

The feminist movement does not capture our hearts. With its privileged status and different reality, this movement of white, middle-class women does not represent the realities we Asian North American women face in our homes, workplaces, or churches. Amid the tension between cultural and theological worlds, we have no particular movement with which we may identify. We are apt to be theological and cultural orphans. The following pages voice the peculiar struggles of Asian North American women on the front lines of Christian leadership. Estranged from the feminist movement and blocked by our own ethnic groups, we women of Asian heritage seek our own identity and integrity, our own call to being. And we understand this call for Asian North American women to be a call from God, a call into the body of Christ.

This chapter focuses on the treatment of Asian professional women both in the workplace and in the church. It analyzes factors that wound and divide the body of Christ. Power and authority issues are daily struggles for women who are pioneering in a man's world. Power dynamics exist in every relationship because relationships encompass gender, ethnicity, class, and generational aspects. In *Power and Innocence*, Rollo May analyzes the basic human need for power and the impact on the human being in its absence. I will use his five levels of power as a framework for ethnic, gender, class, and generational issues. They are:

1. the power to be;
2. self-affirmation;
3. self-assertion;

4. aggression; and

5. violence.

These power dynamics interact and weave together the tapestry of one's life cycle. May offers wise counsel: a healthy community pays attention to both individual and collective attitudes toward power dynamics.

The Power to Be

The expression "the power to be" is the demand for basic survival, as indicated when a newborn baby cries or reaches out its arms. To not express this basic need for survival is considered abnormal. The power to be is an essential element in the development of personality. May stresses that when this power to be is denied, "neurosis, psychosis, or violence will result" (1972:40-43).

The minority professional women's triple marginality—being a woman instead of a man, being the minority instead of the majority, and being marginalized among women—induces alienation and pain. The philosopher Kierkegaard empathized with the affliction of women when he said that "the misfortune of women is that at a given moment they are all important, while the next day they are completely unimportant" (Gutierrez 1989:166). This often causes women to seek their affirmation from males rather than females. These women perceive that men control power.

Hyun Sung, a Korean American in her first year in the workplace of a Christian organization, suffered as a woman in a man's world:

> In my loneliness at the workplace, I sought some friendships with mainstream women. In this competitive environment, I found it difficult to move beyond superficial cliché relationships. Especially when my work was productive, they ignored me. Jane, a white woman with an influential position in the finance department, has been with this organization for more than ten years. Jane gives all her time and energy to the powerful male leaders while

ignoring me. She shields her time from women with potential by not returning their phone calls or by canceling
appointments at the last minute. Jane herself is very
reactionary when she experiences this same treatment
from the male leaders.

Why do women like Jane who already have enough clout
continue to seek solidarity with powerful males? It appears
that self-interest overrides a desire to empower those of like
gender. When women seek affirmation from men it can be
understood as a strong desire of the powerless to identify
with the powerful. This negates the power to be women.
Women thus spurn one another, treating colleagues as objects of competition. Gordon Allport (quoted in Tachiki
1971:75) warns that a minority person's hostility and denial
of his or her minority culture may produce internalized
"racial self-hatred." He illustrates the observation of Jews in
Nazi concentration camps:

Studies of Nazi concentration camps show that identification with one's oppressor was a form of adjustment. . . . At
first prisoners tried to keep their self-respect intact, to feel
inward contempt for their persecutors, to try by stealth and
cunning to preserve their lives and their health. But after
two or three years of extreme suffering many of them found
that their efforts to please their guards led to a mental
surrender. They imitated the guards, wore bits of their cloth-
ing (symbolic power), turned against new prisoners, became
anti-Semites, and in general took over the dark mentality of
the oppressor.

Allport points to two consequences of self-hatred: violence
and a derogatory attitude toward one's own group. The strong
attempt to identify with symbolic America depicted by the
mass media contributes to the crisis among minority groups.
Asian North American young people internalize white American physical images as symbolic power.

Thus minority people do not give value to another minority
professional unless that person is widely recognized. When
Asian professional women meet new people, they find them-

selves in the "noncategorical" category and feel like nonbe-
ings.

The Denial of a Female's Being

Wendy is an ordained minister in her thirties who looks
younger than her age. She shares her struggle in trying to do
ministry in a congregational setting:

> People who do not know me treat me as a secretary and
> tell me to make copies for them. Once they find out that I
> am a pastor, they often cannot hide their surprise and do
> not know what to do with me. Unless I become a nationally
> known figure, this experience will continue. The flip side
> of this is in the case of the male. A friend of mine is not a
> pastor. Yet, with his tall height and gentle appearance,
> people call him a pastor. Ironically, he has to correct people
> that he is not a pastor.

How can a female minister overcome her social disposition
in a world of power images? Since both Eastern and Western
images of authority are external and shaped by the dominant
groups, men and women need to work together harmoniously
to bring perceptual changes in order for Asian North American female leadership to be accepted. When society does not
provide suitable images for their positions, women like Hyun
Sung and Wendy undergo endless embarrassing encounters
with people in both the minority and dominant cultures. This
absence of categories for Hyun Sung and Wendy makes it
difficult for people to recognize their legitimate power to be.
Consequently, women on the front lines are haunted with a
stronger sense of homelessness in an already homeless postmodern world. We need tremendous inner strength in order
to continue our struggle against nonbeing as we journey
toward a sense of dignity.

Self-Affirmation

We all have the basic need to be affirmed for who we are
as well as who we are becoming. Our self-consciousness is

shaped by the affirmation of others. This is why the cry for
recognition becomes our cry as Asian North American women
(May 1972:41).

Ambiguity As a Mechanism of Degradation

Esther, with a Ph.D. in theology, teaches at an Asian North
American seminary. She expresses her "nonbeing" treatment
by an administrator at that seminary:

> I am popular among the students because I add a fresh
> teaching style. One year when I asked for the class sched-
> ule, an administrator replied evasively, "We have not de-
> cided our schedule yet." I said that I would like to teach
> during the spring quarter. When I called back two weeks
> later, the man said that the schedule had been completed
> and that I was not scheduled to teach in the spring. I told
> him I had been counting on teaching in the spring and had
> arranged my other schedule around it. The man simply
> gave the phone to his coworker and delegated his response.
> The man under him took the blame and apologized.

Why did the administrator, also an ordained pastor, avoid
answering Esther? He felt no obligation or accountability to
a woman no matter what her position. Female status is
overruled by power and by position. Gender hierarchy com-
pelled by the face-saving mechanism of Asian culture height-
ens the degradation experienced by women. When a verbal
agreement is not kept, it is easily covered up by a verbal
apology, which avoids an honest and responsible answer.
Being treated with ambiguity feels more painful than a direct
assault because it uses a "nonbeing" treatment. The administrator did not view Esther as important enough for him to
need to explain his mistake.

Verbal agreements rather than written contracts give no
protection for someone like Esther. This cultural form of
communication relies heavily on the relational dimension in
decision making rather than on factual information. Esther
often thinks of how an Asian man in her position would be
treated. She feels she has been treated like a ghost.

Conditional love—based on certain conditions being met—is self-diminishing rather than self-affirming. The woman who is forced to respond to conditional love sets out on a course of destructive competitiveness. Her self-affirmation is taken by others to be a diminishing of them. She in turn is diminished by them (May 1972:41).

When self-affirmation meets resistance, we move on to the next level, self-assertion. But many women find it difficult to assert themselves because of patriarchal, cultural, and theological blockades. Instead, some women find it easier to use manipulation to gain power to be rather than to assert themselves directly. For Asian females, triple marginality afflicts our humanity. On the one hand, in our attempts to earn legitimacy in professional work, we face ambiguity from the dominant white society—we get token treatment. On the other hand, in the decision-making processes, we also suffer ambiguity, resulting in exclusion, as in Esther's case.

Gender As a Tool: A Sign of Neuroses

In the workplace women observe how other women behave in interpersonal relationships with the opposite sex. Wendy observes how her coworker Sally, a Christian education director, interacts with men differently than with women. Wendy shares her experience:

> When I try to talk with Sally, she normally keeps it brief. When she talks with male coworkers, I notice that her tone of voice changes. Her countenance is open and accepting. She usually gives eye contact to males as if to draw their attention to herself. Her body gesture is inviting and far more personal. This contrast makes the working relationship with her difficult.

Sexual Charm

Why are feminine qualities reduced to a sexual charm? What is the impact on the society when more females are involved with the public sector? Our fast-paced society drives people to take shortcuts in every aspect of life. Climbing up the career ladder is no exception. The flip side of women being oppressed because of gender and race is the manipulation of feminine characteristics. Sexual charm becomes a handy way of dealing with the male dominant hierarchy. Some women maximize this biological trait to achieve whatever goal they have. When women choose this route, they alienate other women or fall into competition with each other. Then every woman loses.

We need to guard against this easy access to power at the expense of degrading who we are. If society rewards those who focus on integrity and morality, our humanity need not be sacrificed by the powerful force of compromise.

Sexual Harassment

The reverse of the use of sexual charm is sexual harassment done to women by the male power holders. In the workplace many women find themselves in vulnerable situations from day to day. The fine line in drawing the proper physical boundary varies and puts both males and females in confusion. Knowing their jobs are at stake, many women find it extremely difficult to confront uncomfortable physical treatment from their male bosses. While white females have a clear definition of sexual harassment, the Asian community has only blurry boundaries.

> In an Asian North American congregation, Julie, a Christian education director, felt a prominent church lay leader pat her on the rear. At first she did not know what was going on. He repeated his behavior several times in spite of her verbal disapproval. Then Julie started observing him patting other women in the church. When she finally shamed him in front of the people by calling attention to his action when he did it, he finally stopped touching her. Julie was fully aware of the consequences. Ever since her confrontation in front of others, when Julie has tried to get the session's approval for church matters, he has blocked it.

Must women like Julie abhor their own sexuality in order

to function as leaders in Asian North American churches? Not in Julie's case. She refused to sacrifice her power to be for the sake of ministry. She refused to degrade herself in order to serve the church. Janet Hagberg rightly advocates that the powerless seek action against dehumanizing experiences. She says, "Women, minorities, and certainly the poor ... may feel more of the chronic powerlessness that can over time be demoralizing unless they take some action on their own behalf" (Hagberg 1984:xxiii).

Self-assertion

Self-assertion is more overt than self-affirmation and is therefore a stronger form of behavior. A woman who is able to assert herself is healthy.

Assertiveness Versus Aggressiveness

Often a female's assertiveness is labeled aggressiveness by the male who defines feminine qualities. After all, female assertiveness contradicts the traditional evangelical theological stance of women being submissive. This theological oppression of women's humanity is far more difficult to change than cultural oppression. Out in the world, women's lifestyles have been liberated due to rapid cultural change. However, the constant use of male-centered eisegesis of biblical passages in the church serves to harass many women. Thus a large number of Christian women suffer a more severe internal conflict than non-Christian women. The following story of Mei gan expresses this pain.

"But you're a woman." As a staff person in a parachurch college campus fellowship group, I often have been affirmed through a recognition of my gifts for ministry. But sometimes the response is that "this is great, but you're a woman." When I teach effectively or make a significant contribution, credit is given that I as a person can do well, but when I do not speak or teach well, it is often blamed on the fact that I am a woman.

Must a woman compartmentalize her being and her gender? Gender discrimination is hard to bear because it is an ascribed status, not an achieved status. We did not choose our gender; therefore, we do not bear responsibility for being female. Rather than have legitimate authority deriving from our ministry, Asian North American women are evaluated according to how well we serve the image of the submissive woman. This is the injustice of gender inequality.

Letting the Men Look Good

Jun Myung, a 1.5-generation Korean American is very bright and has natural leadership qualities. She shares the internal dissonance in her leadership role at church:

> I am so burnt out and frustrated with this special inter-church young adult conference. In the middle of the conference preparations, the president of the young adult group moved away. As the vice president, I had to proceed in leadership alone. I received a cold-shoulder response from the group, especially from the guys. They were laid-back, passive, and apathetic because they did not want a woman to be active. I was in tears. They said that they felt burdened when they saw me. They feared that I would give them a job or ask them for help. One guy told me that people who grew up in the United States do not like to be told what to do. They get rebellious even if they were going to do it anyway. He added that "men do not like to be told by a woman what to do." When I asked him about the work to be done, he replied, "Just leave it. Don't worry about the work."

How can people make sense of conflicting subcultural norms in the early stages of immigrant life? Does "making men look good" take precedence over a woman serving God? As Asian North American women acculturate, the strongly held value of women's submissiveness is at stake. Ironically, the rate of Asian women's acculturation into American society is quicker than men's because, at least externally, American society affirms gender equality. June's conflict in serving the church is indicative of the widening gap of gender in-equality for Christian women in the immigrant church. Our acculturation into American culture and our active service in the church challenge the core male-dominant structure.

Even when the young adult males in Jun Myung's case had no desire to assume leadership themselves, they blocked a woman's willingness to take the leadership role. In this particular group, a "let the boat sink" mentality prevailed.

Blaming the Victim

Anne has finished her M.B.A. and started her first job with a Christian business corporation.

> I seem to be a token Asian woman in this Anglo-Christian corporation, hired in order to portray multicultural stand-ards. Since this is my first job in an American business corporation, I do not understand the terms by which the corporation evaluated me. After six months, I still had not gone through orientation. Due to financial troubles, work-ers are overworked and receive low pay. Consequently, the competition for survival is severe and individualism is reinforced. This has left me totally confused. Toward the end of the first year, I started feeling bitter because the executives were measuring me against experienced senior workers. I was criticized because I did not meet the quotas according to experienced standards. When asserting my needs for getting the same opportunities as senior workers against whom I was measured, I ended up being labeled as "pushy."

How can the powerless express their experience without being judged by the power holder's norm? Anne experiences another form of hierarchy, called corporate classism. Her presence itself, as the only minority woman, creates discom-fort in the dominant group. When Anne tries to voice her reality, of which the dominant group has no clue, she is viewed as being out of line. Anne, knowing her basic need to be is not being met, starts asserting herself only to be per-ceived by the corporation as aggressive.

Liberation theologian Leonardo Boff accurately observes
that life at the margins screams at you (1989:40). The condition that causes screaming is rarely noticed by the people at
the center, who only once in a while hear the screaming and
feel uncomfortable. The question of who is causing the
screaming is rarely addressed. Ignorant of the working conditions of the people outside the inner circle, life in the
corporation continues, and the wheels of injustice grind on.

William Ryan states that "the generic process of blaming
the victim is applied to almost every American problem" of
inequality—class, race, and gender (1992:365). However, this
is not limited to the American society. It is a universal
phenomenon and its roots are declared in Genesis: the fallen
nature of human beings. But people do not make the theological connection. Expressions of our triple marginality and
oppression fall on deaf ears, and our behavior is labeled as
aggressive. We are employed because of our gender and
ethnicity, not only because of our qualifications. When we are
employed as mere tokens by the dominant institutions on the
basis of our gender and ethnicity, we feel all the more marginalized.

The categories of the dominant group by which we are
assessed exclude us. We feel a triple injustice is being done
to us because of the already-biased categories of gender and
ethnicity. The first injustice is in the fact that we Asian
professional women experience criticism for going against
the traditional gender hierarchy in our own community.
Second, we therefore feel a severe internal conflict concerning who we are. Third, we experience a different form of
exclusion from the dominant culture, a tokenism based on
our gender and ethnicity. Inadvertently, when the personal
dimension is mentioned, it is our personality defects that
allow the inequality structures to have free hands to work
against us.

Confronted with these triple exclusions, some Asian professional women cry out and are blamed for our crying out by
the power holders as well as by their own ethnic group. The

root cause of our cry is not considered, and the symptom, crying, is condemned. This triple marginal experience, unfortunately, affirms the "blaming the victim" theory. When an Asian woman is a token in the dominant institution, there is no category for her, so she is labeled with categories from the dominant culture. This stereotyping is a form of victimization.

Anne, in her thirties, faces double patriarchalism from her own ethnic group and from the dominant group. Her own ethnic people do not want to identify with her when they can identify with the prestigious dominant professionals. The flip side of this is that the minority group accepts the dominant group's deviation from traditional values while rejecting the females from its own group. The dominant power holders deny even the hint of sexism and racism. The power elite disclaims gender and ethnicity issues and makes personality the focal issue. Thus the powerful place blame on the powerless. The heightened awareness of sexism and racism by the powerful is covered up. Frequently, this "blaming the victim" power structure leaves the burden of empowerment up to the powerless. The victim has to find her own relief.

Alienation through "In Betweenness"

Multiracial Asian North American women Naomi Southard and Rita Nakashima Brock affirm in "The Other Half of the Basket" the lonely marginal reality of Asian North American women in ministry:

> The personal experience of being marginalized and alienated from Western and Eastern cultures is magnified in our professional struggles. An Asian American woman in ministry has crossed significant barriers of culture and tradition in order to fulfill her calling (1987:138).

The Asian American professional woman's energy is diluted because there is no dependable foundation on which to stand. The lack of power to be and the inability to fit into the image of either the minority or the dominant cultural group strip the woman of authority and legitimacy. Such women are driven to a constant effort of job performance and ethnicity- and gender-related energy consumption. In other words, it requires a superwoman to survive in the professional world as a minority female while being criticized for being a super-woman!

In the play, *The Death of a Salesman,* the outcry of Willy Loman's wife calls us to treat fellow humans as human:

> Attention must be paid. . . . Even though "Willy Loman never made a lot of money. His name was never in papers . . . he's a human being. . . . So attention must be paid" (May 1972:41).

Like Willy Loman's wife, minority people sometimes per-sonalize another minority's unjust experience and assert it for themselves. May describes this as an indirect asserting of ourselves.

Aggression

Following May's understanding, aggression is a built-in emotional reaction that results from the violation of one's self-assertion. A psychological cause of aggression is the denial of a healthy response to one's assertion. The following story about Keiko describes how female assertiveness is perceived as aggressiveness by most Asian females, which stems from the blending of both cultural and theological partriarchalism.

> There was a forum on Asian North American Ministry at a local church. The panelists were Asian North American males. When the subject turned to the issue of female leadership, typical Christian jargon was expressed by a male professional. "Women should be silent in the church. This applies today because biblical truth does not change with time." At this, an Asian North American female pro-fessional disagreed. The male erupted at the female's dis-agreement.

Should women be silent in the church at all times? Why were women allowed to prophesy in the New Testament (Acts 21:9; 1 Corinthians 11:5; Luke 1:46)? Can theology and hermeneutics be done free from stereotypical cultural and social grids? No one in the audience, which included other Asian North American professionals, made any comments. In fact, here is the response to Keiko from an Asian North American female friend who attended this forum and had discussed it with other Asian North American women: "It made us uncomfortable to see two Asian professionals arguing. You should not have confronted an Asian male in front of a big group."

In this scenario, many Asian females saw the Asian male's emotion acceptable while the Asian female's disagreement with the Asian male in public was perceived as inappropriate. When female assertiveness is perceived as aggressiveness even by Asian females, this stems from the double dosage of cultural and theological patriarchalism.

In fact, Harriet Goldhor Lerner articulates in *Dances of Anger* that we do not even have terms that describe male anger as negative while many terms exist for female anger (1985:2). Female anger is trivialized while male anger is legitimized. For Asian Christian females, one more pseudosacred dimension, theological patriarchalism, silences us. We not only are culturally homeless, but we are theologically homeless as well.

Lerner explains the underlying factor behind the criticism and fear of female anger. She distinguishes the guilt-conscious woman from the anger-conscious woman. "Why are angry women so threatening to others?" Lerner asks.

Angry Women Are Threatening

If we are guilty, depressed, or self-doubting, we stay in place. We do not take action except against our own selves and we are unlikely to be agents of personal and social change. In contrast, angry women may change and challenge the lives of us all, as witnessed in the past decade of feminism. And change is an anxiety-arousing and difficult business for everyone, including those of us who are actively pushing for it. Thus we, too, learn to fear our own anger, not only because it brings about the disapproval of others, but also because it signals the necessity for change for ourselves. Is my anger legitimate? Do I have a right to be angry? What good will it do? These questions are excellent ways of silencing ourselves and shutting off our anger (Lerner 1985:3). Lerner stresses that the denial of anger paralyzes the ability to be in touch with one's power to be because anger is a signal of the violation of one's being. Lerner's "challenge of anger" relates to the Asian North American women's condition: "Our anger may be a signal that we are doing more and giving more than we can comfortably do or give. Or our anger may warn us that others are doing too much for us, at the expense of our own competence and growth" (1985:1).

Women like Anne who openly express their anger at men are especially suspect. While affirming anger as a legitimate feeling, Lerner warns us about venting our anger. Venting anger only consumes our energy, pushing us toward rigid stagnation rather than toward clarifying and growth-producing effects on ourselves and others (1985:4).

Is the Woman's Place in the Kitchen?

Asian North American women's folk wisdom explains that the way to gain power in the church is through the pastor's stomach:

> At the church, Pastor Chung is surrounded by the ladies in their forties and fifties who constantly serve food and wait on him. These ladies in return gain informal power in the church through their influence on the pastor. They often change decisions that are made at congregational, committee, and even staff meetings. This creates conflict and chaos at all levels of the church.

What is the legitimate role of a woman in the church? The women who have discovered informal power fall into the role of creating unnecessary church conflict. They also turn one another into objects of competition in order to gain more power from the pastor. The unavailability of legitimate power for women brings malady to an otherwise healthy congregational life.

This unhealthy power dynamic between the leadership and the female laity needs to be addressed in order for the church to model a more healthy family dynamic. Specifically, females need to be given legitimate voices and roles in the life of the church.

Violence

When all the efforts of verbal challenge have no effect, the ultimate result is the explosion of violence. May describes violence in the physical dimension as a failure of reasoning or persuasion (1972:43). Karen is an extremely logical person. A second-generation Chinese American, she shares how her church leadership is dealing with her and her ministry.

> I have applied for an internship at the Chinese church where I attend. The church does not know where to place me because I do not fit the categories for children's ministry or youth work. Merely by being in seminary, I have been labeled as a feminist, an aggressive woman trying to invade "man's territory," or I am looked down upon as corrupted by American society, having strayed from Chinese values and proper ways of behaving as a "good Chinese woman."

An adviser to various pastoral search committees for Asian North American churches as well as other churches in his denomination (which is actually supportive of women in ministry) has often asked some of these committees if they would or have considered female candidates. The frequent responses are, "The thought never even occurred to us," and "Are there any?" When asked what they would do if given a female candidate to consider, the committee members have often said, "I don't know."

At a gathering of people in ministry to American-born Chinese people in the Los Angeles area, among all the women in the group, I was practically the only one who was not a pastor's wife. Being married doesn't help either. I have a married friend in the seminary whose Asian North American husband is reasonably supportive. Many question her vocation and calling, asking her why she needs to do "these things." Some accuse her of being selfish, even of depriving her husband of having children—certainly not conforming to the role of a "good Chinese" or "Asian" wife. Some also question why she needs to raise support and often do not know "what to do with him," since most married couples in ministry fall into the category of joint ministry or of a man in ministry with a supportive wife.

What are churches going to do with the growing number of female Asian North American seminarians? Whether single or married, Asian North American women leaders face a Catch-22 reality both within the church and out in the world. It feels more painful when the church treats us as if we are Martians. This is inhumane treatment of members of the body of Christ.

Fortunately, the marriage of Karen's friend demonstrates the precious partnership of marriage. In Karen's case she has a woman's ongoing awareness of her place in marriage and her calling from God. Ironically, it is a progressive wife who brings awareness to her husband and makes marriage partnership possible.

Catch-22

An Asian North American female teacher in a Christian college was excluded from her own people's gathering sponsored by the college. The Asian North American males on campus excluded her from the planning process completely. When she later found out, she decided to give her input to the official at school who was in charge of this particular gathering. Due to the reasonable nature of her idea, the official agreed to implement it. But at the actual gathering, the plan never materialized. Later she ended up being labeled as one who "wants a prominent place in every gathering." This characterization was spread by the official and an Asian North American male.

How are women on the front line supposed to figure out when the dominant cultural group is going to project its image of Asian women onto us and expect us to conform to its rules? Having Asian North American women faces can be very confusing in the white workplace where gender equality is pervasive externally (in the form of rhetoric) but not internally. It is like being in an invisible war zone. At least in Asian North American churches there are blatant signs and discussions about gender inequality everywhere that require no second-guessing.

A twofold stigma of Asian North American professional women occurs when the white society embraces Asian and Anglo patriarchalism in its attitude toward the female. The Asian North American male's chauvinistic influence on the dominant power holder (the white male) excludes female input in order to be "culturally correct." Furthermore, both males interpret the female's desire for inclusion as power hunger.

When the Asian North American teacher mentioned above wanted to be included in her own ethnic gathering at school, the power elite excluded her. Then the dominant power structure blamed her for not being supported by her own community. At their own convenience, the measuring stick changes from the paternalistic to the egalitarian college criterion. When she has opportunities to utilize her expertise, she is told she is not experienced enough. When it comes to her less-experienced areas, then she is measured by different criteria.

Does My Culture Count?

Janet, the teacher's seminarian friend, is upset with the denial of who she is in the curriculum at the seminary where the multiculturalism rhetoric is at its peak.

> I am so angry at being stereotyped from both sides. My question never makes it as a question. I always have to listen to an answer that is not about my question. I feel violated.

Should a desire to be included be a crime against the status quo? This cry for inclusion, this cry for the power to be, is left unanswered. A false answer is attempted, one which labels the crier as "pushy." After the cry sifts through the patriarchal power grid as a hunger for power, it boomerangs back upon the one who cries out and leaves her wounded by her own cry. This is worse than a cry that falls on deaf ears. The victim is blamed. This "blaming the victim" syndrome is the root of Asian North American female suffering.

Shared Stories Build Community

The sharing of our stories is the beginning of discovering ourselves and of connecting ourselves with others:

> Once we see ourselves in others and others in ourselves through our shared stories, our perceptions become enlarged and we realize that we are all marginal. This enlargement of perception through mutual affirmation opens the way for the building of community in diversity (Hertig 1993:16).

In sharing our stories toward the building of community, theological identity is crucial. Theology is never done in a vacuum but always in the context of everyday life. Beneath our gender disparity lies a theological bluff that alienates not only women but also men. Those who inflict pain are violated in their humanity as much as those who receive pain. However, sharing in our humanity, we encounter others' stories, and others become us. In order for Asian

North American women's integrity as human beings to be restored so that we may find our own community as well as the larger community, a gender-inclusive theology needs to be lived out at the congregational level. It is time for Asian North American churches to embrace the lonely cry of Asian North American women on the front lines.

To carry out this noble task, the exclusive "either/or" paradigm needs to be shifted to the "both/and" paradigm. Understanding occurs when we are in dialogue with the different perspectives. Ironically and fortuitously, Asian concepts can provide some of the resolution to the problem of male power over female lack of power. A fresh application of the circle of harmony found in *yin* and *yang* suggests complementarity, mutuality, and reciprocity. The "both/and" perspectives in which males and females complement one another and bring out the fullness of God's image may open the way for better dialogue between race, gender, and class. As we begin to understand the plight of the frontier women with the triple interlocking web, we will avoid hasty, narrow, reductionistic evaluations.

We also need to read the biblical stories afresh in order to sort out the cultural baggage of long-held Western paradigms of theology and sort through our Eastern paradigms so that we may balance and expand our theological journey. This theological journey is for everyone. People of all different cultures will be connected as human beings without losing cultural and individual uniquenesses that fulfill the image of God.

Asian North American women are very concerned about the connections between personal experience and theology. Theology has to be a lived-out discipline in the power of the Holy Spirit, which ought to build, not divide, the community. This requires a paradigm shift in the way we do our theologizing. We all need to be story sharers in order to understand one another. As the biblical stories weave into our stories, we find meaning in the fragmented postmodern world of urban wastelands. We become connected. Furthermore, by creating community, our fragmented reality moves from theological first aid to the healing of wounds. Through intense struggles, Asian North American women strive to make a whole out of fragmented parts.

Let the weaving together of our stories begin.

Questions for Reflection

1. Recall some of your experiences when an Asian North American woman, perhaps you yourself, was treated with condescension or disdain. How did you feel about those experiences? How do you think others in the events felt?

2. What happened when you tried to deal with a situation in which an Asian North American woman was treated poorly? Can you think of positive ways of educating people to change their attitudes and actions regarding the role of women?

3. How can the church address the issue of the role of women?

References

Boff, Leonardo. *Faith on the Edge.* San Francisco: Harper and Row, Publishers, 1989.

Ellul, Jacques. *The Presence of the Kingdom.* Colorado Springs: Helmers and Howard, 1989.

Gutierrez, Gustavo. *The God of Life.* New York: Orbis Books, 1989.

Hagberg, Janet. *Real Power: Stages of Personal Power in Organizations.* Minneapolis: Winston Press, 1984.

Hertig, Young Lee. "Expanding and Balancing Our Horizon." In *Reflections: Korean American Ministry Journal.* January/February 1994, 1–3.

Lerner, Harriet Goldhor. *Dances of Anger: A Woman's Guide to Changing the Patterns of Intimate Relationships.* New York: Harper and Row, Publishers, 1985.

May, Rollo. *Power and Innocence: A Search for the Sources of Violence.* New York: W.W. Norton and Co., Inc., 1972.

Ryan, William. "Blaming the Victim." In *Race, Class, Gender.* New York: St. Martin's Press, 1992.

Southard, Naomi, and Rita Nakashima Brock. "The Other Half

of the Basket: Asian American Women and the Search for a Theological Home," *Journal of Feminist Studies in Religion.* Fall 1987, 135–50.

Tachiki, Amy. *Roots: An Asian American Reader.* Los Angeles: The Regents of the University of California, 1971.

CHAPTER 6

Asian North American Immigrant Parents and Youth: Parenting and Growing Up in a Cultural Gap

By Grace Sangok Kim

Introduction

Especially for immigrant families, the years when the children are adolescents are extremely trying. Perhaps more than any other problem, the question of how parents and adolescent children are to communicate with and relate to each other is most on the minds of Asian North American parents and young people. As noted in the two previous chapters, the issues of power, authority, and relationships boil up to the surface in Asian North American communities. The church is both a place where problems between parents and young people erupt and where resources for guidance and counsel can be made available.

In this chapter, Grace Sangok Kim, an educator experienced in working with Asian North American young people and their parents, has gathered stories of communication gaps and suggestions for establishing communication between family members who love each other but do not have the means of expressing that love so that it is understood and received.

Later, in chapter 10, Kim presents suggestions for youth ministry in Asian North American congregations.

Vignettes of Confusion and Conflict in Immigrant Families

Story 1: The American Dream Becomes a Nightmare

My husband and I decided to emigrate from Hong Kong to the United States about ten years ago. We had an American dream: better educational opportunities for our children.

We were—and are—willing to sacrifice our lives for the future of our children. When we came to the United States, our children were very young, but now our son is sixteen years old and our two daughters are fourteen and eleven.

As we've watched our children growing and rapidly changing, we've begun to have serious doubts about the way children are taught in school. Schools in this country are not strict enough. The teachers don't give much homework. They don't teach young people proper manners, responsibilities, or respect for elders. The students have too much freedom and too many choices. Young people are overly concerned with peer acceptance and popularity. They are interested in their appearance—their hairstyles and fashions. They listen to rock and rap music. Many get into drugs and gang violence. They start to date very early. We are upset, confused, and at a loss as to how to raise our children.

Story 2: Finding Room to Grow

One change I hope I can make about myself this year is in my relationship with my parents.

My parents are very protective of me and don't let me do anything. So to get what I want, I lie and do things against their commands. If I want to go out with my friends, my parents find ways to say no. So in order to leave the house, I make up excuses, as if I'm just going to the store or something. They pressure me to do well in school, and just to get them mad, I do poorly in my classes. When they tell me to do my homework, I just pretend to do it. They don't seem to understand that I need room to grow and in trying to protect me from harm, they've made me become more rebellious. *(A fourteen-year-old Chinese American female)*

Sometimes when I lie, my parents find out. Although they don't get angry, I know they feel hurt and distrust me. I understand that all they want is what's best for me—a bright, happy future—but sometimes it's impossible to obey their orders. I will try to be more honest and open with my parents. I want them to understand what being a teenager nowadays is like, and I also want to understand what being a parent is like. *(A sixteen-year-old Vietnamese American female)*

Marie Lee (1992), a Korean American young woman, published an autobiographical novel, Finding My Voice, *based on her growing up in Minnesota, and described similar inner conflicts as the Vietnamese girl did in the story above.*

Story 3: Living up to Parental Expectations

I am a fifteen-year-old Korean American high school girl. My parents are working hard to make money. My parents, especially my mother, is very critical of many things I do. She thinks I don't dress properly for school and church. I like to wear T-shirts and baggy blue jeans. She thinks I use too much makeup. Actually I don't do anything different from my school friends. My parents expect me to get straight A's in school. I get nervous whenever they want to talk about my grades and my friends. It seems that I can never satisfy them. They have high expectations of me. Sometimes I feel as if I'm in prison. I don't have much freedom at home. I know they care about me and do this for my future. But I feel that my mother is a dictator. I cannot disagree with her or ask her questions. She always talks about how she grew up in Korea, how she obeyed her parents, and how she was taught what is appropriate behavior for girls.

Story 4: A Disappointing Daughter

When I was in China, my mother taught me how to cook, clean house, iron clothes, and sew. Most of all, we were taught how to respect our parents and grandparents. My daughter refuses to learn any of these. She is fourteen years old. She is not polite to us and her grandparents. She does not have good manners. She says that we are too old-fashioned, that this is America, and that she does not have to live with the old culture and customs. I don't know what to do with her.

Story 5: The Children Want to Be Left Alone

My children think that I am an overprotective mother. I love them and care about their education and futures. I do things for them as any mother would do, such as make their beds, clean their rooms, do laundry, and so on. I do not allow them to go out at night because there is no reason for them to go out and waste their time. It is dangerous to go out at night anyway. They think I am not trusting them and their abilities. They don't want me to do things for them. They say that I should just give them enough allowance and that they will take care of themselves in their own way. They say that I should leave them alone.

Story 6: Hard to Talk with Parents

It's hard to talk to my parents. They think I like gangsters and drug dealers. It's just not true. *(A fifteen-year-old Vietnamese male)*

Story 7: No Communication

My relationship with my parents isn't good because of a lack of communication. I have a hard time trying to understand them. So I don't feel as if I can talk to them. Lots of times when I've tried to reason with them, I've felt that they were just shutting me out or getting mad for disagreeing with them. *(A fourteen-year-old Chinese American female)*

A Youth Survey

In 1993 I conducted a survey study of sixty-three teenagers and their parents in an Asian American church in California (G. Kim 1993). The Asian youth survey sample was from twelve to sixteen years in age and about equally divided in gender. The great majority were North American-born and their parents were all first-generation immigrants from Asia.

The subjects were asked to write anonymously on the following questions:

1. How do you feel about your relationship with your parents?

2. Are there many differences between your values and your parents' values?

3. What are your worries?

4. What are the hopes and desires you have of your parents?

Typical and recurring themes in the teenagers' answers to their hopes and desires of their parents include the following:

— Trust me.
— Leave me alone.
— Listen and understand me.
— Don't put me down.
— Don't compare me with others (siblings or friends' children).
— Don't blame me.
— You have too many expectations.
— Accept me as I am.
— Grades are not everything.
— Be more realistic and flexible.
— Don't be a racist.
— Learn English.
— Let me express my real feelings without getting shot back at.

The parents listed the following as the most difficult issues and problems they are experiencing in raising their children:

— bad influences from American society (drugs, teen music and sex, violence, television commercials and shows, etc.);

— inability to understand American teen culture;

— cultural differences;

— children's lack of interest in learning Asian manners and etiquette;

— language and culture barriers;

— poor communication;

— limited time and energy available for children due to long and hard work;

— too lonely and hard a life as immigrants, including feeling cut off from children, in spite of sacrificial work for them; and

— worry and concern about the dating and marriage of their children.

Some Issues Confronting Immigrant Parents and Adolescent Children

We found that raising our children in North America is not easy. In fact, it is much more difficult and challenging than we realized when we left Asia. The multicultural environment with diverse values and traditions is confusing. The democratic ideological emphasis on individuality, freedom, independence, and equality is very different from the way we were raised. These Western ideologies have created new problems for us as parents (G. Kim 1982, 1983-1992).

When we talk about parenting, there is no such thing as "perfect parenting" or the only "right" or "correct" parenting method. Each child is different in personality, and parenting does not work in the same way for all children. We do our best for each child, but we do make mistakes. In recognizing our limitations as parents, professional journals in child development and psychology now write about the concept of *"good enough* parents," not "good parents" or "perfect parents." Also they write about the concept of a "holding environment" (Winnicott 1960), in which a young child can grow freely with a sense of security, safety, and stability rather than confusion and chaos. The primary task of the parents is to provide a holding environment for the child and not so much to "mold" the child.

Most times, our children turn out to be all right. Due to their high respect for academic scholarship, Asian North American students often excel academically. Many of them go to Ivy League colleges. The public image of Asian North American students is that of "a model minority" and "science and math wizards," although such stereotypical expectations can put undue pressure on these students (Suzuki 1989). David Rue (1990), an adolescence psychiatrist, described cases of depression and suicidal behavior among "Asian North American whiz kids."

It is also true that many Asian North American students are motivated to learn an Asian language and Asian culture, including family values and respect for parents and elders. There are many success stories in parenting among Asian immigrants.

However, we have to remember that, for every Ivy League college applicant among Asian North American youth, there are two or three high school dropouts. The numbers of Asian gangs, runaways, pregnant teens, and drug abusers are increasing. Asian North American young people represent a wide spectrum of characteristics and behavior. They cannot be lumped into a stereotypical "model minority" container.

Issues for Reflection

1. Immigrant parents face certain gaps between themselves and their Westernized children. While gaps are experienced in families all over the world, Asian North American families are especially vulnerable to those caused by differences of generation, culture, communication and language, and expectations.

2. The gaps cause common confusions and conflicts in parenting, such as:
   - different expectations of each other by parents and children;

- parents' thinking that their children are being Westernized too fast;
- problems of language and inadequate communication;
- problems of parenting complicated by different cultural values and philosophies;
- disagreements over cultural values for the children; and
- confusion over expressing or teaching cultural values in Asian North American churches.

Integrating Asian and North American Perspectives

As we can see in the stories above and the survey results, parenting and growing up in North America are complicated processes. It is just as difficult and challenging a task to the youths as it is to the parents. The school environment is more loose and less structured than in Asia and offers students many choices of electives and a greater freedom of decisions. Sometimes students may become distracted, unfocused, or overwhelmed. Also they are constantly bombarded with television commercials and other mass media emphasizing youth, sex, fun, violence, and material temptations. They are affected by fashions, video games, and rock and rap music. Peer influence and acceptance are much stronger for the adolescents than the influence and acceptance of parents.

When immigrant parents were growing up in Asia, the school environment was quite strict and structured. All classmates were of homogeneous ethnic makeup. Growing up in that environment was clear-cut and easier. Everyone went through the same things and the school life was standardized. Immigrant parents from Asia tend to project their own school experiences onto their children and expect them to behave at home and school the way they did.

In Asia, people believe in strong family life, with respect for parents and elders. Immigrants grew up in a way of life that has been strongly influenced by Confucian philosophy.

Confucian teachings emphasize self-discipline; self-cultivation (striving for higher education, scholarship, and lifelong education and growth); respect for parents, teachers, the elderly, and ancestors (filial piety); and respect for order, structure, and hierarchy in the family as well as in government and society (R. Kim 1986). The interests of family, group, and collective welfare take priority over the interests of the individual members.

These basic differences in the values and philosophies between Eastern and Western cultures are frequent sources of conflict between immigrants parents and their teenagers (M. Lee 1992).

The following table of traditional cultural values offers some highlights and contrasts.

Traditional values in Asian countries are rapidly changing through Westernization. The whole world is getting smaller with the influence of television, frequent travel and migration, and fast information exchange, resulting in mutual influences of ideas and values. Now there are more overlapping gray areas between Western and Asian cultures. Nevertheless, there are some core differences between the two. These differences often cause misunderstanding and disagreement between parents and Asian North American teens (M. Lee 1992; Kim and Kim 1994).

Traditional Cultural Values

Asian Culture	North American Culture
Family Relations	
• family-oriented	• individual-oriented
• interdependent	• autonomous, independent
• vertical, authoritarian	• horizontal, democratic
• respect for parents and elders	• variable depending on the family
• family loyalty, filial piety	• self-determination and personal happiness
• duty, obedience	• freedom of choice and independence

Life philosophy

- family-kinship bonds, collectivism
- success through self-discipline, will, and determination
- sense of stoicism and fatalism
- reciprocity and obligation

- face-saving and status consciousness
- holistic living in harmony with nature

- individualism
- pragmatism, realizing one's talents and potentials
- sense of opportunism and optimism
- avoidance of obligation (for example, "going Dutch treat")
- doing your own thing, self-satisfaction
- control and conquest of nature

While Asian values (mainly Confucian) have many virtues we can uphold, such as a work ethic, self-cultivation, and respect for family and parents, the virtues also cause some problems with gender roles, rigid hierarchy, lack of flexibility, and lack of respect for individual rights. As Asian North Americans, we need to be liberated from some aspects of the Asian cultural system. That is one of the reasons many immigrants left Asia.

On the other hand, some Asian North Americans feel that Western individualism may have gone as far as it can go. Highly developed individualism may be largely responsible for the breakdown of community, increasing divorce, single parenthood, lack of family cohesion, and the "do your own thing" culture to the degree that the quality of interpersonal life in North American society is declining.

Now, North American companies and businesses are embracing and adopting Japanese and other Asian ways of doing things. They are discovering that the Asian way has a lot to offer and that the Western way is not necessarily the superior way, either in industrial production or in the quality of people's lives.

Asian North American immigrants have been exposed to both worlds. We are in a unique position to have gained insights into both cultures. We can contribute to the development of a new, higher level of integrated and synergistic world-view and values.

Such ideology and philosophy would be less dogmatic or doctrinaire but would include a more harmonious and "both/and" instead of "either/or" approach. It is an exciting time for us to be able to explore a conceptual and practical framework that is both Asian and Western. We are between East and West, between North and South, between the old and the new, and between two languages.

Questions about Cultural Values for Immigrant Parents

1. What do you consider the positive and negative aspects of Asian and North American cultures?

2. In many immigrant families, differences in cultural values and philosophies between Asian and Western views create much confusion and conflict. What should be the parents' value orientation? An Asian way, Western way, half-and-half way, or a hybrid culture? What modifications are needed? How would an appropriate way be found?

3. If you could take the best parts from both cultures and combine or synthesize them, what kinds of values or value system would emerge?

What Would Be the Cultural Values of Asian North American Youth?

What kind of values and world-view are Asian North American youth likely to develop in contemporary North American society? Based on his research on 564 Asian North American adolescents, Professor Young Pai expressed a view that a single alternative perspective—that is, North American versus Asian values—oversimplifies the world in which the Asian North American young people live. He proposed a multidimensional or "web" type of perspective that can give us a much more accurate understanding of the pressures and tensions surrounding our youth. He states:

> The "web" metaphor suggests that our young people live their lives in a very complex network of relationships. Indeed, their world consists of many different intersecting, overlapping, and interacting cultural strands. Asian North American youth must deal not only with differences in Anglo and Asian norms, but with the fact that these standards frequently contradict each other. They must relate to the cultures of their Anglo adolescent contemporaries, their school, the larger American society, their parents, and adult Asian North American community.

The fact that Asian North American youth have few explicit and easily understood rules for thinking and behaving in varying situations exacerbates their predicament. Indeed we can truly say that they are frequently caught up in the tangled web of conflicting norms. Further, we, as Asian North American parents, teachers, and pastors, have not been very helpful to our youth because we ourselves do not yet clearly understand the dynamics underlying the influences of these multicultural strands on our youth and on ourselves (Pai 1993).

Pai proposed Ward Goodenough's notion of the *"private culture"* of each individual. A private culture can be defined as the set of norms according to which a person assigns meaning and significance to the objects, events, and human action of one's private world. In this view, understanding our youth means understanding the content and structure of their private cultures and comprehending the many forces in the youth culture that influence their thinking, acting, and value judgment.

Professor Pai may be according extreme freedom to the individual youth to develop and define one's own *unique private culture*. Indeed, we need to understand their individual experiences of the multiple cultural and psychological dimensions impinging on them. However, I feel that the church and parents can help and guide Asian North American youth to experience and develop bicultural/bilingual (or multicultural) orientations in a way that provides *some* coherent framework or context for the youth. The private culture may not have to be based totally on an individualistic, normless, and amorphous world-view. One can make considerable intentional input in the shaping of one's own cultural identity and world-view. (This issue is covered in more detail in chapter 10.)

Parenting Skills

In a monograph titled "Ten Principles on Raising Chinese American Teens" that came out of the San Francisco Chinatown Youth Project, Evelyn Lee (1988) offers an excellent discussion on parenting issues. She provides several lists of observations and practical suggestions. These lists can help Asian North American parents and teenagers to understand each other better and to improve communications between them. Lee lists teenagers' worries as follows.

Eight Common Worries of Teenagers:

1. getting poor grades—not doing well in school;
2. being afraid that their friends do not like them—feeling left out or alone;
3. getting along poorly with parents or other family members;
4. lacking confidence and belief in themselves and their abilities—being scared of the future;
5. losing a boyfriend or girlfriend—developing relationships with friends of the opposite sex;
6. feeling self-conscious—being concerned about appearance and physical changes;
7. not having enough money; and
8. being confused by the meaning of life—trying to figure out their own values, including church participation.

Different Parenting Styles and Related Problems

Different parenting philosophies and approaches often create different kinds of relationships with children and thus different consequences (E. Lee 1988):

- *authoritarian parents:* maintaining a position of authority demanding obedience;

- *permissive parents:* spoiling and allowing the children to get away with too much;

- *inconsistent parents:* vacillating and often changing the mind without giving reasons;

- *physical punishment:* using physical force, damaging trust and teens' self-respect (parents can be legally charged with physical abuse);

- *self-righteous parents:* neglecting the children's feelings, quickly passing judgment in a self-righteous manner;

- *comparisons:* comparing children with others, especially as a way of put-down;

- *critical / negative parents:* criticizing when the children are not doing well, but neglecting to praise them when they do well;

- *favoritism:* Asian traditions tending to favor sons over daughters and the older son over younger ones; and

- *conflicting authority:* Dad, Mom, Grandpa, and Grandma each giving different advice and opinions.

According to Pai's study, the more the parents are seen as authoritarian, the less likely children are to seek help from parents and the more likely there will be feelings of conflict, disharmony, and less "love in the family."

On the other hand, the more the parents are seen as democratic, the more likely children are to seek help from parents, have fewer feelings of conflict and disharmony, and have greater feelings of "love in the family."

Communication Problems between Immigrant Parents and Their Children

Lack of opportunities to talk. Many Asian parents work very long hours, leaving them little time or energy to talk with the children. They make an effort only when difficulties or crises arise. It is important to make time to talk even when there are no problems. Parents need to know that the quality of time is more important than the quantity of time.

Language barriers and inadequate communication due to the poor command of English by the parents and the children's lack of Asian native-language capabilities. This is a serious and difficult problem. Parents could learn and improve their English. Children could be encouraged to learn their native Asian language not only at home, but also at a language school offered in the ethnic community. But even if verbal conversation is limited, children know whether their parents love them and care for them. Parents can show love and care by nonverbal body gestures, smiles, hugs, and approving voice and facial expressions.

Lack of conversational topics. Parents and teenagers have different backgrounds and interests. Even if they feel like talking, they may not know what to discuss with each other. Some teens like to talk about music, sports, fashion, or movies. But parents may not be interested in these topics or know much about them. The challenge is to find topics of mutual interest, such as stories about school, growing up in different cultures, and hobbies.

Ineffective communication styles. One-way lecturing or preaching will turn off teens. Parents should discuss rather than scold and offer guidance rather than criticism. Talk sincerely with warmth and care.

Ineffective listening. Listen to your teen's opinions and feelings with patience, interest, and active listening skills.

Negative nonverbal communication. Instead of verbally discussing their concerns, some parents may express their displeasure or disapproval by a dirty look, a long sigh, refusing to eat or talk, etc. Children are confused and angered by such nonverbal communication (Tanouye 1991).

Evelyn Lee suggests the following ten principles of parenting as harmonious and sensible approaches for Asian North American immigrant parents (E. Lee 1988).

Ten Principles of Parenting:

1. Understand your teenager's physical and psychological needs.

2. Improve communication.

3. Use appropriate rewards and discipline.

4. Encourage initiative and independence.

5. Provide guidance in your teenager's social life.

6. Encourage extracurricular activities.

7. Know your teenager's school environment.

8. Develop a positive cultural identity.

9. Maintain family harmony.

10. Utilize community resources.

References

Attorney General's Asian and Pacific Advisory Committee Final Report. California State Department of Justice, 1988.

Bilingual Education Book. Bilingual Education Office, California State Department of Education, 1990.

Holt, Daniel D. *The Education of Korean American Youth: Achievements, Problems, and Mental Health Issues.* California State Department of Education, 1989.

_____. *Handbook for Teaching Korean-American Students.* Bilingual Education Office, California State Department of Education, 1992.

Kim, Bok Lim. *The Korean American Child at School and at Home.* Washington, D.C., U.S. Department of Health, Education, and Welfare, 1980.

_____. "The Language Situation of Korean Americans," in *Language Diversity: Problem or Resource? A Social and Educational Perspective on Language Minorities in the United States.*

Edited by Sandra Lee McKay and Sau-ling Cynthia Wong. Cambridge, Mass.:Newbury House Publishers, 1988.

Kim, Grace. *A Plaza of Dialogue*. Seoul, Korea: Young Hak Press, 1988 (in Korean).

_____. "It's OK to Say No." In *Asian Presbyterian Women's Study Guide*. New York: United Presbyterian Church (U.S.A), 1982.

_____. "Dear Grace" (weekly column), in *The Korea Times USA*, 1983–1989, and in *The Korean Central Daily, USA,* 1992-93.

_____, and Luke Kim. "Survey Results of Korean American Youths and Their Parents." Paper presented at the workshop on young people, parents, and communication, San Jose, Calif., August 1993.

_____, and Luke Kim. *Korean American Immigrants and Their Children*. New Faces of Liberty. Zellerbach Family Fund Project. San Francisco: Many Cultures Publishing, 1994.

Kim, Ronyoung. *Clay Walls*. Sag Harbor, N.Y.: The Permanent Press, 1986.

Lee, Evelyn. *Ten Principles on Raising Chinese American Teens*. San Francisco: Chinatown Youth Center, 1988.

Lee, Marie G. *Finding My Voice*. Boston: Houghton Mifflin Co., 1992.

Pai, Young. *Finding on Korean American Early Adolescents and Adolescents*. Kansas City: University of Missouri, 1987.

_____. "A Sociocultural Understanding of Korean American Youth 'Caught in the Web,'" In *Korean American Ministry*. Edited by Sang Hyun Lee and John Moore. Louisville: General Assembly Council, Presbyterian Church (U.S.A.), 1993.

Rue, David S. "Depression and Suicidal Behavior among Asian 'Whiz Kids.'" A paper presented at the American Psychiatric Association Annual Convention, San Francisco, May 1990.

Suzuki, Bob H. "Asian Americans As the Model Minority: Outdoing Whites? Or Media Hype?" *Change*. Vol. 21. November/December 1989, 12-19. Washington, D.C., American Association for Higher Education.

Tanouye, Ellen. *Learning Parental Skills Together in an Asian American Context*. Japanese Presbyterian Conference, 1991.

Winnicott, D. W. "The Theory of the Parent-Infant Relationship," *International Journal of Psychoanalysis*. Vol. 41, 1960, 585–595.

CHAPTER 7

The Asian North American Community at Worship: Issues of Indigenization and Contextualization

By Greer Anne Wenh-In Ng

Introduction

Asian North American congregations face the challenge to affirm their culture and identity as people of Asian heritage. They also are a part of the people of God called into being and given a new life and identity by Christ. Chapters 7, 8, and 9 address this multicultural challenge. These chapters suggest that cultural resources can be harmoniously integrated into the worship, festivals, and traditional church programs of Asian North American congregations. Thus the people can be integrally Asian, North American, and Christian. The church can help people to fulfill the human identity and life that God the Creator designed for all God's children. Such a life is rich in language, art, story, and tradition.

In chapter 7 Professor Greer Anne Wenh-In Ng tells several stories of Asian North American groups who have found ways to witness to God's good creation through their worship and liturgy. Practical suggestions for planning indigenous worship and for finding useful resources are provided.

The Asian North American Community

Walk into any Japanese, Korean, or Chinese American or Japanese, Korean, or Chinese Canadian congregation on a

147

Sunday morning. Except for the fact that the faces surrounding you are definitely Asian, is there anything in the way worship is conducted that makes this different from the service being held at First United Methodist Church or St. Andrew's Presbyterian Church down the road? The hymns, the prayers, the symbols in the sanctuary, the vestments of the worship leaders and the choir—do they give any hint as to the Asianness of these Christians and their faith community? In this chapter we explore our call to bring *all* of who we are into worship—Korean, Japanese, Chinese, or Vietnamese North American as well as Christian, embodying within us the ethos and spirituality, the social and cultural "specialness" of our ancient civilizations. In three contemporary stories we will encounter three different worship occasions and will try to identify what the issues and questions are vis-à-vis our theme. Then we will move on to some theoretical and theological analyses of the issues in each case, concluding each section with some practical suggestions for doing follow-up within our own congregation for those intrigued enough by the topics. Readers are also encouraged to share unresolved questions and issues with like-minded peers.

Story 1:
For All the Saints . . . and All Our Ancestors

Scene I: Pastor Tan's study

Pastor Tan (to herself): Oh dear, Andy will be here any minute to talk over the Halloween night program for the youth group—something quieter, he implied in his phone call yesterday. Last year's got a little out of hand. He was afraid that would frighten off new members like Geok Leng, the new girl from Singapore. "Something informative and not too boring." Easier said than done, my friend. Why, here's the calendar from my home church, with the lunar dates on it. Ah, I see that the end of October is still the ninth moon. I wonder . . . (Hears a knock on the door.) Come in.

Andy: It's me. Got any ideas yet for next Friday? I've hit a brick wall. That's an awful confession for a resourceful youth group leader to make.

Pastor Tan: Ah, but I think I've just made a breakthrough. Here, sit down and tell me what you think. . . . (The two go into close conspiratory conversation for a while.)

Andy (a smile slowly spreading across his face): You know, it just might work. I'll go dig up some facts. See you!

Scene II: The Friday after, Halloween night, at the youth group meeting. Teens in orange and black shirts and slacks are sprawled around the fireplace in Andy's parents' home. Snacks are being passed around.

Andy: And now for the serious part of the evening. (Groans from a few people.) We are going to look at how Halloween connects with similar festivals in our own culture. I give you Pastor Tan.

Pastor Tan: Who can tell me what "Halloween" stands for?

Steve (a teen): That's easy: short for All Hallows' Eve, the night before All Saints' Day, which is November 1, tomorrow. Is that why we'll be singing, "For all the saints, who from their labors rest," on Sunday?

Pastor Tan: That's right. And can anyone guess how our parents' grandparents used to remember their "saints"?

Geok Leng (putting her hand up hesitantly): My grandmother used to visit the grave sites of the family when I was still in Singapore. We didn't sing any hymns, though. She took some of grandfather's favorite food—and always some flowers. She let me go with her most years, around Easter time. I noticed that there were always lots of people at the other sites that day. Some of them would light incense sticks and burn paper money.

Carolyn (another teen): Ugh, what a heathen custom!

Andy: It might interest you to know that the Scandinavian tribes in Europe used to light fires on the hills to show their departed souls the way home. Most cultures in the world have some sort of ritual to commemorate their dead, actually.

Pastor Tan: That day in spring that Geok Leng was

describing falls on the fifth day of April every year: it's known as the festival of the Clear and Bright: "Qing Ming." But there is another date in the fall, the ninth day of the ninth moon by the lunar calendar, on which people can do a similar kind of commemoration. This year, it happens to fall on October 25.

Chung Mun (another teen): Does it have a special name?

Andy: Yes, it's called "Qong Yang," meaning "double nine." In the old days families would take a trip up the hillside for an outing. The outing was done to remember the time that someone, who had received a warning of a coming pestilence, had gotten everyone away from their town by taking them up the hillside. And, sure enough, upon their return they found all their animals dead. After that, they kept up the custom. The visit to the grave sites developed alongside it, because the hills were where most of the graves were.

Terry (another teen): Well, we can't observe anything like that now, because we are not in China, we're in Canada. Besides, we're Christians.

Pastor Tan: We are Christians, yes. But we are also Chinese. We don't stop being Chinese when we join the church. And Chinese people have always tried to remember their ancestors. So how do you think we can hold the two together? Are "saints" limited to members of the church, or can we count our ancestors among them? (Several voices chime in at once.) Wait . . . one at a time. . . . (Discussion continues.)

Scene III: In the driveway. About to enter her car, Pastor Tan is approached by Geok Leng.

Geok Leng: Thank you for the discussion tonight. I was feeling really down because the anniversary of my grandmother's death is coming soon and I knew I couldn't get to visit her grave in Singapore. Now I'll remember her over here when we go to worship on Sunday. I'm glad I joined the youth group.

Pastor Tan: I'm glad too. Good night. (To the night) And thank *you.*

Questions and Issues

Two main types of questions seem to arise out of the above story:

1. To what extent is it permissible or faithful for Christians of East Asian Confucian background living in North America to retain some form of veneration of ancestors and of family members who have died? How do they properly venerate ancestors without being made to feel they are somehow not being true to their Christian faith and practice? Specifically, is it permissible for Christians to honor and remember their ancestors and other deceased family members by:

   a. marking the anniversary of their deaths with some kind of ritual? In the case of Japanese North American Christians, this may include special services at the graveside during the period from forty to sixty days after the funeral.

   b. keeping in some shape or form traditional commemorations of the dead set at specific times of the year, such as Qing Ming (April 5) and Qong Yang (ninth day of the ninth lunar month), these in the Confucian tradition being days to visit ancestors' grave sites?

   c. making specific reference to them during the church's annual celebrations around All Saints' Day?

2. Should East Asian Christians in North America celebrate festivals from their heritage cultures, especially those that still seem to have religious connotations attached to them? Such questions become even more acute in families where some of the members have not converted to Christianity and are still carrying on traditional rituals.

   a. Do the Christian members participate, either voluntarily or when requested or urged? If they do, might they not feel guilty about taking part in something that they think is pagan or non-Christian and therefore contaminating the purity of their Christian faith and practice? Or do they refrain from having anything to do with non-Christian rituals for fear of being accused of practicing "syncretism" (that is, mixing Christianity with non-Christian or pre-Christian rites that smack of superstition)? If they do refrain, do they then feel guilty about severing themselves from the rest of the family and disturbing family harmony on top of failing to honor their ancestors and others of the dead?

b. Is one option to keep the commemoration of the dead and veneration of ancestors as a purely sociocultural phenomenon quite separate from one's religious practice of Christianity?

The Asian North American church needs to help to clarify some of these issues so members can feel more integrated and less guilty about what they have been doing or not doing. Perhaps it even needs to set some new directions toward a "more abundant" way of fulfilling both sets of obligations.

Analysis of the Situation

The theological concerns underlying the questions raised above can be grouped under two concepts: syncretism, defined as "a mixing of two or more religious systems to the point where at least one, if not both, of the systems loses basic structure and identity," and dual religious systems, where "Christianity and another tradition operate side by side" (Schreiter 1985:144,148). Let us examine ancestor worship or veneration in its wider contexts and in light of these concerns.

Biblical, Historical, and World Contexts

Filial piety is definitely not contradictory to Scripture. "Honor your father and your mother, so that your days may be long..." (Exodus 20:12) is among the Ten Commandments. In spite of differences in motivation, the motivation is quite clear. In the Confucian system filial piety stems more from a conviction that parents give one life and therefore deserve all the gratitude, respect, and honor one can render them; hence the corollary, for males, of continuing the family line by passing on this life to future generations. Confucian cultures specifically extend this honor and respect to parents and parents' parents, etc., going back many generations.

Such veneration is not unique to Confucian cultures either. In African cultures the veneration of ancestors is very much alive today and is, in fact, one of the thorny issues the church needs to face, since it permeates all social practice and cannot just be dropped upon people's conversion. And, of course, historically, the idea of "remembering the saints" developed out of the many pre-Christian rites of commemorating the dead practiced by northern European peoples. Such an emphasis, however, is absent from contemporary Western culture, which in general shies away from facing death itself and from connections with the dead. Such neglect is definitely felt as a gap in the cultural-religious life of East Asian North American Christians.

Historically, the Vatican's Chinese Rites Controversy (1610–1742) has had the unfortunate lasting effect of proscribing practices of "ancestral worship," making it out of bounds for Chinese, Japanese, and Korean Christians as well as for Chinese Christians living in Vietnam and other parts of Southeast Asia, even long after the prohibitions have been lifted by the edicts of 1936 and 1939. (For an excellent account of this history, see George Minamiki's *The Chinese Rites Controversy from Its Beginning to Modern Times*. For studies on ancestor worship in Korea and Japan, see works cited in the references at the end of this chapter.) Missionary efforts in the nineteenth and twentieth centuries have generally followed the "Christ against culture" stance and required converts to dissociate themselves from the cult, whether practiced at home or in a temple. This attitude has persisted in spite of the clear pronouncements in the papal instructions of 1935–36, in which the meaning of both ancestor worship and the Confucian cult are acknowledged to have evolved over the years into more of a social, familial, and civil nature and therefore have become merely "cultural and secular" rather than remaining religious.

Syncretism and Dual Religious Systems

The term "syncretism," the mixing of two or more religious systems, had its origin in the Mediterranean world ("syn-Crete") around the beginning of the common era, where competing cults were constantly being assimilated into one another and being reshaped into new forms. From a Christian point of view, syncretism has always been looked upon negatively by a church tradition that holds to ideas such as "no other name" except that of Christ and "outside the church there is no salvation."

In our present discussion, the dual religious system that this obtains is the form Schreiter characterizes as "double belonging," the kind that occurs in Asia "where a particular religious tradition and citizenship in a nation are seen as inextricably bound up, . . . in which religious patterns are so deeply woven into a culture that it is no longer possible to discern easily what is religion and what is culture" (1985:148). Just as it is almost impossible for a Thai or Burmese person not to be Buddhist, it is almost impossible for a Chinese, Korean, or Japanese person, whether in Asia or the diaspora, not to be somehow inextricably Confucian, Taoist, and possibly also Buddhist in some way. Within this reality, veneration of ancestors would be a potent element of the Confucian strand of East Asian culture in the category of "dual religious systems." However, as has been suggested above, it is unlikely that present-day East Asian Christians in North American retain any significantly religious connotation in their desire to honor and respect ancestors. Filipino liturgical scholar Anscar Chupungco perceptively pointed out that whereas new converts usually overzealously go the other way and "refuse to adopt pagan rituals or even architecture, the Chinese converts [in the seventeenth and subsequent centuries] could not be persuaded to abandon the ancestral rites, for these were part and parcel of their life as a people" (1982).

One might raise the question of whether the equivalent *chesa* practice in Korea, or the enshrining of ancestral tablets in the local Buddhist temple in Japan, is as secularized as the Chinese practice has been made out to be. If not, this would be a more cogent case for considering the validity of dual religious systems in the contemporary scene. It is clear that in Japan itself, for instance, dual or triple religious allegiance poses no problem for most people.

For Whom Are Syncretism and Dual Religious Systems a Problem?

Are syncretism and dual religious systems a problem mainly for those parts of the universal church whose world-view is "either/or" (which would include most of the churches in the Western world) rather than those members whose culture and world-view are able to contain "both/and"? The furor over the powerful worship conducted by Professor Chung Hyun Kyung, the Korean theologian, at the Seventh Assembly of the World Council of Churches in Canberra (1990) would indicate a resounding yes. Cries of "Syncretism!" and "Heresy!" greeted her invocation of the spirits of *han*-ridden or deeply suffering people of the past and her making use of rituals that included aboriginal drumming and Korean shamanistic vestments. Yet, as she asks so cogently in her book *Struggle to Be the Sun Again: Introducing Asian Women's Theology* (see references), "Who owns Christianity? Is Christianity unchangeable? What makes Christianity Christian?" This fear of syncretism by Western theologians assumes that "Christian identity is an unchangeable property they own . . . a [sort of] copyright of Christianity." And yet, she points out, that is a fallacy if the main goal of people's faith is not doctrinal purity (or, we might add here, liturgical purity) but their survival and liberation and that people need to choose "selectively life-giving elements of their culture and religion, woven into religious meaning" (1990:114).

Therefore, are syncretism and dual religious systems a problem mainly for those whose religious history and experience is grounded in an exclusive and proselytizing monotheism (that is, Western Christians) rather than for those who have always lived in cultures characterized by religious pluralism, as the majority of Asian Christians have? The same would hold true for inheritors of the Asian ethos, since that plural religious world-view is so inextricably woven into their cultures that one cannot separate the two.

For whom are they a problem within the "younger churches," including East Asian North American churches? Is it the religious leaders, clergy, and trained theologians anxious to uphold the doctrinal purity they have imbibed from missionary and theological school, or the ordinary faithful, practicing members? Actual conversations with church members reveal that they either feel such things are not a problem or, if their church prohibits such practice or thinking, would like to be able to bring the questions out into the open and talk about them, since they are matters unresolved in their religious life.

Finally, why is the mixing of pagan religious elements into early Christianity from Hellenistic, Germanic, Celtic, and Syrian systems not a problem, whereas religious and cultic elements from outside Europe, such as those from native aboriginal cultures (both North and South American, Pacific, and African) and the highly developed and literate systems in Asia (Buddhism, Taoism, Hinduism, etc.), seem to pose such a threat? Do we detect a trace here of cultural/religious/political imperialism as well as a trace of good old Christendom supremacy?

Being on the Way: Implications for Ministry Practice

1. Do these issues of syncretism and dual religious practice speak to the current situation in your congregation? What examples do you have of people struggling with this topic? If you are not sure what is going on, you may want to do some discreet asking around or provide a nonthreatening opportunity

for members of an existing fellowship (adult, youth, or women's) to open up conversation on this topic. The approaching first anniversary of the death of a senior member of a family, or of an elder of the church, might be a natural trigger. Working in pairs, record and, if possible, classify the type of practices already in place. Does any of it surprise you?

Here are two actual examples of dual religious practice—one from a congregation, the other from an individual. The congregational example comes from Buena Vista United Methodist Church in Alameda, California. The worship service on the first Sunday of every month includes a memorial component, when members and families lift up the names of individuals whose anniversaries of death occur during that month. Besides flowers, special prayers are offered on behalf of those individuals.

The personal example comes from a young adult, born in the United States, who recalls how his mother used to take him each spring (probably around Qing Ming), as the oldest son, to visit the grave of his father and to remember all the ancestors. His mother would take along food, flowers, incense sticks, and paper money, displaying the former and burning the latter. Now that he is no longer living at home, he tries to remind himself to make this observance (much more simply, he admits) at least once a year.

2. After you have collected some basic information and statistics, you might want to hold discussions with individuals and groups whom you discern to be ready. Readiness quite often depends on how far people already are into their Christian faith identity. As a rule, new converts are more clear-cut about not mixing traditional cultural-religious forms with their newly embraced faith systems. You could use story 1 ("For All the Saints . . .") as well as people's own experience to start off, making use of some of the questions from the "Questions and Issues" segment and sharing some of the insights from the "Analysis" segment where appropriate. Bringing the topic into open discussion is in itself significant. It allows those who have been wondering whether they could

even think of such a possibility to engage in some informed searching and reflection. It also reassures those who may have been anxious over their "orthodoxy" to get help in wrestling with their doubts.

How does a congregation or an individual decide when to take the risk to experiment with expanding the Christian concept of the communion of saints to include one's ancestors? When people bring the question up themselves, that is one indication. At the same time, readiness also depends on how grounded and, therefore, secure people are in their Christian identity. In this connection, Paul's stance toward whether or not to eat food sacrificed to idols (1 Corinthians 8:1-13; 10:23-33) is instructive. "All things are lawful," he declares, "but not all things are beneficial ("expedient" in earlier translations). . . . not all things build up"(10:23-24). "Take care that this liberty of yours does not somehow become a stumbling block to the weak" (8:9). The analogy with ancestor veneration is helpful. There need to be stages of education and raising consciousness, not an abrupt innovation without preparing people for it. Individuals and families who already practice such combining of rituals could act as storytellers and examples, bringing this topic to open discussion.

3. A further issue concerns the traditionally male centeredness of the Confucian ancestral-veneration cult. The cult requires that only male descendants have the right and duty (specifically the oldest son, in the more strictly observed Korean rites) to hold such "sacrifices." Women's roles traditionally have been limited to the preparation of food and other such mundane (not sacred or ritualistic) responsibilities. In the more egalitarian ethos of general North American culture, the church needs to critically assess this custom. As anthropologists point out, cultures are not static but evolve and undergo changes in response to what else is happening around them. It is therefore not likely that even such a time-honored tradition as Confucianism can remain static. With the strides made by the women's movement in societies

all around the globe, churches will do well to reevaluate the part women and girls play as they formulate new ways. For instance, by now it would be unthinkable not to include mothers as well as fathers among one's ancestors or to restrict responsibilities of commemoration to sons only. This needs to be explored in any discussion of the topic.

4. What are some actual *liturgical resources* churches and families will need to try out this new approach? Here are some suggestions for starters:

a. Music and hymns: write new verses to "For All the Saints" to include the ancestors who have gone before. These could include "ancestors in the faith" special to your congregation or the Asian North American Christian community as a whole. The *New Hymnal of the China Christian Council* contains an indigenous hymn for such occasions. (An English version of this hymnal is currently being produced.)

b. Ancestors (from the community as well as the family, see below) can be included in prayers of petition and intercession. Special prayers, such as litanies, can be developed for the congregation and for families, leaving appropriate spaces for names to be filled in. The time even may come when, after these have been tried and found useful, these ideas and worship aids get shared in liturgical publications of the wider church as a contribution from the Asian part of the Christian community.

c. The educational programs of the church could develop study units on honoring ancestors. "Ancestors" could incorporate the idea of "all the saints/sages/elders" by including members of the faith community and even one's ethnic community in additional to those in one's own family. For instance, young people could be encouraged to find out about their forebears and about those early pioneers who were never able either to marry or bring their families to live with them in North America; it was their struggles that

paved the way for later generations. In this way a
wider sense of community may be fostered that acknowledges the kinship between Christians and non-
Christians across Asian North American history.
Also, in addition to local "saints," a well-known one
for the Asian and Asian North American community
could be lifted up not only in local faith communities, but across denominational and geographical
lines. Two such that come to mind are the Reverend
Tim Oi (Florence) Li, the first woman to be ordained
in the Anglican communion in the world, and Don-
aldina Cameron, a tireless mission worker among
the "lost" Chinese women in the San Francisco area,
for whom San Francisco's vital inner-city mission,
Cameron House, is named.

Story 2: Happy Sixtieth Birthday, Dr. Lee!

Dr. Oon Jung Lee flipped over her calendar pensively. Why,
in another month her birthday would be here—no ordinary
birthday either, but her sixtieth! As everyone knows, the
sixtieth birthday is the most important birthday in a person's
life. By the sixtieth year you have completed a full cycle of
life. For the first time you would allow your adult children to
make a big fuss over you, bringing all *their* children along to
the feast. How well she remembered her oldest sister's celebration in Seoul. Unlike similar happenings in North America, you didn't have to keep your plans a secret either. Was
that only five years ago?

Oon Jung smiled ruefully. There wouldn't be anything
close to that kind of celebration for herself, that's for sure.
For one thing, she was now far away from Seoul. For another,
there wasn't any son or daughter or grandchildren whose
special responsibility it was to celebrate it for her, since she
had remained true to her girlhood vision of pursuing a career
even at the risk of ending up an "old maid." Did she do the
right thing? She had always thought so. But faced with the
prospect of an uncelebrated sixtieth birthday, she wasn't so

sure now. Ah, well, on with these articles. The big medical conference was in three weeks; she would hardly have time between that and her own big day to feel sorry for herself.

The big day came at last, falling on a Sunday. Bright rays streamed in from the east, lighting up Myung's stained glass window card from Chartres like a blessing. When she got to church, things were pretty much as usual. No one seemed to remember enough even to wish her verbally "Happy Birthday." She settled into her favorite pew as the familiar hymns began.

Halfway through the announcements, Oon Jung perked up. What was this? Was Pastor Yoon out of his mind? He was announcing an open invitation for the congregation to gather after church in the church hall "in order that we may as a community of faith help to celebrate a very important occasion: the sixtieth birthday of our respected and beloved sister, Dr. Oon Jung Lee."

In a daze she stood up to acknowledge the honor. In a daze she followed fellow parishioners, now bursting with "Happy Birthday!" around her, into the church hall. Why, what a transformation! Festive crepe paper and balloons were strung across the beams. Up front a festive table was spread with all her favorite dishes. She was led to the seat of honor, there to be addressed by the president of the young adult group.

"On behalf of the young adult group, and indeed of all of us here at Grace Church, I want to say how privileged we are to be your family as you reach this important milestone of your life. Your example has given us—especially us women—impetus and courage to carve out a path for ourselves. Others of us are your spiritual children because for so many years you have shared the Good News with us in waiting rooms and classrooms. We bring our children to join in this celebration, for they are also your grandchildren."

One after another they came, these "grandchildren," shyly handing her all sorts of homemade presents. The Sunday school superintendent, whom she had mentored long enough to see blossom from a confused "1.5-generation" teenager to a self-assured member of the law profession, stood beaming nearby, nodding encouragement. Then came the young people, actually thanking her in public for the insights and gifts of debate they had exchanged with her! Now it was the adults' turn. Last of all came the gray-haired ones, her seniors, welcoming her into the company of the officially wise. "Am I wise?" mused Oon Jung. "I feel as if I am only just beginning to know about life."

Someone's camera flashed, grace was said, and the young emcee announced, "Let the feast begin!" There were more flashes as she obligingly posed with clusters of people. These pictures will come in handy to send to her siblings; they will never have to pity her for her lack of family ever again.

Reflection, Questions, and Discussion

Intersection of the cultural/secular and the sacred/holy

In this story, the congregation as a substitute family helped a single adult without children of her own celebrate a life-cycle milestone highly significant to all three East Asian cultures. Was this appropriate involvement for the church? Does this differ substantially from the part the church plays at other life events, such as marriage or death, acts imbued with both pastoral concern and spiritual significance?

Some might object to the church's involvement for fear of being co-opted by the culture, citing the parallel of following the culture's celebration of, for instance, Mother's Day or Father's Day. In that particular case, one option is to acculturate, giving secular celebrations a Christian overlay such as renaming Mother's Day into "Christian Family Sunday." Yet how successful are such attempts? Are they even necessary? As the Asian component of the body of Christ in North America, can we not claim the freedom to celebrate in our culture specific customs and life-cycle milestones with integrity? Just as the ancient Israelites evolved rituals of blessing for many occasions appropriate to their culture, can we not do so in our time and context?

Perhaps the difference lies partly in the fact that these are the customs and traditions of minority cultural and ethnic groups on this continent, not the customs and traditions of the dominant culture. The issue would then become an issue of power. Or it could be that these cultures are seen basically as non-Christian if not outright "pagan." The issue here would then be a fear of syncretism again.

Or it could be that some of these occasions (diaspora events such as refugee settlement or immigration to a new location) are simply outside the experience of the average dominant church. The issue would be one of context and relevance or irrelevance.

I would like to suggest that pastorally, theologically, and spiritually, it is important for Asian North American churches to do some hard thinking on these issues. We need to question the current tendency, for most of us, to keep our Christian faith and spirituality and our cultural and traditional observances in watertight compartments, relegating the latter to purely private, social, secular, cultural spheres.

Pastorally, the church as the community of faith has a responsibility to stand with individuals and families in their life crises and special milestones. The wider church through the ages has endorsed this in its ministries of pastoral care and in the significant involvement in times of marriage and death. I simply want to suggest including additional occasions required by our particular contexts.

Theologically, if the psalmist's "the earth is the LORD's, and the fulness thereof" (Psalm 24:1, KJV) and "the LORD shall preserve thy going out and thy coming in" (Psalm 121:8, KJV) are expressions of a genuine faith and hope, then they can be appropriated by the Asian North American inheritors of that faith tradition. In applying such faith statements and prayers to our particular situation, we will be affirming the incarnational nature and universality of this one Holy One.

Spiritually, affirming individuals and families in their

crisis situations and life-cycle milestones provides resources to strengthen their spiritual life and faith journey. It signals to them not only that the church is with them in a compassionate, caring way, but also that such life events have a spiritual dimension. When this dimension is made visible, the church witnesses of the presence of God in people's lives, and the people have an opportunity to enhance and deepen their relationship with the "ground of their being."

One interesting contemporary parallel in this search for attending to particular ritual needs may be found in the growing creativity of women's rituals. Some of these do not claim to be specifically Christian, since the women's movement cuts across religious affiliations (for example, one of the groups studied in Charlotte Caron's fascinating *To Make and Make Again: Feminist Ritual Theology;* see references). Others are attempts of groups of women within the ecumenical community seeking to address their location and context seriously (Procter-Smith and Walton 1993). Once-suppressed groups, whose special identity and needs traditionally have been merged in the universal church and rendered invisible, are everywhere standing up to develop rituals that are life giving to themselves. Asian North American Christians can learn much and take courage from these movements.

Weddings and funerals

Weddings and funerals are often attended by family, friends, and members of one's ethnic community who may not be members of any Christian faith persuasion. What tensions might arise on such occasions?

a. Weddings do not as a rule pose too much of a problem, since all church weddings are by definition "Christian" in form—that is, ritualistically. All Asians accept the fact that a Western-style wedding will require white for the bride instead of red, exchanging some kind of vow or covenant between the couple, and so forth. In some cases cultural customs are kept (for instance, the Chinese bride changing into a traditional red bridal dress and "pouring tea" to her new parents-in-law and female in-laws). These are sufficiently clear as being sociocultural customs rather than religious rituals. Where awkwardness may arise is when non-Christian family members and friends find it difficult to follow the service or when inappropriate wedding music, including a vocal solo, is selected. At other times, non-Christian family members in positions of authority might want a Western-style wedding by a clergyperson held in an inappropriate setting.

b. Funerals seem to cause much more confusion, both for the bereaved family and the Christian presider. This derives from the fact that funeral practices seem to be the one area in which "dual religious systems" are most in evidence. Some are sociocultural customs pure and simple, such as wailing aloud (a widespread custom in Eastern cultures). Some are comparatively innocuous, such as giving out candy (to take away the bitterness of grief and ill luck of coming in contact with the dead) or "bowing three times" to pay respects to the deceased before a picture or the casket itself. Others, however, are parallel religious practices, such as the observance of the seven "sevens," on each of which paper constructions of life's goods such as houses, cars, and furniture are burned to meet the needs of the newly deceased in the other world. These are usually performed by Taoist priests. It hardly ever happens that a Christian family in North America would adhere to these customs. However, it is not inconceivable that individual Christians may find themselves in the situation of having to pay respects where relatives or friends do observe them. When such perplexed Christians come for counsel, how should the church advise them? A guideline to bear in mind echoes what is applicable to cases of ancestor veneration: clarify the religious significance of each ritual, steering away from attributing divine powers to human customs, and discerning where attendance at certain rituals might become a "stumbling block" to the faith of other members of one's Christian community.

Developing Rituals for Special Occasions
Specific to Asian North Americans

What other special occasions in the life cycle could the church help members and their families celebrate? There are variations specific to Japanese, Korean, and Chinese cultures, although many, as we have seen, are common. Take the celebration of birthdays as an example. Japanese culture seems to attach a great deal more importance to specific years in addition to highlighting the sixtieth. North American Japanese congregations, therefore, might want to adopt or develop appropriate prayers for children when they reach the ages of three, five, and seven years, if particular families have preserved this tradition. Some of these have already been made available in translation (such as the Sierra Mission Area "Asian Ministers' Language and Cultural Seminar" resource *Worship Handbook for Japanese American Christian Lay Leaders and Ministers*, p. 50). The same goes for ages nineteen, twenty-three, and thirty-seven for females and twenty-five, forty-two, and sixty-one for males as important "periods in life when it is necessary to evaluate one's life" (Ibid., p. 51). Chinese and ethnically Chinese Vietnamese Christians might appreciate the church's involvement in the celebration of a baby's first "Full Moon" banquet—for female as well as male babies. All three cultures probably pay as much attention to "teaching the unborn" (*tai jiao* in Chinese); appropriate prayers and spiritual exercises for pregnant mothers might be a direction to channel a congregation's liturgical creativity to address this need.

Here is a sample list of life-cycle occasions to get you started. These are ones specific to Asian individuals and families and do not include regular life-cycle events from birth to death commonly celebrated across most cultures in North America.

a. Personal occasions:

- "teaching the unborn" for pregnant mothers—and older siblings and father, and grandparents;
- birth and the giving of the newborn's culture-specific

name in its heritage language (where parents and grandparents are not able to do so, bilingual members of the congregation could help out);

- first day officially at school, using a green onion ("*qong*" in Chinese is a homonym for "intelligent," "bright"); and
- becoming an aunt or an uncle for the first time. Explain the specific relationship to the young person and point out the location in one's family tree.

b. Communal occasions:

- moving into or away from a congregation;
- emigrating or immigrating; and
- chief breadwinner leaving family behind to a new job location, sometimes back in the original country.

c. Other occasions (add your own to this list).

Some of these occasions already may be in place in individual lives and families; but the church may not yet recognize them in its community life. This could happen at Sunday worship or in fellowship groups or church school. The church could encourage groups and individuals to provide worship resources in the form of thanksgiving prayers, blessings, petitions for guidance, exercises for personal devotion, and so on. New music, hymns, and movement liturgies could be created to express the many different emotions inherent in them. Judicatories, denominations, and denominational Asian caucuses or a group such as PAACCE may be requested to provide leadership or finances to support their development. One example of such a resource is *Celebrations and Rituals for Church Families* (see suggested references).

Story 3: A Mochi Communion

It was the fifteenth anniversary celebration of a "home-grown" North American group, the Pacific Asian American and Canadian Christian Education Ministries (PAACCE). Throughout the morning there had been a recalling and remembering of origins and past achievements, a hard look-

ing at present realities, and visioning about the challenges
of the future. Now it was time to draw these threads together
in a closing liturgical celebration, culminating with Holy
Communion.

The Eucharistic prayer, shared by the celebrants, sounded
familiar. At the words of the institution, "This is my body,
broken for you, do this in remembrance of me," however, what
was lifted up was not a loaf of ordinary bread, but a white
Japanese style *mochi* or glutinous rice cake. Flashes of surprise, then delight, passed round the room, as those present
served one another in the centuries-old rite. As the service of
thanksgiving drew to a close, a newsprint was unrolled for
the singing of the final hymn. Once again, knowing smiles lit
up, for the words were familiar yet also different:

> Now thank we all our God
> With hearts and hands and voices,
> Who wondrous things has done,
> In whom all PAACCE rejoices,
> Who for fifteen springs and falls,
> Has blessed us on our way
> With countless gifts of ministry
> To celebrate today. . . .

It was a fitting close to a culturally affirming day.

Questions and Issues

It is my guess that writing new words to a time-honored
hymn, which seems to be an accepted practice in the church
at large, would present no theological or liturgical problem
but that the substitution of Japanese rice cakes for bread in
communion may raise charges of "unorthodoxy," of "indis-
criminate inculturation," or even of "heresy." Two issues,
however, are closely related: contextualization, an attempt
at rendering the liturgy more relevant to the context in which
it takes place, and indigenization and inculturation, an attempt to make elements of the liturgy more culturally appropriate to the group that is engaged in that worship.

In this story, only one element (substituting a more culturally relevant substance in place of the usual bread at communion) came under the heading "inculturation." Other elements (for instance, art and symbols, songs and music, readings apart from Scripture, church decorations and architecture), however, could come into play in the preparation of regular Sunday worship services in East Asian North American congregations. The central concern here is this: how does a particular people or community render praise—"doxology"—in its regular worship life and express its fullest self utilizing its cultural riches without violating the boundaries that signify its Christian identity?

Analysis

One of the strongest spokespersons for the church's responsibility to take up this question is Roman Catholic liturgical scholar Anscar Chupungco, himself a Filipino Christian. "Liturgical adaptation," Chupungco declares, "is a theological imperative arising from the event of the incarnation" (1982:87). The fact that Christ became human in a specific culture (Jewish) gives us "the assurance that in his resurrection he can, even today, incarnate himself in different races and cultures through the faith of the church . . ." (Chupungco 1982:59). Chupungco goes on to add that "the refusal to adapt amounts to a denial of the universality of salvation" (1982:87).

Not only among Asians in North America, but also among "global" Christians in the Third World has the vexing question of substituting a more familiar or culturally appropriate symbol for the bread in Communion come to the fore again and again. One hears of coconuts being used in the South Pacific (coconut meat for bread and coconut juice for wine) or prune juice and *chipati* (the bread that is the staple food) being used in India. We know that at the Last Supper, Jesus was engaged in a Jewish rite, that of the Passover, which he transformed or inculturated into a central Christian symbol by giving new significance to recognized symbols of his own culture. A liturgical scholar like Anscar Chupungco would say that in matters of "exterior forms" such as what to use for baptism or Communion, one must distinguish between "those elements which are essential to the definition of the rite itself and those which are contingent on the cultural milieu and are consequently not indispensable to the essence of the rite" (1982:71). He places water for baptism in the former category and bread and wine in the latter, since wheat bread and grape wine are "dependent on the agriculture of the place and the eating habits of the people." (1982:71) In fact, in some places in the world these food items are not native to the local culture and therefore not only unfamiliar, but also unavailable. Or they may be socially taboo, as consuming alcohol in public places is in Buddhist cultures. One could add that Methodists also share in this sentiment and, in fact, have been able to substitute natural unfermented grape juice for the biblical fermented kind. On this score, it would seem that using a culturally more appropriate food item such as *mochi* (or rice or coconut) would not cause theological difficulty. However, to eliminate or change the gesture of "breaking" the bread, theologically signifying the sacrificial giving up of Jesus' body, would not easily be justified.

At the same time one could point out that, in order to be in continuity with symbols sanctioned by centuries of use in the Christian church, such substitution should not be made without weighty and sufficient reason. And perhaps it should not be made in ordinary, run-of-the-mill Sunday worship, only on special occasions and maybe on more informal occasions such as retreats and events with smaller groups. Here we could use profitably Schreiter's guidelines for contextualization, one of which states that, as far as possible, what remains after the change should still be in continuity with the wider Christian community's practice (1985:117-121).

Being on the Way

1. *Playing detective* (you can do this by yourself, but it's more fun to get a few others or members of an existing church group):

a. Look around your worship space—the sanctuary and its surroundings. What evidence of indigenization do you see? Are your stained glass windows a bit out of the ordinary? A Japanese American church in Los Angeles had erected one commemorating all the World War II internment camps. Does one wall have a couplet hanging down, true Chinese style, with brush calligraphy black on bright red? Did your banner makers use embroidery on brocade instead of burlap or felt? Is there a sample of Asian Christian art—for example, one of the Watanabe prints or a paper cut from China—in the pastor's study, the church library, or the office?

b. Look more carefully at the art used. How much of it is the usual Christian art, such as Lamb of God with a cross, Greek letters alpha and omega, bread and cup, and the like? Did you unearth any specifically cultural symbols and art forms, such as a goat instead of a lamb, a dragon instead of a lion?

c. Go over the music used in your services—not just the words or printed hymns, but also anthems sung, musical instruments used, styles employed, and so on. To what extent were these from the congregation's cultural heritage rather than the traditional European repertoire?

d. Go over some orders of service. What kind of innovative components have been introduced from time to time—things not usually set in the order in your denomination's official worship book? Is there a special life-cycle celebration peculiar to your culture?

e. Does anybody recall a worship occasion when readings were included that were relevant to the theme but were not from Scripture? These could include classics from your culture, passages from the writings of contemporary Asian and Asian North American theologians, and quotes from poetry and novels.

f. What other evidence of indigenization and contextualization of your worship resources, style, and form could you uncover?

g. Go outside and have a good look at the church building. If it was a building designed under authority of the congregation, did the building committee of those days incorporate any architectural style, symbol, or landscape feature that is specific to your culture of origin? Some churches have moon gates. Others have green tile roofs. Still others include a goldfish pond in the compound. Obtain the book *The Place Where God Dwells* (see suggested references) to see what churches in Asia have done. If your congregation is going to build or rebuild in the future, be sure to explore this aspect fully before you finalize your plans.

2. *Debriefing:*

a. Sit down with your fellow sleuths and talk over your experience. How do people feel about their discoveries—or lack of them? Was it "Wow, I didn't know we had all that!" "Wonder why I never noticed it before?" "I don't know—seems a bit fishy and not altogether 'Christian' to me"? What else? What were your own feelings?

b. Select one or two items and discuss some of the following points:

- Do people recall whether this item has "always been there," or was a recent venture? Who introduced it, and was there easy acceptance or much resistance at the time? What insight does that give you about how to introduce such elements? For example, adequate preparation of the congregation might be one idea, and getting various church groups and individuals, especially "movers and shakers" involved early so they could have a say in the decision might be another.

- Is there any particular item or element you do

not currently practice or have but would like to try? Brainstorm strategies on how to go about it. Whom will you involve: which choir to sing a particular number, whom to select for an appropriate reading? It would be important to work closely with the regular worship planners, whether a worship committee or others.

3. A few *resources* you might find useful as you go about your debriefing include:

- *Hymns from the Four Winds: A Collection of Asian American Hymns;*
- *Sound the Bamboo; and*
- *The Bible Through Asian Eyes* (see suggested references).

References

AMECEA Liturgical Colloquium. *Liturgy: Toward Inculturation.* AMECEA Pastoral Institute. Eldoret, Kenya: Gaba Publications, 1986.

Caron, Charlotte. *To Make and Make Again: Feminist Ritual Theology.* New York: Crossroad, 1993.

Chung Hyun Kyung, *Struggle to Be the Sun Again: Introducing Asian Women's Theology.* Maryknoll, N.Y.: Orbis Books, 1990.

Chupungco, Anscar J. *Cultural Adaptation of the Liturgy.* New York, Ramsey: Paulist Press, 1982.

_____. *Liturgies of the Future: The Process and Methods of Inculturation.* New York, Mahwah: Paulist Press 1989.

_____. *Toward a Filipino Liturgy.* Quezon City, Philippines: New Day, 1976.

Francis, Mark R. *Liturgy in a Multicultural Community.* Collegeville, Minn.: The Liturgical Press, 1991.

Geffre, C., and J. Spae, eds. *China As a Challenge to the Church.* Concilium: Religion in the Seventies. New York: Seabury Press, 1979. See especially: "The Chinese Religious Sense" by Julia Ching, 19–25; "Theology in the Age of China: Evangelisation and Culture" by Claude Geffre, 75–87; "How Can One Be at the Same Time Authentically Chinese and Christian?" by Stanislau Lokuang, 88–91; and "Can One Be Truly Christian and Chinese at the Same Time? Point of View of a Christian from Hong Kong" by Edmond Tang, 93–95.

Greeley, A. and Baum, G., eds. *Ethnicity*. Concilium: Religion in the Seventies. New York: Seabury Press, 1977. See especially the following: "Ethnic Groups and Church Attendance in the United States and Canada" by John Simpson, 16–22; "The Babel Story: Paradigm of Human Unity and Diversity" by Bernhard Anderson, 63-70; and "Reflections on Ethnic Consciousness and Religious Language" by John Shea, 85–90.

Japanese Presbyterian Worship Handbook Committee. *Worship Handbook for Japanese American Christian Lay Leaders and Ministers*. Sierra Mission Area Asian Ministers' Language and Cultural Seminar, Sacramento, Calif. 1981.

McCabe, Joseph V. "The Challenge of Inculturating the Liturgy," *Liturgy*. Vol. 6, no. 1, Summer 1986, "The Church and Culture," 9–13.

Minamiki, George, S. J. *The Chinese Rites Controversy from Its Beginning to Modern Times*. Chicago: Loyola University Press, 1985.

Ng, Greer Anne Wenh-In. "The Dragon and the Lamb: Chinese Festivals in the Life of Chinese Canadian/American Christians." *Religious Education*. Vol. 84, no. 3, Summer 1989. "Liturgy and Religious Education," 368–383.

(No author listed.) *Liturgy and Inculturation*. Lutheran World Federation, 1994.

Payne, Jennie Winsor; Char Burch; and Larry Walter, eds. *Celebrations and Rituals for Church Families*. San Francisco: Family Life Committee of the Parish Life and Work Commission, Northern California Conference, United Church of Christ, 1988.

Power, David, and Luis Maldonado, eds. *Liturgy and Human Passage*. Concilium: Religion in the Seventies. New York: Crossroad, 1979.

Procter-Smith, Marjorie, and Janet R. Walton, eds. *Women at Worship: Interpretations of North American Diversity*. Louisville, Ky.: Westminster/John Knox Press, 1993.

Schmidt, Herman, and David Power, eds. *Liturgy and Religious Traditions*. Concilium: Religion in the Seventies. New York: Seabury Press, 1977.

Schreiter, Robert J. *Constructing Local Theologies*. Maryknoll, N.Y.: Orbis Books, 1985.

Smith, Henry N. "Ancestor Practices in Contemporary Hong Kong: Religious Ritual or Social Custom?" *Asia Journal of Theology*. Vol. 3, no. 1, April 1989, 31–45.

Smith, Robert J. *Ancestor Worship in Contemporary Japan*. Stanford, Calif.: Stanford University Press, 1974.

Stevick, Daniel B. *The Crafting of Liturgy: A Guide for Preparers.* New York: The Church Hymnal Corp., 1990.

Uzukwu, E. Elochkwu. *Liturgy: Truly African, Truly Christian.* AMECEA Pastoral Institute. Eldoret, Kenya: Gaba Publications, 1982.

Suggested References on Asian Festivals and Customs and Asian and Asian North American Liturgies and Rituals

Committee on Chinese Customs and Rites, Singapore Federation of Chinese Clan Associations. *Chinese Customs and Festivals in Singapore.* Singapore: Singapore Federation of Chinese Clan Associations, 1989.

Japanese Presbyterian Worship Handbook Committee, Sierra Mission Area, Asian Ministers' Language and Cultural Seminar. *Worship Handbook for Japanese American Christian Lay Leaders and Ministers.* Sacramento, 1981.

Loh, I-to, ed. *Sound the Bamboo.* Manila: Christian Conference of Asia, 1992.

National Federation of Asian American United Methodists. *Hymns from the Four Winds: A Collection of Asian American Hymns.* Supplemental Worship Resources 13. Nashville: Abingdon Press, 1983.

Payne, Jennie Winsor; Char Burch; and Larry Walter, eds. *Celebrations and Rituals for Church Families.* San Francisco: Family Life Committee of the Parish Life and Work Commission, Northern California Conference, United Church of Christ, 1988.

Takenaka, Masao. *God is Rice: Asian Culture and Christian Faith.* Geneva: World Council of Churches, 1986.

Takenaka, Masao, and Ron O'Grady. *The Bible through Asian Eyes.* Auckland, New Zealand: Pace Publishing in association with Asian Christian Art Association, 1991.

_____. *The Place Where God Dwells: An Introduction to Asian Church Architecture.* Auckland, New Zealand: Pace Publishing in association with Asian Christian Art Association, 1995.

Wong, C. S. *A Cycle of Chinese Festivities.* Singapore: Malaysia Publishing House, 1967.

CHAPTER 8

Festivals: Celebrating Community, Story, and Identity

By Ellen Tanouye

Introduction

*Ellen Tanouye, a pastor in a Japanese American congrega-
tion, tells in story form how a congregation witnessed of its
identity and practiced Christian community through the celebration of an annual festival. Based on the report of the
church bazaar described in chapter 3, this story presents the
power of festivals to help young and old to know themselves
as members of the community who have a unique identity and
a common set of values.*

*This chapter reflects Asian North American propensities
for story, ritual, roles and responsibilities, communal events,
and the transmission of tradition through participation in
festival and ritual.*

Festivals

Festivals are celebrations that bring people together on
joyous occasions. They lift up and affirm specific persons or
events. They draw together a community to mark a change
or transition in the life of that community. Festivals can mark
a change in seasons (such as winter to spring) or a transition
within the life of an individual from one stage to another
(such as marriage, adulthood, retirement, or graduation).
Festivals also center on the story of a particular community—

its past, its relation to the present, and its vision into the future. Festivals celebrate community identity. Knowing who you are, to whom you belong, and what you believe and value are important in celebrating your identity within a community. Two stories, adapted from actual events, are told in this chapter. As you read them, you will undoubtedly recall similar events in your own congregation.

The first story is about the discovery of festival within a particular congregation's midst and how a church may be able to reclaim its sense of cultural identity and value through the tracing back of one particular festival activity. The story recalls the tracing of history that one pastor was able to do in his congregation. (This is a recasting of the factual account told in detail by Michael Yoshii; see chapter 3, "The Buena Vista Church Bazaar.")

Festival in Our Midst

It was time for the chicken teriyaki sale committee to plan its fund-raiser again, and the members wanted the pastor there for advice and support. Pastor Yosh was puzzled at the unusually strong commitment to this project. It wasn't a big fund-raiser—rather modest in money raised, in light of all the work involved in preparing, cooking, and selling the *teriyaki obentos*. It had been going on for decades, and now the main organizers, buyers, and cooks were mostly retired folk who were generally too tired to do other church projects and were beginning to show weariness about chicken teriyaki too. But the constancy of the annual event kept Pastor Yosh wondering why. This year he resolved to figure out the underlying reasons.

First, Pastor Yosh went to Jack, the head cook of the chicken teriyaki project, to find out what he could. Jack was, as usual, in his backyard, tending to his bonsai plants. They seldom got the chance to talk, so Pastor Yosh knew it would take a while before he could get to the point and ask the needed questions. Several hours later, Pastor Yosh reflected on the information he had gathered. Apparently the story began when the men of the church had heard about another chicken teriyaki sale across the bay and had gone over to that church to check out the equipment. They'd gotten plans for building the huge cement block barbecues that were built back then in the 1960s. The men had made their own metal grills that were custom-fit for the structures. One of them, Sam, had welded together the huge grills and made them sturdy enough to last a lifetime, maybe more. But none of the men who had originally built the barbecues were around anymore. Most of them had died, and a few had gone to live with their children in places far away.

Next, Pastor Yosh contacted Sumi, the head buyer and organizer of the chicken crew, which was made up mostly of women. Sumi was busy cooking at home, canning homegrown fruits and vegetables for herself and her family. A couple of grandkids crawled around the kitchen, playing happily with the plastic containers and pots and pans in the bottom drawers. Pastor Yosh sat through several cups of tea and homemade *manju* (a sweet rice snack) before he was able to gather the information about the chicken teriyaki sale. The plot thickened at this point because it turned out that the marinade was a secret recipe that had been kept within another church for years and years. Somehow, a clever and resourceful woman from Pastor Yosh's church had managed to obtain the recipe and, to this day, no one except that one church in the whole Bay Area and Pastor Yosh's church have such an excellent recipe for chicken teriyaki. The marinade is surpassed by none.

As Pastor Yosh sipped his tea and watched Sumi's grandkids play happily on the floor, Sumi's aunt happened to enter the kitchen and join in on the conversation. The aunt was eighty-five or so and a bit hard-of-hearing. She didn't speak much English. Sumi did some interpreting and the aunt revealed some surprising new information. So, by the end of the afternoon, Pastor Yosh had gathered a whole new set of data that he had never heard of before.

Pastor Yosh drove back to the church, wondering about the

things that had been shared by those women. First of all, he had discovered that the chicken teriyaki sale used to be held in the spring, not the summer. As he'd questioned the older aunt, he'd found that there was another event in conjunction with the fund-raiser. To his surprise, he found out that the event had originally been a March 3 festival for girls. This festival was a Doll Festival, and someone from the church had provided a doll set for display years ago. This woman even had old photographs of the display at the church, with the dolls and other ornate decorations elegantly placed on each of five tiers. The chicken teriyaki sale had come about after the annual Doll Festival had become a church tradition, eventually replacing the Doll Festival and becoming an annual fund-raiser. Pastor Yosh had uncovered a wealth of tradition evolving from a simple event of the church!

Implications

Although Pastor Yosh's congregation had scant memory of the Doll Festival, he was able to uncover this celebration, which apparently had existed before World War II and continued until sometime after the war. The fact that it no longer existed is significant. The fact that Pastor Yosh rediscovered it and perhaps will reclaim the festival as part of the cultural heritage of the church is also significant.

The second story about an annual church event takes place in another Asian North American congregation. It, too, suggests the importance of festivals and rituals as meaningful cultural events in the life of a church. Here the festival is more obvious and apparent, yet its intent and significance remain to be discovered and articulated by this particular church family. This is a festival of making *mochi,* or pounding rice. It occurs yearly in the Japanese household and signifies the ending of one year and the anticipation of another. *Kagami mochi*, decorative rice balls, are put on display in homes to bring in the New Year as well as to represent the symbols of good health, prosperity, and long life. It is quite a physical ordeal that takes place over the course of several days and can involve as many as fifty people. The following story describes this particular festival as it took place in one congregation.

The Mochi *Project*

Pastor Rob had deliberately dragged his feet on acting on a certain agenda item for the church governing body—the *mochi* project. He didn't want to cancel the event entirely, but he knew that other members of the session, especially the *Sansei*, wanted to focus on more "spiritual" activities. So he was delaying the process of selecting a *mochi* project chairperson for as long as possible. But tonight he had to bring it up under old business for sure.

"Well, let's look at this item of old business—the *mochi* project," Pastor Rob started off with hesitancy. "Did you ask last year's chairperson about serving again, Tad?"

"Yes, I did," said Tad, "and Ken told me that because of his health problems, he couldn't do it this year. But he found somebody to take his place: Jim Sakamoto."

"Great—thanks, Tad," said Pastor Rob with a sigh of relief. "So, will someone make a motion to elect Jim as chair for the *mochi* project?"

"So moved," piped in Nancy, clerk of session.

"Is there a second?" asked Pastor Rob.

"Second," replied Tad.

"Any discussion?" asked Pastor Rob, hoping that there wouldn't be any.

Sure enough, Gwen, the Christian education chairperson spoke up. "Don't you think that it's an unspoken obligation for all of us to participate in making *mochi*? I'd feel guilty if I didn't support the project. But I have a feeling we'll all be kind of exhausted, since it's right after Christmas and all. I mean, it might have been important for the church a long time ago, but my family doesn't even eat the stuff!"

"Besides, " added Jeff, another *Sansei* elder, "it's mostly a cultural thing for us as Japanese Americans, but many of our younger folks who have to do the hard work aren't even

Japanese; they're Korean or Chinese or something else. What value would they find in having to do this project?"

"Well, we've always done it in the past," contributed Nob quietly. Nob was a *Nisei* elder. "And it's not so much the *mochi* that's at stake, but I think it connects us with who we are as a church family and where we've come from." For Nob, who hardly ever spoke up, this much talk was in itself a statement.

"Any other comments?" asked Pastor Rob. Silence hung over the room, but it seemed clear to all the elders that Nob's statement carried a lot of weight.

"All those in favor say, 'Aye.'" said Pastor Rob quickly.

All twelve elders said, "Aye."

"All those opposed?" asked Pastor Rob more confidently. Silence filled the air. Pastor Rob felt relief spreading throughout the room.

"Well then, motion carried," stated Pastor Rob cheerfully, with hope in his voice. "Tad, could you talk to Jim and get that committee organized?"

"Sure—no problem," said Tad agreeably.

The *mochi* project got some attention each Sunday at worship during announcements a month before the event. The announcements were low-keyed, with no pressure, and the announcer made it clear that it was an optional event: you could come and participate if you wanted, but you didn't have to; you didn't have to buy the ten-pound minimum order of mochi, only if you wanted to. So the evening before the event, it was surprising and almost shocking to see so many men gathering at the church. Not only were there the same people as last year, but there were others too!

There was an unspoken, unwritten commitment from the church family around this particular activity, starting with the men. It could be seen in the older men who never directly stated how important the event was but somehow got that message across by volunteering to keep the all-night vigil. In previous years they had complained and wanted the younger men to take their place. This year no complaints were lodged;

they just showed up at midnight as in years past. This year the younger men showed up as well, from the *Yonsei* sons of the *Sansei* to the young adults and older *Sansei*, making it a bigger crew than ever.

The gathered crew talked and laughed well into the night, working together and sharing stories. The younger ones got out their rented videos and unrolled their sleeping bags. They talked and laughed some more, working together and sharing their lives. They rinsed and drained the barrels of rice, which had been washed and soaking from days before. At 3 A.M. they began to heat the fires so that the first batches of rice would be ready to form at 6 A.M. Right after the first batches of rice were put to steam over the fire, one of the *Sansei* men prepared a hearty breakfast for everyone there. Somehow, gathering around the table and eating together bonded them in a special way—without words but with a significant effect upon them all.

"Hey, Mark! You sure seem hungry, even in the middle of the night!" joked Dan, one of the *Yonsei* children, addressing his brother, who was wolfing down some rice and Portuguese sausage.

"I wouldn't talk! Look at your plate!" retorted Mark, in fun. Indeed, Dan's plate was as full, if not fuller, than Mark's, and Dan ended up polishing off all the rice and sausage on his plate in no time.

As the men and boys ate, there was some conversation about the food and more talk about the game on television this past week. They enjoyed each other's company, and they shared the common interest of sports as a topic of conversation. It began to be quiet, as the younger boys dropped off to sleep in their sleeping bags and the older men went off to tend to the fire.

At 6 A.M.sharp, the women took over. This year there were the faithful and steady *Nisei*, the *Nichigo*, who speak only Japanese, and the early-rising *Sansei*. This year for the first time, there were a couple of *Yonsei* children who helped in the process of cutting, shaping, cooling, and packaging. Each person had a responsibility.

"Come on, Jennifer, try it!" encouraged Mitsie, an older *Nisei* woman who was a veteran at forming the *mochi* balls. "See, you just keep your hand like this and keep it moving, like this." She explained it all patiently, showing Jennifer how it was done properly.

As Jennifer tried it, it was clear that the hot *mochi* was shaping into a wrinkly, oblong football—all wrong and too large. "Oh, gosh," blurted out Jennifer in distress, "I'm no good at this."

Mitsie came around to Jennifer's side and did the forming alongside her. As Jennifer got the hang of the process, a tiny crack of a smile came on both Jennifer's and Mitsie's faces. They knew, in that moment, that a tradition of shaping had been somehow passed on, despite Jennifer's clumsy initial attempts, and they had both been a part of that special moment.

"All right, Jennifer," said Mitsie gruffly, not wanting to get emotional over the experience. "You'd better hurry up and finish this row. You don't want it to get too cool."

"OK," said Jennifer agreeably, and she proceeded to shape the *mochi* with new confidence.

The elders of the session expected the annual activity of *mochi* making to die out this year. Initially it had been done as a service for other Japanese American churches in the area and for the church families who didn't have the equipment for making the *mochi* each year. Several elements of festival and ritual are apparent in this story, and the following discussion will draw upon the observations made in this account. More was happening than an overnight cooking and early-morning shaping of *mochi*.

Characteristics of Festival

A. *A festival is regular and recurring.* If there is a festival or ritual that is claimed by a congregation, it will be apparent to the church family as well as outsiders viewing the event that it is indeed a regular and recurring activity within the life of the church. Expectation and anticipation are often a part of the recurring nature of rituals, and the attitude of looking forward to an event was an integral part of the *mochi* project described above. The recurring and regular nature of the act itself was somehow important to church folks. Making the event seem optional or unnecessary was a strategy that the church officers thought would make it disappear from the church calendar. Not so!

Furthermore, when the people gather each year to repeat the festival or ritual, the younger participants learn—by doing—from the older ones. Over the years, many stories are told, many lessons are learned.

B. *A festival gathers and incorporates.* This rice pounding certainly had the effect of gathering the older, experienced folks together and also of incorporating new members into its activity. The fact that the sons of a *Sansei* male, young adults, plus the *Sansei* themselves were there spoke to a need for gathering intergenerationally and incorporating younger males. Even among the women's responsibilities, new and younger faces appeared at every station of activity—the cutting, the drying, the weighing, and the packaging.

Gathering and incorporating are both vital parts of any festival or ritual.

C. *A festival is identified and articulated among the community and gives identity to the participants.* The event of making pounded rice is identified as a cultural activity of welcoming in the New Year. Annually we welcome in the incarnation of our Lord and Savior at Christmas, and annually Japanese American Christians welcome in the New Year by gathering as a church family for this intergenerational activity. Each person participating in the event can articulate the purpose of the activity: the welcoming of a new year. And most important, each participant receives an identity shared by the entire group.

D. *The festival is a covenant renewal and rehearsal.* The church officers had originally thought that the elimination of obligation to produce *mochi* for other churches would allow this activity to die out. Surprisingly, the *mochi* committee members decided to continue the activity, and the rest of the church family rallied around them to support the project. It was unspoken that the *mochi* making was the symbolic act of promising to be with each other in the coming year as a church family. It served as a covenant renewal for the church as a family, to welcome in the *oshogatsu* (New Year) in relationship with each other. As the various stages of *mochi* pounding took place, there would be stories shared about past years and how it had been long ago—without the machinery, purely by hand. Funny incidents would be recalled, and times of extraordinary happenings would be memories brought out and shared with pleasure and pride.

E. *A festival is corporate, with people acting in relationship to each other.* It was a test of this church's cultural identity to allow the project to exist purely because of its ritual and corporate nature, not because of a financial or product-oriented need (such as a fund-raiser). It was wonderful that the response of the church family was so positive and so affirming. Not only did all the generations of folks come out to support the *mochi* project, but the fellowship and bonding that occurred during the event made it a valuable time of sharing and storytelling. It was fascinating that this event drew younger folks who were not Japanese American or even Asian American and that they, too, listened with interest to the stories being shared. Thus the relationships existing among the church family were strengthened because of this one event. The church officers took notice of this response in amazement.

The best part about the corporate nature of the festival was that, as a church body celebrating the coming of a new year, the pastor was able to preach on the topic of a new year and framed the *mochi* event theologically for the people. Articulating the event theologically added validity and importance to *mochi* making. The pastor's intentional drawing of the cultural and the theological together in the sermon enabled the people to acknowledge *mochi* as this church's ritual of expressing hope in a new year. The *Mochi* Festival also was a life-affirming, congregation-building festival.

Asian North American Congregations As Festival Congregations

Asian traditions of festivals are part of our cultural heritage expressing who we are and where we come from. Sharing stories of how and why festivals were celebrated can be extremely healing and revealing for individuals as well as for groups of people in the church. As seen above, some festivals or rituals come to be celebrated by the church family almost by rote, before they are either claimed by the group as a whole or forgotten or replaced by something else. In the case of the *mochi* project, the ritual was clearly affirmed as a valid and integrally important ritual of the church that expressed who the members are as a people. In the earlier case of the chicken teriyaki, the festival of *Hinamatsuri* had been forgotten and overlaid with a chicken teriyaki fund-raiser. As the pastor of the church has uncovered a wealth of information about the history of that particular festival in the church, the congregation may be able to reclaim that festival as their ritual that connects them back to a history where the dolls had a significant role in the identity and life of the church.

One wonders what the dolls could share in their stories of being displayed yearly in the church before World War II and what it felt like to be locked away in a basement during the trauma of the war years. Finally, when the dolls have their "resurrection" experience as the Doll Festival is restored, they will tell many a story about the past festivals and see with their doll eyes how much change the church has gone through. The girls looking up at the dolls will be different somehow from those before the war. They will be *Yonsei*, racially blended, Asian North American, or perhaps not Asian at all. And yet the look of love and wonder that will fill the girls' eyes will somehow be the same. As the dolls look back at the girls, they will remember who they are as special decorative dolls. These dolls have the privilege of being a part of that special *Hinamatsuri* of identity and belonging. They will tell marvelous stories.

Questions for Reflection

1. What are some stories you can tell of how an Asian North American congregation conveyed its identity and values through a regular event such as a church bazaar?

2. What are some specific ways identity and values are conveyed through such events?

3. How do congregations instill a sense of community among their members?

4. How do children and youth come to know the church as a community of faith?

5. Does your congregation engage in storytelling? How can storytelling enhance identity and community?

CHAPTER 9

The Church As Mediator between Cultures

By Ellen Tanouye

Introduction

The Asian North American congregation forms individual and group identity and forges communal ties through its festivals, bazaars, and similar special events, many of which are observed year after year. The congregation also is a setting for people of different generations and cultures to come together. Not that all congregations succeed as mediators of generational and cultural conflicts; but the stories by Ellen Tanouye in this chapter evoke for the church the possibilities for a ministry of mediation between cultures.

The Church As Mediator

The community of God demonstrates the love and nurture of its people by the kinds of caring relationships it fosters among people. In Asian North American congregations, one of the tasks of caring is to mediate between two cultures, the Asian and the Western. Relationships need to take into account the cultural characteristics that create unique bonds between generation and class, language and education, parents and children. The ways relationships are developed, maintained, and transformed reflect the ways in which culture is mediated and preserved within the church community. This chapter presents examples of cultural diversities that affect the community of God and suggests how relationships of caring are developed, particularly those with strong values attached to them.

Let us visit a small but growing Japanese American church on a Sunday morning. Many activities are happening involving many people. A sense of family bonding is present within the church walls and, in fact, numerous extended families are a part of this congregation. The congregation is housed in an old converted cottage that has been expanded and added onto, but recent growth has prompted the leaders of the church to consider moving into a new facility where space is not such a limiting problem. Recently they have been approved by the city to add more parking spaces to their property because parking is a continual problem, especially on Sundays.

Don wakes up early on Sundays. It's his favorite day of the week. This is the day he gets to be with his best friends in Sunday church school, and he smiles just thinking about it. As Don's family van enters the church grounds, he sees many cars already in the parking lot. His family, like most of the young families, are usually not early to church. His grandmother's car, on the other hand, is already there, and he glimpses a car door opening next to him. His best friend, Eric, is getting out. So as soon as Don hops out, both he and Eric race up the steps of the back door to the church, not even waiting for their families. They are greeted in the kitchen by a couple of older women who are busy fixing tea and crackers for the fellowship hour. Both of the children mumble a quick, "Hi," and make their way into the social hall with their echoing footsteps. They mischievously peek into the sanctuary where the Japanese-language service is in full swing. Thirty pairs of eyes are on them as they open the door a crack. They listen a few seconds to the voices singing in a language they don't understand. Giggling, they slam the door and run off to the nursery, where their teachers are setting up their activities for the Bible story and lesson.

In an adjacent room, Don's and Eric's parents are congregating, chatting over freshly brewed gourmet coffee and

croissants. Unlike the older generation's Bible class next
door, this class has a relaxed style with lively discussion
among the parents and the leader about parenting as a
Christian family matter. They enjoy each other's company
and spend a lot of time joking and laughing. Humor seems
to be an essential part of this gathering. Back in the
sanctuary, the Japanese-speaking folks have finished their
worship of praise and singing and are deep into a Bible
study. They have no table to gather around because they
need none. The pastor speaks and the participants listen
intently. The air is serious and there is no discussion. The
lesson is good, and people nod their affirmations quietly.

In the atrium is still another Bible study in session. This
class of older women is more comfortable in the English
language but prefers a teaching style that is more Asian
and directive. There is plenty of laughter in this setting
too, since the teacher is quite entertaining, and humor
masks the serious nature of the lesson. Eric's grandmother
is in this class, and she's hoping that the answers she has
written in her book are acceptable.

In the vignettes above are several examples of diversities
within the culture that are mediated by the church. Each
diversity holds a tension between two extremes, East and
West, young and old, English and Japanese. If one group did
not affirm or accept another group's way of doing things,
conflict over the differences could emerge and create a break
in harmonious relationships. By acknowledging and affirming diversity within the culture, the church is able to have
peaceful coexistence among the groups of the church family.
By allowing and serving the diverse elements of its congregation, this particular church is able to nurture several
generations of Japanese Americans and their family networks within the same community of God.

Immigrants and North American–born Asians

There is no clear demarcation between the immigrant and
North American-born in the church setting described above.
Most of the immigrants are comfortable in the Japanese-

language service, but there are a few younger immigrants who tend to associate with the English-language crowd. The immigrants who have married Anglo-Americans also tend to associate with the English-language folks.

First/Second or Third/Fourth Generations

In this particular congregation there are two kinds of first-generation Asian North Americans: those who immigrated to America in the early 1900s and have dwindled to a few in number, and the younger, more recently immigrated folks who have a quite different cultural experience. The second-generation folks, the *Nisei*, are mostly the children of the older *Issei* immigrant generation and are mostly in their sixties and seventies. English is their first language, but they prefer the more Asian style of education in which the teacher does the majority of talking. The third generation of Asian North Americans are the children of the *Nisei*. They are the baby boomer generation who were born after the internment years (during World War II, when Japanese North Americans were placed in internment camps) and know little about the suffering and racism that their parents went through. They know few Japanese words or ways and prefer a democratic style of education. Don's and Eric's parents are of this generation. The fourth generation tend to be a blended group of children who have one parent of Japanese ancestry, the other parent being either Asian or Anglo. They, too, only know English but surprisingly feel more comfortable in this Asian North American church setting than in the primarily Anglo school and neighborhood settings. Don is *Yonsei* with both parents who are *Sansei*, and Eric is *Yonsei* with one parent who is *Sansei* Japanese and one parent who is *Sansei* Chinese.

English or Japanese Language

The Japanese language tends to be lost by most families of the next generation. *Nisei* generally speak mostly English and use very little of their Japanese. Recent immigrants tend to pick up English as a second language pretty quickly, especially since their children likely speak mostly English. Don's and Eric's grandmothers can speak Japanese but use mostly English with their families. The *Sansei* have lost the Japanese language except for a few words, and the *Yonsei,* or fourth generation, have no clue what Japanese is like as a language. Thus Don's and Eric's parents speak Japanese with no fluency and with an American accent, and Don and Eric only know Japanese from the foods they eat or certain television programs.

Eastern or Western Style of Education

The Eastern style of education is effective in the church setting for the *Issei*, the new immigrants, and the *Nisei*, but not the *Sansei* or *Yonsei*. This style is effective because it allows the participants to accept the knowledge from the *sensei,* or teacher, without revealing ignorance on their part. The transfer of information is basically one-way, and the participants have great respect for the teachers of the church. With Western styles of education, participants have to be actively engaged in the learning process or they will easily lose interest and be bored. The *Sansei* and *Yonsei* have a great need to have dialogical learning so that they can challenge the teachers about the information they are learning. Interestingly, however, even these generations of Asians can sometimes switch to the Eastern style of education when it appears that they can learn the information easily by listening. They, too, do not want to reveal their ignorance of the subject matter and will tend to be quiet rather than volunteer wrong information.

Hierarchal or Democratic Class

Unlike language or style of education, class consciousness tends to be blended rather than hierarchal. The *Issei* and new immigrants tend to be more aware of class and role distinc-

tions among the church members. Each time someone becomes engaged, it is common for immigrants to send away to
Japan for the family background information to see whether
or not this potential partner is acceptable to the bride's or
groom's family. As the *Nisei* and *Sansei* and *Yonsei* join the
ranks, the distinction of class is more blurred. Most *Nisei* in
North American society were relegated to less than their
potential in terms of their careers. Don's grandparents, for
example, were a gardener and a housekeeper. This lack of
opportunity tended to flatten out an otherwise hierarchal
class distribution of *Nisei*. There are even fewer socioeco-
nomic indicators separating the *Sansei* and *Yonsei* because
of their emphasis on higher education and professional careers. Most *Sansei* are part of the middle class or upper
middle class in terms of income, lifestyle, and values. Both
Don's and Eric's parents went to good schools and earned
professional degrees. The democratic approach to class fits
the *Sansei* and *Yonsei* well because they have been successful
for the most part in doing well in society. However, there are
subtle barriers to climbing up the ladder of success. For
example, the "glass ceiling effect" in many companies and
institutions prevents nonwhites from ascending to the top of
their companies.

Parent-Child Gap

If the church is seen as the mediator of the diversities
within a culture, the perennial parent-child gap is an area
where gentle and patient mediation can take place in a
church setting. Often the parent-child gap does not become
an issue in the family until the child reaches adolescence. At
adolescence, the primary area of development centers on the
process of identity formation. This process involves not only
searching for answers to the question "Who am I?" but also
to "What do I believe and value?" and "How are my relationships reflected in who I am?" Many times this process pits
child against parent. The following story describes a case of
a parent-child gap during adolescence:

Matthew knew that his parents placed high—perhaps enormously high—expectations on him in school. He was bright, but he had the reputation of being a "nerd" in school, like many of the Asian North Americans in his classes. That meant it appeared to his fellow students that he studied hard, and Matthew was not quite sure that he liked that part of his identity. Although he didn't get straight A's, he usually could escape his parents' disapproval and criticism by the time report card time rolled around. This semester, though, was a struggle. His algebra grades had dropped to the level of unacceptability—deep trouble! Not only that, the homework was becoming overwhelming. Things finally exploded in the spring, when the grades came out. Matthew managed to hide the report card for a couple of weeks, but the guilt was becoming unbearable. Then his best friend inadvertently mentioned the bad grades to Matthew's mother. Suddenly the parent-child gap seemed like an infinite chasm. Not only did Matthew's parents react negatively, but Matthew also had not been able to bridge the gap of communication with any sort of self-confidence or self-esteem.

The parent-child gap is a developmentally common one, often occurring in isolation within a family. These kinds of problems are not shared among the church family because of the possibility of bringing shame upon the family. In one particular situation Matthew and his parents were part of the church family and ended up sharing their predicament with their pastor and close friends. Through much discussion and careful thought, the parents and Matthew were able to work through their parent-child gap caused by a basic lack of communication and trust. The parents ended up spending time tutoring Matthew. This time allowed them to regain the kind of communication and relationship that brings healing and restoration.

Grandparents As Mediators

Grandparents can be the most wonderful, richest source of cultural information. A wealth of stories and tales about days past exists. They can link their grandchildren with the past by sharing their traditions and histories in story and in deed. Passing on traditions is a process that requires a great deal of patience and time. Usually grandparents have more time to spend with their grandchildren because they are retired from their jobs. The opportunities for mediation of cultural diversity are greater. The following story portrays the fullness and richness of a grandparent-grandchild relationship as the two do a household task together:

> Joy watched her grandma carefully preparing the evening meal. Her hands flew quickly as the words also flew out of her mouth, so Joy had to pay close attention to keep up with her grandma's stories and her cooking. The lettuce had to be cut first, before the fish, and there was a certain way of placing the cut pieces upon the plate so that it would look attractive.
>
> "But, Grandma, why can't I help you with the fish?"
>
> "No, my child, your hands will get too fishy and you are too young for this. Just watch."
>
> So Joy watched and listened while her grandma told her about the art of cutting *sashimi* in the proper way. She would interweave her instructions with stories of her own childhood, of growing up on the beaches of Japan, of eating such fresh fish it would still seem to be moving. Joy just loved to see the *sashimi* come out so beautifully, and she loved the smells, even if her grandma didn't approve of her getting it on her hands. She could hardly wait until she would be old enough to make the dish herself. She smiled to herself as she anticipated the evening meal.

In this story, Joy's grandmother taught her not only about a cultural skill in cooking; she also shared with her the precious history of her own life story that was related to the cooking activity. Joy's mother was extremely busy working outside the home, so she hardly ever spent this kind of time teaching her daughter about cultural traditions or telling her stories from the past. Joy's grandmother, on the other hand, loved to cook and tell stories—the more the better. She enjoyed the presence of her granddaughter and often shared more with her than she had with her own children.

Church As Peacemaker and Community Builder

As families grow and develop in the church, the church family also grows and develops. With growth and development come changes that lead to differences and can often develop into conflicts. When these differences and conflicts arise, it is up to the church (and church leaders) to resolve them in a compassionate and understanding manner. Often feelings get hurt and words get misunderstood because of miscommunication. The church must always be aware of its role as peacemaker and assume its role as community builder. The following story occurs in some form in many churches and may strike a chord of similarity in yours:

Ann was excited because it was her first time to be asked to help on a church committee. She had to work the day of the all-church potluck, so she thought she would pick up a cake at the local bakery. Luckily, she got off work early, so she had the extra time to bake a cake from scratch before she left for the church. Her stomach sank as she saw the huge sheet cake that filled the dessert table in the social hall. Did she hear wrong when Helen had talked about what to bring? She turned to Helen, who was busy arranging her own salad dish on the other table. Maybe she had heard wrong. Ann was so embarrassed that she felt like going home. As she tried to decide what to do, she felt a hand on her shoulder.

"Don't worry, Ann," Carol said gently. "Some of us really love chocolate, so I'm sure your cake will disappear in no time."

"Gosh, I feel so dumb," said Ann. "I didn't know we were only supposed to bring salads." "It's OK, really," reassured Carol. "They might have mentioned it in the women's meeting last Thursday, but I remember you came in a little late because of your work schedule."

"Oh well, I guess I'll stay anyway," Ann said. "Can I help in setting up the tables?"

Ann is a new member in this Asian North American church. She has no family ties to the church, so she is just beginning to make relationships within the church family. The all-church potluck could have been a potential conflict situation if Carol had not seen Ann's distress and reassured her of acceptance. Helen, who had initially contacted Ann about the potluck, had given her the correct information. However, later the committee decided to order a sheet cake and have people bring salads instead. Instead of calling Ann to tell her about the change, Helen assumed that Ann would ask someone who had been on time to the meeting. Helen always disapproved of people who were late to meetings because she herself was always early to meetings. She also was a little resentful of Ann because Ann had been asked to be on the fellowship committee, one that Helen had been on for many years. Helen felt a little threatened by Ann because she seemed so competent and confident. Helen wished that she could be as self-assured. Since Ann worked full-time and had a family and a busy schedule, Helen was disappointed that the committee would choose her instead of someone like herself, a retired, older person who had lots of time on her hands as well as lots of experience. Fortunately, where Helen was not forthcoming with helpful information, Carol was able to step in with a helping hand for Ann.

A church needs peacemaking and community building within the church family. Although it seems that such behaviors should occur naturally, they don't. It is important to have church members like Carol, who saw a potential conflict and handled it quietly and peacefully. Perhaps in the future, interactions and conversations with Ann will reveal information about Helen and her resentful attitude toward her. The mediating church needs a few perceptive troubleshooters like Carol. This kind of peacemaker and community builder often bridges gaps between people that can turn into ugly rifts. Carol may possibly bridge the communication gap between

Ann and Helen and also come up with a way to diffuse Helen's resentment and help Helen to find a way to use her gifts constructively.

Mediating Cultural Differences in Your Congregation

1. As you reflect on these small incidents in an Asian North American congregation, do you recognize them? Similar reactions and interactions happen all the time, usually in quiet, subtle ways.

2. Who in your congregation notices when two different people or two diverse groups come into contact?

3. Who knows enough of the Asian and Western ways, or the old and the new ways, to be a communicator and a community builder?

4. Who teaches people to be bridges between cultures?

CHAPTER 10

Asian North American Youth: A Ministry of Self-Identity and Pastoral Care

By Grace Sangok Kim

Introduction

The final cluster of chapters in this book takes an even more practical turn than the previous chapters. This section provides specific ideas, program possibilities, and methods of ministry for achieving a heightened sense of community in Asian North American congregations.

Educator Grace Sangok Kim, who wrote about immigrant parents and adolescent children in chapter 6, now writes about adolescent identity formation and a ministry with youth that nurtures the formation of personal identity and personal faith. Kim provides information about the unique personal and family situations and the social contexts that challenge Asian North American youth. These youth are confronted by ethnic and racial confines that often marginalize them. Can these cultural characteristics also provide for young people a sense of identity and belonging? This chapter suggests youth ministry approaches and programs that lead the youth to bicultural integration and identity and membership in a multicultural society and church.

Who Am I?

A Case Study

Mr. Bong Hwan Kim is currently executive director of the Korean Youth and Community Center in Los Angeles. Mr.

Kim was interviewed by Professor Elaine H. Kim regarding his life experiences growing up in the United States. The following is an excerpt from Elaine Kim's chapter on Mr. Kim titled "Between Black and White" (1993).

I came to the United States when I was three years old. My father had come before us to get a Ph.D. in chemistry. He had planned to return to Korea afterward, but it was hard for him to support three children in Korea while he was studying in the United States, and he wasn't happy alone, so he brought the family over. He got a job at a photographic chemical manufacturing company in New Jersey, where he still works after almost thirty years. He never made it past the "glass ceiling." I view him as a simple person who must have been overwhelmed by the flip side of the American dream they never tell you about. There was never a place for him in America except at home with family or maybe at the Korean church. Both my parents were perpetual outsiders, never quite comfortable with American life.

The New Jersey community where I grew up was a blue-collar town of about 40,000 people, mostly Irish and Italian Americans. I lived a schizophrenic existence. I had one life in the family, where I felt warmth, closeness, love, and protection, and another life outside—school, friends, television, the feeling that I was on my own. I accepted that my parents would not be able to help me much.

I can remember clearly my first childhood memory about my being different. It was the first day of kindergarten, and I was excited about having lunch at school. My mother had made *kimbap* (rice balls rolled up in dried seaweed) and wrapped it all up in aluminum foil. I was eagerly looking forward to that special treat. When the lunch bell rang, I happily took out my lunch. But all the other kids pointed and gawked. "What is that? How could you eat *that?*" they shrieked. I don't remember whether I ate my lunch or not, but I told my mother I would bring tuna or peanut butter sandwiches for lunch after that.

I have always liked Korean food, but I had to like it secretly, at home. There are things you don't show to your non-Korean friends. My father spelled his name "Kim

Hong Zoon." The kids at school made fun of his name. "Zoon?" they would laugh. They called me "Bong" because "Bong Hwan" was too hard to pronounce. As a child you are sensitive. You don't want to be different. You want to be like the other kids. They made fun of my face. They called me "flat face." When I got older, they called me "Chink" or "Jap." It made me feel terrible. I would get angry and get into fights.

They used to say, "We consider you to be just like us. You don't seem Korean." That would give rise to such mixed feelings in me. I wanted to believe that I was no different from my white classmates. It was painful to be reminded that I was different, which people did when they wanted to put me in my place, as if I should be grateful to them for allowing me to be their friend.

I wanted to be as American as possible—playing football, dating cheerleaders. I drank a lot and tried to be cool. I convinced myself that I was "American," whatever that meant, all the while knowing underneath that I'd have to reconcile myself, to try to figure out where I would fit in a society that never sanctioned that identity as a public possibility. Part of growing up in America meant denying my cultural and ethnic identity, and part of that meant negating my parents. I still loved them, but I knew they could not help me outside the home.

Once when I was small and had fought with a kid who called me a "Chink," I ran to my mother. She said, "Just tell them to shut up." My parents would say that the people who did things like that were just uneducated. "You have to study hard to become an educated person so that you will rise above all that," they would advise. I didn't really study hard. Maybe I knew somehow that studying hard alone does not take anyone "above all that."

I was a natural athlete, and I enjoyed every kind of sport during my high school days. My parents encouraged my interest in sports, indulging and nurturing my boyish and manly enthusiasm by sparing no expense whenever I needed equipment. Probably sports saved me from complete lack of self-esteem as an Asian growing up in New Jersey in the early and mid-1960s. Through sports, I got lots of positive feedback and was able to make friends with white boys, who respected my athletic abilities, even though I was Asian. In high school I was elected captain of the football team, and my girlfriend was the captain of the cheerleaders. My grades were not particularly good in school. My parents were upset, but I didn't pay much attention to them.

When I got into college, I experienced an identity crisis. Because I was no longer involved in sports, and because I was away from home, I no longer felt special or worthwhile, and I became depressed. I hated even getting up in the mornings. Finally I dropped out of school.

I decided to go to Korea, hoping to find something to make me feel more whole. Being in Korea somehow gave me a sense of freedom I had never really felt in America. It also made me love my parents even more. I could imagine where they came from and what they experienced. I began to understand and appreciate their sacrifice and love and what parental support means. Visiting Korea didn't provide answers about the meaning of life, but it gave me a sense of comfort and belonging, the feeling that there was somewhere in this world that validated that part of me that I knew was real but others outside my immediate family never recognized.

After spending a year in Korea, I returned to finish college, and then I packed up and headed for California. I had always wanted to go to the West Coast, not only because of the mystique of California "freedom," but also because I heard that Asian Americans had a stronger presence there. I wasn't much into career planning. I wasn't looking forward to getting a job in the mainstream labor market, but I was anxious to find out what the "real world" was like.

Questions for Reflection

1. What kind of identity problems did Mr. Bong Hwan Kim go through? What helped him the most?

2. What seem to be Mr. Kim's definitions of self-identity and ethnic identity?

3. What are the strengths and weaknesses of the "melting-pot" and "salad bowl" theories for dealing with ethnic and racial differences in North America?

4. What are the needs and aspirations of the "1.5 generation"?

5. What conceptual models of ethnic identity development and processes would be helpful to Asian North American people?

Toward an Asian North American Identity

Melting Pot or Salad Bowl

North America is historically a nation of immigrants and a multicultural society. Because early European settlers and immigrants constituted a majority of the population, the cultural and ideological orientation in North America has been Eurocentric. The nation has advocated the *melting-pot theory* as a model of assimilation. A melting pot, like homogenized stew, is possible among Euro-Caucasian immigrants through their mixed marriages because of similar physical traits, skin color, and fundamentally European background.

However, the melting-pot model cannot work for all minorities unless wholesale interracial marriages occur in North America, as was once suggested by Arnold Toynbee, a British historian. As long as there are differences in outward appearance, people tend to be categorized, classified, and put in a pecking order according to skin color and physical characteristics (Kitano 1977).

An alternative model of a multiethnic and multicultural society is that of a *salad bowl*. Each ingredient in a tossed salad retains its own color, texture, taste, and individual identity. In such a society the sum total of all the ingredients becomes a multi-ingredient national identity without the individual parts losing their identity. And as a salad dressing serves to blend the ingredients together in unity, so, too, must the various members of a multiethnic culture come together;

otherwise each group might vie for power and control, with a risk of developing militancy and even Balkanization.

Development of Self-Identity

What is identity? Baumeister (1988) defined the criteria for identity as those characteristics that result in a consistent, continuous person over a period of time, and in differentiation from others.

Our identity is the total sum of our being and the entirety of what we are—that is, the totality of our physical, mental, emotional, social, legal, cultural, and spiritual dimensions, including conscious and unconscious thought processes and feelings (Kim and Kim 1993). Self-identity is a multifaceted and dynamic process. Many factors and dimensions interact with each other, contributing synergistically or sometimes conflictually to the development of identity. Some aspects of us are given and beyond our control. For example, in *biological identity,* we don't have much control over birth; birth order; gender; color of skin, hair, and eyes; and other aspects of physical appearance. Nor can we control various genetic factors, including hereditary dispositions, talents, and certain medical conditions. We are born with these givens and have no choice but to accept or deny them. We may be grateful for and happy with our natural endowments. Or we may lament and complain—feeling sorry for ourselves for the way we are—or resent God and our parents for bringing us into the world this way.

However, identity does not form entirely by itself. Other characteristics can be acquired and cultivated with conscious effort. Identity formation is an active process in which we can participate intentionally. Following are specific dimensions of identity that we can directly affect:

a. *Legal identity, including citizenship, naturalization, Anglicized legal name, marital status, and ethnicity of our spouse.* Our birthrights, such as citizenship, royal family status, inheritance of title or wealth, are also part of legal identity. Some are beyond our control, but others can be modified legally.

b. *Social identity, such as professional, occupational, or achievement-related identity.*

Social achievement often helps define one's identity as perceived by self (self-concept) and others (social status and public image). Academic degrees and professional titles, for example, may contribute toward positive self-esteem and public perception.

c. *Psychological identity.* Psychological and emotional life experiences greatly influence the shaping of identity, especially in one's relationships with parents or caregivers, siblings, peers, teachers, and role models during the early developmental phases. Also, attitude toward one's own ethnicity is influenced by positive and negative experiences of ethnic culture and affiliation, such as family and community rituals and celebrations, stories, the examples of elders or racial discrimination, alienation, marginality, emotional and physical harassment, and lack of empowerment.

However, social conditions do not always affect individuals in a uniform way. How an individual perceives reality subjectively is just as important as, if not more than, the objective reality itself. Much seems to depend on how individuals interpret their situation and on their capacity to adapt (Hurh 1993).

Thus our attitudes toward, and interpretations of, our subjective experiences, whether positive or negative, influence greatly the outcome of our psychological well-being. The more we feel powerless, the more we feel the locus of control is beyond us, the more we are victimized. The concept of "empowerment" becomes an important factor in psychological identity.

d. *Cultural identity.* The family transmission of cultural traditions, values, customs, and rituals has a powerful influence on the development of cultural identity. The degree of interest in and desire to learn our own ethnic/cultural heritage, history, and language is something we can cultivate. This helps us understand and identify better with our ethnic roots. Attending ethnic churches and summer camps on ethnic culture, visiting the Asian country of origin, and meeting relatives can all enhance a positive identification with our own culture.

e. *Religious / political / ideological identity.* Another dimension of our identity can be shaped and defined by what we believe religiously, politically, or ideologically. A certain description or label—such as Christian, Buddhist, atheist, Communist, Black Panther, feminist, or environmentalist— may tell us something about the person associated with that description and how others perceive him or her.

Life Phases and Identity Development

In a conference on "transitional generations" held in the San Francisco Bay area, 1.5 and second-generation Asian American young adults shared their own journeys of identity development (D. Kim 1993; Park and Sohn 1993).

When they were children, peer acceptance and approval were very important to them. They were sensitive to being different from peers because they were afraid of being ridiculed. They wanted to be like white children. They felt more secure and accepted when they felt they were like their peers and didn't stick out. During their elementary and junior high days, they tended to deny or reject their racial ethnicity and wanted to be like their dominant white peers.

Their experiences were similar to the findings of Pushkin and Veness (1971, in Baumeister) in their study that children are quick in comparing themselves with others and in discerning similarities and differences among themselves, especially in any physical appearance that stands out. Young children can be rather cruel and discriminating to each other, engaging in name calling, racial slurs, and verbal and physical threats. These can be ways of establishing some kind of pecking order among themselves.

When these young adults reached late teens or college age, their identity questions surfaced more acutely as they began to date and also as membership in the college fraternities and sororities became an issue on account of ethnicity. They began to think about their identity more seriously for the first time. Steady courtship with a person of different ethnicity and a plan for a possible marriage did precipitate serious identity crises and questioning and/or resolution, not only within themselves and their partners, but also with parents and family members.

By the time they reached young adulthood, they felt easier accepting their ethnicity, accommodating their bicultural orientation with more or less a positive resolution. They noted that by the time they grew to be adults, their immigrant parents were also changing. Parents became more mellow and willing to accept their children's way of life, whether it was more Western or bicultural. The earlier conflicts over cultural issues between the parents and growing children were resolved significantly toward a more mutually acceptable accommodation.

Population characteristics are changing rapidly with the recent influx of Asian immigrants to Canada and the United States, especially in California. In this new environment, Asian North American youth may not feel as isolated or different from their peers as before because there are now so many peers who look like them. This phenomenon will need further observation and study as to how the new multicultural environment will affect identity development.

Stages of Ethnic Minority Identity

Derald Sue and David Sue (1990) developed a theory of the stages of ethnic minority identity development that is supported by the personal experiences of Douglas Kim, Karen Park, and Matthew Sohn previously listed. The stages are described below.

a. *The conformity stage.* Asian North American children like to conform to their white peers. They may have negative feelings about themselves and have some feelings of self-hatred with regard to their own racial ethnicity.

b. *The dissonance stage.* As teenagers, they begin to experience cultural confusion, conflict, or identity crises. Denial begins to break down, which leads to questioning. They are in conflict as a result of disparate pieces of information or experiences that challenge their current concepts. This stage frequently occurs among late teens and young adults who are rebellious against their parental and ethnic values and yet are beginning to think about their ethnic identity; it is sometimes precipitated by dating.

c. *The resistance and immersion stage.* Asian North Americans begin to reject, or react against, the dominant white society and their values as having no validity themselves. Common feelings during this stage are guilt, shame, and anger. Now they begin to show some endorsement of their own ethnicity and culture.

d. *The introspection stage.* Loyalty and responsibility to their own ethnic group and family and a desire for personal autonomy come into conflict. They begin to recognize that there are many elements in the white society that are very functional and desirable, yet there is confusion as to how to incorporate these elements into the ethnic culture and values. An introspective mood sets in and leads to more questioning and searching.

e. *The integrative and awareness stage.* Those in this stage attain a synergistic and integrated bicultural orientation that is more realistic and workable for them.

Derald Sue cautioned about limitations in proposing this kind conceptual model. The model can serve as a conceptual framework to help us understand the process and development, but in reality the development does not consist of a neat progression of stages. There are overlaps and mixtures of the various stages with many other factors involved.

Modes of Asian North American Cultural Identity Orientation

There is a tendency for an Asian North American to adjust to one or a combination of the four modes of cultural identity and values: assimilation, traditionalism, isolationism, and bicultural integration. They are described in the following table (Kim and Kim 1993). This is a modified version of a similar paradigm previously proposed by Sue and Sue and Kitano and Daniels (1988).

Ethnic Cultural Identity and Adjustment of Asian North Americans

(modified from the Kitano and Daniels [1988] model)

High

Assimilation

- Mainstream
- More American than ethnic
- Associates mainly with white friends and people
- Culturally assimilated, but physical appearance still remains a barrier

Bicultural Integration

- Bicultural perspectives
- Maintains active contact with both cultures
- Biculturally comfortable and competent
- Can easily move in and out of both cultures
- Synergistic integration in value orientation

Low   **High**

Isolationism

- Disillusioned and uncomfortable in both communities
- Withdrawn from both communities
- Loss of cultural identity
- Isolated and individualistic existence

Traditionalism

- Emphasis on Asian culture and tradition as the better way of life
- More comfortable in the ethnic enclaves
- Rejects American values and avoids white people

Low

Mainstream Euro-American Values and Identity

Assimilation. This mode is represented by a person who is eager to assimilate into the dominant white American mainstream. The person tends to associate with white peers and avoid Asians. He or she rejects Asian culture and values. The person may have negative feelings about being an Asian or may feel that he or she can succeed in the country only by becoming a member of the mainstream society.

Traditionalism. This is the mode in which the person believes that adherence to Asian cultural values and lifestyles is very important, even at the risk of rejecting mainstream Western values and white peers. He or she is proud of being an Asian, associates with Asian friends, and maintains an Asian lifestyle.

Isolationism. In the mode of isolationism, the person is withdrawn from both Asian and Caucasian cultures because he or she feels uncomfortable in or rejected by both communities. He or she may feel "decultured" and prefer to live an individualistic life without any involvement in either community.

Bicultural integration. In this mode of orientation, the person feels comfortable and competent in biculturalism. Whether or not the person speaks the Asian language of his or her origin, he or she has a positive self-concept as an ethnic Asian and can move in and out of both cultures and communities with ease, flexibility, and appropriate cultural behavior. The person views bicultural orientation as an asset, not a liability. His or her life is understood as having been enriched by bicultural and multicultural experiences.

This kind of person may be called an "international," "global" or "cosmopolitan" person (Hurh 1993). The bicultural orientation is an ideal, desirable, and attainable goal for 1.5 or second-generation Asian North Americans, although it will not be easy to attain.

Again, this model is only a conceptual scheme to contrast the different modes of cultural identity and value orientations.

There are overlaps, differences in degree, and changes over time in a person's cultural orientation. We should avoid pigeonholing a person in a rigid manner.

Questions for Reflection

1. What is meant by *bicultural* orientation?

2. Attitudes of bias and prejudice against other ethnic minorities are common among Asian North American immigrant parents. How will these attitudes influence their children?

3. What are the roles parents can play in enhancing the positive ethnic self-identity of their children?

4. How can ethnic Christian churches help young people experience and develop a more positive self-identity as Asian North Americans?

The 1.5-Generation Asian North Americans

The term "1.5 generation" emerged in the Korean American community several years ago, and now it is being used in other Asian North American communities. The term refers to Asian North American immigrants who accompanied their parents to the United States when they were young (early and middle adolescence) and who are now functionally bilingual (Hurh 1993). Although they are technically first-generation immigrants like their parents since they were born overseas, they can be differentiated both from their parents (first generation) and their American-born offspring (second generation) because of their young age at the time of immigration. The sociocultural characteristics and psychological experiences of these *preadult* immigrants are so distinct from either their first-generation parents or their American-born second-generation contemporaries that they deserve separate analysis (Hurh 1993).

These 1.5 adolescent immigrants go through unique circumstances and different sets of sociocultural-psychological adaption in their life in the United States. Two possible modes of personality adaptation may emerge among the 1.5 generation: the *cosmopolitan* and the *marginal* (Hurh 1993).

Those with the *cosmopolitan* personality emerge from the positive resolution of biculturalism and ambivalent self-identity and display creativity, motivation, leadership potential, and active participation in both ethnic and mainstream communities, as in the case of Mr. Bong Hwan Kim described earlier. They can take advantage of their bicultural and bilingual orientation by playing a bridge role between first-generation adult immigrants and second-generation Asian North Americans.

The *marginal* personality type is a product of the negative resolution of the bicultural tension and conflict, and manifests unresolved ambivalence or denial in personal identity, hypersensitivity, social isolation, a lack of feelings of belonging, and feelings of powerlessness and insecurity.

Strengthening the Cultural Identity of Asian North American Youth

As mentioned previously in the section on cultural identity, there are many ways in which parents and churches can help Asian North American youth strengthen their interest in Asian culture and develop their cultural identity. The following suggestions are offered to help the Asian North American youth increase their interest in Asian culture and values (E. Lee 1988):

a. *Provide learning opportunities and motivation.* Youth programs in ethnic Christian churches can provide opportunities for cultural identification. Parents can read Asian storybooks to young children and cook Asian ethnic food together with them.

b. *Be actively involved in Asian or ethnic culture.* Participate in community cultural events, and attend summer ethnic culture and leadership camps. Enroll children in martial arts classes, calligraphy lessons, dragon dances, fan dances, or traditional ethnic dance classes. Attend Asian movies and Asian arts

museums to develop and stimulate their interest in
Asian culture and arts.

c. *Expose children to Asian culture, especially the culture and people of their country of family origin.* Finance teenage children on a trip to a summer
culture program in an Asian country, to meet relatives in the native country, or to visit an ancestral
village. Or finance their university language-learn-
ing programs.

d. *Make children proud to be part of their Asian family.* Observe cultural customs and rituals, such as
New Year's or Moon Harvest Day celebrations,
Christmas dinner, or a landmark (for example, sixtieth) birthday celebration. Do things together to promote the importance of family. Often these kinds of
family events and experiences are deeply etched in
children's memories. Share your family background,
childhood experiences, immigration story, and hard-
ships with teens (but not in a way that denigrates
Americans). Let teens get to know their grandparents or significant relatives—those living in North
America as well as those in the native country. Tape-
record oral histories of grandparents together with
teenagers. Talk about Asian culture, arts, philosophy, and famous or well-known people who have
made important achievements and contributions in
different professional fields. Also talk about ordinary, hardworking Asian North American people in
restaurant, laundry, and other small businesses and
in the labor market.

e. *Set an example.* Instead of merely talking about the
Asian culture endlessly or forcing children to learn
against their will, demonstrate in daily attitudes
and behavior what is valued and appreciated in the
Asian culture. Children will gradually learn to respect what parents and relatives value and practice.

f. *Promote family harmony by helping children think*

of the family first. Problems arise when each family member thinks only of himself or herself. When each family member makes an effort to be considerate of the others' needs, feelings, and points of view, it enhances family harmony. Let children know that a happy and strong family life is emphasized by the Asian culture.

g. *Visibly express the love and affection between husband and wife.* The overt expression of love and affection between a husband and wife, especially in front of children, is not part of the traditional Asian culture. But this is a Western practice parents may well need to learn and adopt. And a willingness to adopt such a Western practice provides a good model for our children to observe and emulate in their future marital behavior. There is nothing intrinsically wrong with a husband and wife overtly demonstrating their love and affection in the family. In fact, in some Asian North American families, young children have expressed their worry that the parents do not love each other or will divorce because they have never seen the parents holding hands or kissing. It is also important for children to see their father treating their mother as his equal, not as an inferior because she is a woman, as Confucian teachings of hierarchy may have been understood. In North America, Asian parents need to adopt the democratic values emphasizing gender equality.

h. *Have fun together as a family.* North American-born teens tend to view Asian culture and traditions as "too serious," "too stiff," "too formal," "too hierarchal, with no sense of humor," and "no fun." It doesn't have to be that way. Asian North American families can have lots of fun and playfulness and do things that are enjoyable and relaxing. Families can play more games and sports, go on picnics, and travel together.

The Role of the Church for Young People: Youth Ministry with Racial/Ethnic Minority Adolescents

In the booklet *A Colorful Community: Ministry with Racial/Ethnic Minority Youth*, David Ng (1991) wrote an imaginary but realistic case of a youth ministry program that supports an Asian American teenager:

A Case Study:
A fourteen-year-old Vietnamese girl, Xoan-Mei Tranh, growing up in a new and strange land

Xoan-Mei was born in a refugee camp in Thailand, and her family came to the United States as refugees. Her brother, six years older, was killed by a land mine in Vietnam. She has three American-born younger siblings who are now eight, six, and three years old.

Xoan-Mei's journey of identity formation is taking many of the twists and turns common to most teenagers. However, her road is more difficult and different from that of many North American adolescents. She is a person of racial/ethnic minority and Asian cultural background.

She is aware of her body changes—something all adolescents experience. She is also aware that she will not be as tall or physically built as the Anglo girls at school or as women who are portrayed in movies, television shows, and glamour magazines. Her mind is also changing. She is now raising more questions about herself, her white peers, and how things are done in the United States. Given her home situation, many of these questions are internalized. She knows better than to ask too many questions of her parents, especially of her father.

She is also keenly aware that she thinks differently from her Caucasian classmates. Her family has a religious background that is Buddhist, even though they are now Christian. Their social ethics are Confucian; their philosophy of life is Taoist.

Her parents grew up with the religious attitude that life includes much suffering, which must be overcome through enlightened attitude and perseverance. Becoming spirit (not just becoming spiritual) is a goal of life. Xoan-Mei and her siblings are taught that they are not to do anything that will bring shame to their parents and family, or even to their country, Vietnam.

Whether or not she realizes it, her world-view is that of *yin-yang*. All of life is in balance and harmony. Opposites are held in creative tension: male/female, positive/negative, good/evil, strong/weak, bitter/sweet, growth/decay, day/night, hot/cold, and so on. Every item and every aspect of life is connected and balanced in a harmony of life that embraces both forces. This Asian "both/and" view of life contrasts greatly with the Western "either/or" way of viewing, which tends to force a choice for or against.

In contrast to her Anglo peers, who are taught to be independent-minded and decisive or even aggressive, Xoan-Mei grew up learning to be accepting of "fate" and a life of harmony and moderation and to avoid conflict. So she seems not at all "assertive" to the Anglos and, in fact, she appears too passive to her friends.

She is puzzled about her observation that to many of her classmates, their families seem almost unimportant. Outside activities and organizations often take precedence over family life and obligations. Xoan-Mei, however, lives in a family system that is top priority. Her life is dominated by her family and family values. The family is her main unit of relationship. Her parents have authority over her. Now that her older brother is dead, she has assumed authority over and responsibility for her younger brothers and sister. Decisions are made in light of what is good for the family. No one is an independent agent making a decision solely for the individual. Her decisions about studying, spare time, college, career, and even marriage are communal decisions.

Years from now, Xoan-Mei may look back on this pervasive

family system and be glad for its support. But right now she harbors ambivalent feelings because, in her surge toward identity formation and personal independence, she feels constraints of family pressures. Sometimes what is supposed to be good often is bad, at least in terms of personal freedom and self-esteem. It seems to her that they always have a family celebration the same night there is a school football game or dance. At school many of her classmates are friendly, but sometimes she has unfortunate incidents in which she is called derogatory names. Occasionally Xoan-Mei thinks to herself, "Anglo kids don't have to go through any of this."

Frequently she feels unwelcome and that she is barely tolerated in this new country. She is uncertain and wary about her future economic and social opportunities.

Xoan-Mei experiences multiple pressures and stress: being an adolescent in search of identity, living in a family with some difficulties in communication and cultural values, being a refugee in a majority culture that wittingly and unwittingly asserts dominance over her. These are not easy years for Xoan-Mei. At times she feels discouraged and frustrated.

For all this, St. Patrick's Church in her neighborhood is the only bright spot in her life—one very positive experience for Xoan-Mei and her family. Only four blocks from her apartment, St. Patrick's is a place of comfort, acceptance, and hope. This church has members and leaders who offer pastoral care and nurturing programs that have enabled people like the Tranhs to feel that they are persons of worth, respected and loved.

While not perfect, the approach to youth ministry at St. Patrick's is exemplary in three aspects. It is based on sound *theological and ecclesial* foundations. It has also a sympathetic understanding of the *developmental tasks* of the church's adolescent members. And of great significance for the racial/ethnic minority members of the church, St. Patrick's has an appreciation for the *unique situation* of these people.

Theological and Ecclesial Foundations and Pastoral Care of Youth Ministry

David Ng (1991) emphasized that each church needs to seriously reflect on the basic question "Why youth ministry?" It's not enough to say, "We do it because we have always done it." Theological themes are rich with potential for informing us as to why we do youth ministry. Among many themes are those of *creation, personhood, community, faith, and mission.*

God's creation: The programs and opportunities for study in youth ministry can help young people to know the world as *the good creation of God and to know themselves as a part of that creation.*

This understanding of themselves and their world provides a basic framework for understanding life's purpose. Identity formation includes the forming of a sense of self in relation to God, to one's life, and to the things of life. Young people need to think through for themselves the reason for their existence and the way they relate to all else in the world, including other persons, nature, and the rhythm of birth, growth, work, and death. To know God as the Creator of all of this and Giver of life, talent, and purpose provides a basis for having a positive, purposeful view of life and of self (Ng 1991).

Personhood: Personhood—personal, individual identity in relation to others—is framed by this positive view of creation. The church, through its tradition and particularly through the messages of the Bible, can give the model of fully realized humanity: Jesus Christ himself. In Jesus Christ each person's own identity as a human being is defined and challenged toward fulfillment. Identity formation is a big issue for every adolescent, and the church's theology has at its core the richest resource for persons searching for identity.

Community: Another large part of the church's story of creation is that we are made to live in *community.* To be human is to relate to other humans (and to all of creation) in a loving manner, giving and receiving love and nurture. To do youth ministry is to involve young persons in a community of meaningful, nurturing relationships. As adolescents go through their explorations of what they know about themselves, God, and the church, it is timely for the church and community to walk through with them on this faith journey toward the discovery and affirmation of personal faith. Adolescents, with newly honed skills of inquisitive and abstract thinking, can be critical and analytical and can recast older, more naive perceptions of God into fresh understandings of a God of grace who gives life, offers forgiveness, and calls for commitment. Young people are notorious for being hard questioners of all things, including the doctrines of the church. In youth ministry we are glad for these questions and doubts, and we thank God that we have the privilege of working with teenagers during their critical time of faith development. Thus the youth grow in the community of faith.

Mission: Mission, vocation, call, discipleship, and similar ideas provide further rationale for doing youth ministry. Driven by the need for identity formation, young people will ask, "What is life's meaning?" and "What is the meaning of *my life?*" Each young person is to be challenged, through youth ministry, to see creation and life purpose and to respond in commitment to fulfilling this purpose. Youth ministry presents the challenge of vocation and mission.

Certainly other significant theological themes can be considered as bases for building an approach to youth ministry. Sexuality, gender, social and economic justice, peacemaking, world peace, stewardship of the global environment, and other topics need to be understood theologically and their theological implications presented to young people. Whatever a church lists as its theological issues, the important point is that its ministry with youth is grounded in solid theology.

Ecclesial concerns for youth ministry: Related to theological concerns are the ecclesial—those concerns that have to do with enabling young people to become active and productive members of the body of Christ. A congregation needs to develop youth ministry that not only invites young people to become Christians, but also to invites them to fully participate in worship and serve God as a full member of the community of faith.

Many Asian North American immigrants and their children who are new members of a congregation have not grown up as Christians or been baptized. The church can help them feel comfortable participating in worship services, some of which may not be familiar to them, including communion and baptism. In youth classes, programs, and special activities such as retreats and field trips, worship is explained, often through guided instruction and participation. Nurture and Christian education are a required part of any youth ministry program.

Developmental aspects of youth ministry: Youth ministry can be structured on the framework of adolescent development. The major task for young persons, especially those in early and middle adolescence (ages twelve to fifteen), is to form a sense of identity that is satisfying to the self and to significant others, such as family and peers. In that undertaking, young persons take stock of the values and practices that were handed down by family, school, church, and other institutions. Using more developed modes of thinking, including the propensity to question and to think hypothetically, adolescents rely less on the ways and thinking of the past. More and more they choose for themselves what to think and do. The movement is toward independence (Ng 1991).

During this developmental stage, two skills that need to be learned are relationships and decision making.

Developing relationships: We all know the tremendous influence of peers at this age.

As a young person strives for independence, there is a natural desire to avoid the ties and control of earlier relationships, such as with parents and other authority figures. Too often, peers impose new forms of authority over one another. When an adolescent's peer group is a gang, the control those peers exert can have dangerous or even violent results.

So much of relationship building, especially intimacy, is a new experience to the adolescent that many do not know how to relate, or they feel insecure and frightened. Worse, the examples offered by secular society and the dramatic inter-personal relationships depicted in popular television programs are often characterized by one-upmanship, score keeping, deceit, hurt, jealousy, selfishness, self-aggrandizement, pleasure-seeking immaturity, manipulation, and exploitation. Youth ministry may be a place of hope and better alternative models for teenagers who need to escape the tyranny of a gang or peer pressure on sex, alcohol, and street drugs. They need to learn how to relate to each other in a more healthy and loving way. Teenagers seek meaningful peer relationships in an environment of caring, acceptance, and support. Youth ministry must be a *relational* ministry.

Decision-making skills: It is imperative for a young person to learn the skill of decision making. Implicit is the power to make decisions for one's self. As that power is gained, there needs to be a development of the ability to make good decisions. Some of this is the nitty-gritty ability to define the question or issue, lay out the facts or factors, and then to choose. The logic of making decisions is available to most teenagers, and rational procedure can be practiced. But we all know that there is more to decision making than logic. Through role-playing and case studies, young people can exercise how to choose from various options and evaluate consequences of the options. Reflection and evaluation, and the possibility of trying again, all are a part of teaching the skill of decision making.

Organizational Models in Youth Ministry

To establish youth ministry for Asian North American young people, several models can be considered (Lee, Chu, and Park 1993):

- The first and most common model is the English-speaking
  Asian North American youth ministry within an Asian
  ethnic church, such as a Chinese, Korean, or Vietnamese church. Sometimes the ethnic church attempts to
  play multiple roles, with an emphasis on teaching Asian
  language and history. Through a language and culture
  school program, the church hopes to strengthen the
  young people's ties with the Asian culture and ethnic
  language. It may have the risk of watering down education for faith. Other problems include the fact that often
  the teachers have only a basic command of English and
  conduct the Sunday school class using teaching methods
  that they grew up with in Asia. The young people who
  are educated in an American school system frequently
  lose interest in classes conducted with Asian teaching
  methods.

- The second is the semi-independent Asian North American
  youth ministry based on or sponsored by an Anglo church.

- Third is the entirely independent English-speaking "Pan-
  Asian American" church composed of members of 1.5 or
  second Asian North American generations of different
  Asian national origin. Second-generation Asian North
  Americans are less bound by their ancestral Asian nation-
  ality and its cultural traditions than first-generation immigrants, and they do work well with other Asian North
  American youth. There are churches of this category in
  San Jose and Rosemead, California, but the numbers of
  such churches are few at the present. However, there is
  great need and potential for the establishment and growth
  of this kind of church in the future.

- Fourth is the ministry sponsored by a parachurch organization entirely outside a traditional church structure.
  Such models include university campus ministries, Campus Crusade, and "student church" associated with a college campus (for example, University of California Davis
  Korean Student Church). They are usually nondenomina-
  tional and primarily student-oriented and have an ad-

vantage of drawing students, regardless of their denomination.

Concluding Suggestions on Youth Ministry

David Ng suggests nine actions for congregations in support of Asian North American young people:

1. Have a biblical-theological and sociological base for ministry with racial/ethnic and cultural minority young people.
   - Be informed by theological understandings of creation, community, personhood, faith, and mission.
   - Describe your young people sociologically.

2. Find out about your young people.
   - Ask them to tell their own stories.
   - Listen, listen, listen.
   - Visit, visit, visit.
   - Find out their needs.

3. Be a community of support.
   - Support the young people as they try to be Christian.
   - Have one-to-one and small-group ministries.
   - Be an extended family.
   - Make the church a place of rest, haven, and comfort.

4. Offer wholesome alternative activities.
   - Provide recreation and sports.
   - Offer study halls, tutoring, and counseling about education.
   - Challenge young people to serve others.
   - Involve young people in work and service projects.
   - Offer field trips and other activities away from the neighborhood.

5. Serve as guarantors and role models.
   - Enact "aunt and uncle" roles.
   - Help young people to relate to others.

6. Stress vocation and mission.
   - Develop the leadership of the young people.

- Work with a core group of youth.
- Challenge individuals to reach their potential.
- Insist on mission and service.
- Challenge and guide regarding vocation and career choices.

7. Relate identity and culture.

- Deal directly and often with ethnic and racial identity and affirmation.
- Deal with justice issues, such as racism and poverty.
- Challenge the young people regarding vocation and mission to their own people.

8. Help with spiritual formation.

- Help the young people find appropriate spiritual expression.
- Encourage them to worship with the community of faith.
- Find a spiritual support group for yourself.
- Share your spiritual quest and discoveries with the young people.
- Expect weariness and guard against burnout.

9. Expect to learn from the young people and to be enriched by them (Ng 1991).

References

Baumeister, R. F. *Identity: Cultural Change and the Struggle for Self*. New York: Oxford University Press, 1988.

Hurh, Won Moo. "The 1.5 Generation: A Paragon of Korean American Pluralism," in *Korean Culture*, Vol. 14, special issue 1993, Los Angeles, Korean Culture Center.

Kim, Douglas. "Korean American Identity." Panel presentation at Korean American Student Conference (KASCON VII), San Francisco, March 1993.

Kim, Elaine H. "Between Black and White," in *State of Asian American Activism and Resistance in the 1990s*. Edited by K. Aguilar-San Juan. Boston: South End Press, 1993.

Kim, Luke, and Grace Kim. "Transition Generation." *SKIPA Journal*. Vol.1, no.1, Sacramento, Calif., March 1993.

_____. "Searching and Defining Korean American Identity in Multi-Cultural Society," in *Korean American Women: Tradition to Modern Feminism*. Edited by Y. I. Song and A. Moon. Greenwood Press, 1995.

Kitano, H. L., and R. Daniels. *Asian American Emerging Minorities*. Englewood Cliffs, N.J.: Prentice-Hall, 1988.

Lee, Evelyn. *Ten Principles on Raising Chinese American Teens*. San Francisco: Chinatown Youth Center, 1988.

Lee, Marie G. *Finding My Voice*. Boston: Houghton Mifflin Co. 1992.

Lee, Sang Hyun, Ron Chu, and Marion Park. "Second Generation Ministry: Models of Mission," in *Korean American Ministries: A Resource Book.*" Edited by Sang Hyun Lee and John V. Moore. Louisville: Presbyterian Church (U.S.A.), 1993.

Ng, David. *A Colorful Community: Ministry with Racial / Ethnic Minority Youth*. Network paper no. 41. New Rochelle, N.Y.: Don Bosco Multimedia in Conjunction with the Center for Youth Ministry Development, 1991.

Park, Karen and Matthew Sohn. "Perspective of Second Generation Child and Parent." Panel presentation at Transition Generation Workshop, San Jose, Calif., January 1993.

Presbyterian Church (U.S.A.). *My Identity: A Gift from God*. New York: Presbyterian Church (U.S.A.), 1984.

Sue, Derald and David Sue. *Counseling the Culturally Different: Theory and Practice*. New York: John Wiley and Sons, 1990.

Yu, Keun Ho, and Luke Kim. "Psychosocial Development of Korean American Children," in *Psychosocial Development of Minority Children*. Edited by Johnson-Powell, Morales, Yamamoto. New York: Brunner-Mazel, 1979.

CHAPTER 11

Asian North American Relationships with Other Minority Cultures

By Greer Anne Wenh-In Ng

Introduction

Asian North Americans and their congregations are tempted toward isolation. For some it is the fear of encounters with strangers whose language and customs mystify and confuse. For others it is a weariness with the constant struggle against the racism or arrogance of the dominant culture in North America. Admittedly, some Asian North Americans keep to themselves because of their own feelings of racial and cultural superiority.

Greer Anne Wenh-In Ng, a Chinese Canadian seminary professor whose ministry has bridged several languages, nationalities, and cultures, lifts up the vision of a church that acknowledges differences and connects the different peoples into a common Christ-centered community. Several strategies are described for countering the "dominant agenda of 'divide and conquer' that pervades society today."

Relationships with Other Minority Cultures

Scene I: It was breakfast time at a conference for racial/ethnic minority women in Toronto. Members of the steering committee could be seen huddled around one of the tables, in close consultation. The concern? An African American participant had been greatly disturbed on opening night to find white women among the circle. "I had expected this conference to be for racial/ethnic minority women only. I walked in and here were these white faces. I want to let you know that any place with a white face is not a safe environment for me." This was a dynamic that the planning committee, consisting primarily of Asian Canadians, had not anticipated.

How were members of the steering committee to handle the situation? Should they try to explain to their black sister the rationale for including these particular white women— that some actually came from minority European communities within the denomination, while the rest (the Anglos) were all in one way or another engaged in ministry with ethnic minority congregations? Should they acknowledge her concern but keep to their original design anyway? Or should they risk upsetting their well-thought-out plans, bring this matter to the whole community gathered there, and let the participants themselves come up with suggestions? After much agonizing over different alternatives, they opted for the third choice. The communal decision was to adopt the suggestion, put forward by the white women themselves, that they form their own small group from then on.

The conference continued in that manner, ending on a "high" with a creative and meaningful worship experience the final morning. The evaluations showed that participants appreciated the way the conference was conducted as well as the content and the sharing. As for the planning committee, the members realized they had learned a crucial lesson— never universalize for other minority groups their own experience as Asian Canadians. In this case, although both Asians and blacks in North America experience racism, the corporate history of African Americans had been one of enslavement, not just colonization and discrimination, so the reaction to whites was very different. Everyone at the conference learned how important it is to learn about these historical differences, so that they could be sensitive and honor others' experiences and perspectives.

Scene II: At an educational institution a meeting was in progress to develop a program for Native American ministries. The one Asian member of the group soon noticed that whenever she began pointing out some similarity between Native American cultures and Asian cultures, she was almost always immediately silenced with, "But you can't apply Asian values to the Native American context. Native American cultures are very different. . . ."

She also noticed that those who so rudely interrupted her were invariably white, Anglo male members of the group, never the Native American members themselves. This made her muse, " What makes white persons assume they have the right to speak for Native American persons in this way? Is this a case of imperialism, racism, sexism, or all of the above?"

Reflection on Issues

1. *Each minority group has its own history.* It is important to point out that "learning about one another" goes beyond getting to know one another's customs, festivals, traditions, food, and so on in a sort of multicultural fair. Learning that stops there does not differ much from the limits the dominant culture sets in learning about all of us. It turns out to be a kind of cultural voyeurism, a paternalistic treatment of other cultures as being "exotic."

In her book *Sisters in the Wilderness: The Challenge of Womanist God-Talk* (see references), theologian Delores Williams provides an excellent resource for us to learn one special strand of the history of African Americans—that of black women both before and after the American Civil War from their own records, in their own words, and from their own perspectives. This is a strand usually not included in general black history or theology and is a good reminder that in order to be able to respect others, we need to distinguish the differences even within a group. For example, Japanese, Korean, and Chinese North Americans want to be known in their own identity and histories. The increasing visibility of

Asian American and Asian Canadian novels, art, plays, and films is one way of reciprocating this responsibility on our part to fellow minority citizens.

Having colleagues and friends from other minority groups, too, helps break down racial/ethnic/cultural stereotypes, but it is not enough. Getting to know one another's group histories helps to guard against the "some of my best friends are African American (or Hispanic American, etc.)" syndrome, one that would admit personal relationships but still preserves unflattering stereotypes toward other groups as a whole.

2. *Are Asian North Americans racist toward other minority groups?* Feelings of superiority certainly exist; all cultures are ethnocentric. Members of ancient civilizations that boast of thousands of years of history before the coming of Christ have a tendency toward feelings of superiority. There is a tendency to treat all "foreigners" as "others" with terms such as "white devil" (or "white ghost," after Maxine Hong Kingston) or to label African Americans as "black devils." One place where such attitudes are most transparent is in intermarriage. Most East Asian parents would tolerate almost anything other than one of their children marrying a non-Asian; even an interethnic alliance (a Korean marrying a Chinese person, for instance) is preferable to marrying a non-Asian. To acknowledge this is to admit attitudes of prejudice and discrimination.

Racism, however, is technically only possible when one group has the political power to impose unjust social arrangements and laws to the systematic disadvantage of another group. In this strict sense, so long as one group lacks such power, they cannot be said to be racist toward another. Where such power does exist (for instance, economic power), the danger of actualizing one's racist tendencies becomes real. Are Asian North Americans, those so-called "model minorities," in that danger at this historical juncture vis-à-vis some other more disadvantaged groups such as African Americans and Hispanic Americans? It would be Utopian to pretend that tensions do not exist between Asian Americans and those two other minority groups in the United States. The 1992 riots in Los Angeles, involving the two aforementioned groups pitted against operators of inner-city stores in South Central who happened mostly to be Korean American, are a sober and horrific reminder.

3. *Minority groups can relate horizontally instead of vertically.* And yet, are there not other factors at play when minority groups relate to one another? The phenomenon in scene II above might furnish a clue. By suppressing the opportunity for two minority groups to relate horizontally, the dominant group and its individuals hold on to power to remain the center. As in the case cited, when the groups do succeed in getting together to consider their situations and cultures, they often find that they share many common values in contradistinction to the white Euro-American dominant culture. Significant examples are the priority of the community over the individual, the viability of kinship networks and the concept of a nonnuclear family system, respecting and honoring age, and the tradition of venerating elders and ancestors. A vivid example of cross-cultural dialogue may be seen in an exciting venture sponsored by a major denomination several years ago, resulting in an illuminating volume titled *Out of Every Tribe and Nation: Christian Theology at the Ethnic Roundtable* by Justo L. González (see references). This book represents the thoughts shared by some seventy minority persons in a series of roundtables over several years. These people found numerous deep-rooted similarities of cultural values and styles.

As a rule, minorities find themselves dealing more often group to group with the dominant culture or competitively with one another, as when they fight for multicultural grants from the government or a denomination. Unless they are intentional about seeking out other racial/ethnic minority cultures to relate to, they end up being in a weakened position when negotiating with dominant forces. "Dividing and conquering" may not consciously be a strategy adopted by the dominant group, including institutional establishments, which are mostly white/Anglo, but as an often-adopted practice, it certainly succeeds in keeping minority groups powerless. Part of the reason is that when each group is compared to the ideals and standards of the white/Anglos, the former inevitably comes out the loser, since the standards were set by the latter.

Minority women have certainly found this to be true in their struggle to participate in the women's historical project. They've found that the tendency of most white feminists to speak for them has deprived them of a voice and rendered them either tokens at meetings and consultations or else totally invisible. In recent years, therefore, African American, Hispanic, Native American, and Asian American women have opted for interconnecting among themselves rather than always being the ones in the margin. (See some examples of such work, *This Bridge Called My Back: Writings by Radical Women of Color* and *Inheriting Our Mothers' Gardens: Feminist Theology in Third World Perspective,* listed in the references.)

One advantage of standing horizontally in solidarity with one another is that we now have a better chance of producing a "critical mass" that the dominant group finds harder to ignore. Another is that we can gain encouragement as well as learn tactics (or not to repeat mistakes, which is just as important) from one another. To be in solidarity does not negate or play down differences; it emphasizes, as Korean theologian Yong-Bock Kim put it, the action of "interlinking, like a chain of arms, across those differences because our goals point in the same direction—fuller humanhood and life for each one in the people, the *minjung*" (1993 T.V. Moore Lectures, San Francisco Theological Seminary, April 1993).

Being on the Way: Strategies and Suggestions

Some possible strategies have already been alluded to in the foregoing section—learning to know one another's stories, breaking down racial/ethnic/cultural stereotypes, owning up to one's ethnocentrism and admitting the danger of racist tendencies, resisting the dominant agenda of "divide and conquer" and taking steps to relate to one another intentionally, and getting acquainted with one another's publications. Here I will simply make a few possible ministry and program suggestions to supplement what your own congregation or group has already tried.

1. *Develop educational opportunities* to learn one another's stories and histories—pulpit exchanges, visits to one another's churches, joint leadership programs—across ethnic and racial lines both within and across denominations. One denomination is asking an Asian American pastor to serve two part-time positions: one in his own ethnic group and one in an African American congregation. Vacation Bible Schools, church camps, and youth groups present some further opportunities, provided there is attention paid to nurturing the ethnocultural specificity of one's particular community of faith.

2. *Make creative use of one another's resources.* For example, hymns, anthems, or congregational singing could be a strategy that involves the whole worshiping congregation. Many of the new hymnals by the denominations now include hymns from around the globe, often in Romanized versions of the original languages. Another example is readings from one cultural tradition's oral or literary store. If possible, invite members of that group to do the reading or storytelling in church, a study group, or Sunday school.

3. *Be aware of the efforts at cross-cultural and multicultural education* that are already going on in school boards and other institutions or other contexts. Demand more-inclusive texts in history and children's social studies. An excellent example of looking at American history from a minority perspective is Ronald Takaki's *A Different Mirror,* which includes the histories of Native Americans, Mexican Americans, and the many immigrant peoples. Adult study groups in churches could dip into Justo González's two-volume *History of Christian Thought,* which includes what once was

relegated to the realm of mission history. These volumes have been translated into both Korean and Chinese. (See References.)

4. *Learn about one another and about other Asian North Americans.* Have you ever tried to learn another Asian language not for academic purposes, but to be able to worship in the Asian North American church down the road? This would be helpful especially for immigrant congregations with their original languages. We Asian North Americans need to learn about one another so that within the community of Christ we may counteract some of the divisions brought about by painful historical events. There are denominational Asian caucuses and organizations such as Pacific American Center for Theology and Strategies (PACTS), Pacific Asian American and Canadian Christian Education Ministries (PAACCE), and Asian and Asian American Women in Theology and Ministry (AAWTM). You may want to reach out cross-ethnically both within your own denomination and across denominations.

5. *Get involved in joint action and advocacy* in social concerns, such as ministry with battered women and the provision of shelters or fighting against international tourist sex exploitation of children and women of Asia. For some, these ideas may provide a new direction; for others, they will be confirming what they have already started. Can you share what your church would like to try or has successfully done?

It is important for members who come from these cultures to be reminded that Native American/aboriginal, African, and Mexican/Mayan cultures have existed all those years too. Transmitted in an oral rather than a written form, these cultures contain wisdom and deep spirituality that are proving to be indispensable in teaching the rest of the world how to live in peace, justice, and in integrity with all creation.

References

Albrecht, Lisa and Rose M. Brewer, eds. *Bridges of Power: Women's Multicultural Alliances.* Philadelphia, Santa Cruz, Calif., Gabriola Island, B.C.: New Society Publishers, 1990.

Elizondo, Virgilio. *The Future Is Mestizo: Life Where Cultures Meet*. Oak Park, Ill.: Meyer Stone, 1988.

González, Justo L. *A History of Christian Thought*, 3 volumes. Nashville: Abingdon Press, 1987.

———. *Out of Every Tribe and Nation: Christian Theology at the Ethnic Roundtable*. Nashville: Abingdon Press, 1992.

Herzberg, Dorothy Chave. *Frameworks for Cultural and Racial Diversity*. Toronto: Canadian Scholars' Press, 1993.

hooks, bell. "Choosing the Margin As a Space of Radical Openness." In *Yearning: Race, Gender, and Cultural Politics*. Toronto: Between the Lines Press, 145-153.

Hutchincheon, Linda and Richmond Marion, eds. *Other Solitudes: Canadian Multicultural Fictions*. Toronto: Oxford University Press, 1990.

Legge, Marilyn J. "Elided Voices in Canadian Women's Fiction: Hearing Women's Commitments to Authentic Life." In *The Grace of Difference: A Canadian Feminist Theological Ethic*. Atlanta: Scholars Press, 1992.

Lorde, Audre. *Sister Outsider: Essays and Speeches*. Freedom, Calif.: The Crossing Press, 1984.

Moraga, Cherrie and Gloria Anzaldua, eds. *This Bridge Called My Back: Writings by Radical Women of Color*. New York: Kitchen Table Press, 1991.

Ortega, Ofelia, ed. *Women's Visions: Theological Reflection, Celebration, Action*. Geneva: World Council of Churches Publications, 1995.

Peter-Raoul, M., L. R. Forcey, and R. F. Hunter Jr., eds. *Yearning to Breathe Free: Liberation Theologies in the U.S.* Maryknoll, N.Y.: Orbis Books, 1990.

Russell, Letty M. et al., eds. *Inheriting Our Mothers' Gardens: Feminist Theology in Third World Perspective*. Louisville: Westminster Press, 1988.

Takaki, Ronald. *A Different Mirror: A History of Multicultural America*. Boston: Little, Brown Co., 1993.

Thistlethwaite, Susan Brooks, and Mary Potter Engel, eds. *Lift Every Voice: Constructing Christian Theologies from the Underside*. San Francisco et al: Harper and Row, Publishers, 1990.

Williams, Delores. *Sisters in the Wilderness: The Challenge of Womanist God-Talk*. Maryknoll, N.Y.: Orbis Books, 1993.

Decision Making
and Conflict in the Congregation

By Virstan B. Y. Choy

Introduction

*When Asian North American congregations try to resolve
conflicts by using styles and methods common to Western
people and institutions, differences often are not resolved
and may even worsen. The methods of the West usually are
not appropriate for people and congregations nurtured in
Eastern thought forms and protocols of behavior. Chapter
12 describes five cases of decision making and conflict
resolution in Asian North American congregations. The
reader is invited to consider how conflict could be dealt
with realistically and creatively in an Asian North
American fashion. The analyses of these cases present
some surprises that reflect new findings the author and
his colleagues made in their research on conflict management in Asian North American congregations.*

*The author, Virstan B. Y. Choy, participated in a research
project for the Alban Institute in Washington, D.C., regarding appropriate conflict-management approaches in Asian
North American congregations. Choy teaches and directs
the field education program at San Francisco Theological
Seminary. He has had extensive experience as a pastor,
judicatory executive, and participant in denominational
and interdenominational committees and projects. The
strategies offered in this chapter are not better than other*

strategies for conflict management, but they are appropriate for Asian North American congregations. These ways of relating, considering, and deciding honor Asian cultural perspectives and sensibilities.

Decision Making and Conflict in the Congregation

Relationship to God brings us into relationship with other Christians. For most Christians these relationships occur in the form of Christian community we call congregations. This chapter examines factors and dynamics at work as relationships come together in a congregation when it makes decisions about its life together. What Asian North American cultural predispositions and postures influence the ways we relate to and decide about the life of the congregation?

In terms of ministry and Christian education concerns, what predispositions and postures are keys to understanding decision-making differences and conflicts in Asian North American congregations? How might such understandings be used by the leaders and members of these congregations to improve their addressing of such conflicts? How might such understandings be used by non-Asian North American denominational leaders in working with Asian North American congregations in more culturally sensitive and relevant ways?

These questions are especially significant at moments when the interactive nature of Christian community is most evident—whenever decisions need to be made about the common dimensions of Christian life together: worship, mission (its purpose or direction), use of the congregation's resources (money, people, facilities, or ideas), even the structures and process of decision making itself.

Many Asian North American congregations include immigrant as well as North American-born members of three and sometimes four generations. They need to communicate in more than one language or dialect. Complications of Christian community are experienced when certain kinds of decision-making questions emerge out of the life of the community. These questions sometimes are problematic and even conflict inducing:

- Given the different language or dialect groups in our church, shall we worship in one bilingual (or trilingual) service or in separate language-group services?
- Given the immigrant as well as North American-born persons living in the community our church seeks to serve, and given our limited resources, what is our congregation's vision for its ministry? What should be the priority direction for the mission of our congregation?
- Given the many needs of the different generations and language groups in our church, should we be searching for a bilingual pastor or a first-generation Korean-speaking pastor and an English-speaking youth leader?
- Given the many needs and programs in our congregation, what should be the priorities for our pastor's time commitments?
- Given the increasing numbers of 1.5-generation and second-generation children in our church, should Sunday school classes be taught in Taiwanese or in English? Should Taiwanese history and culture be included in our church's education program?
- Given the needs of the different people in our growing congregation, should our fund-raising campaign be dedicated to constructing an elevator for transporting the *Issei* members to the different levels of the church building or to expanding the number of classrooms for the increasing numbers of *Yonsei* children in the Sunday school?
- Given the different generations represented on our church board, do we adopt the younger generation's proposal that we evaluate the performance of the pastor each year, or do we maintain the older generation's

attitude that any evaluation of our spiritual leader by laypersons is inappropriate?

Continuing the practice established in preceding chapters of this book, we shall:

- begin with stories and cases;
- encourage your questions as you read and examine these experiences;
- move from questions to analysis from an Asian North American perspective;
- reflect upon how Asian North Americans are "on the way" in this aspect of Christian community; and
- offer some emerging observations about decision making and conflict management in the Asian North American living out of Christian community.

Community Decision Making and Community Conflict Management: Some Case Stories

We now examine stories of decision making and conflict in Asian North American congregations. What do these cases tell us as well as teach us about being in Christian community in distinctively—if not uniquely—Asian North American ways? Some cases are intracultural (describing interactions between or among Asian North Americans); some are intercultural (describing interactions between Asian North Americans and persons of other races and cultural traditions).

The following questions may help to focus your examination of each case:

Personal Reflection Questions

1. Are the interactions between the persons in these stories similar to or different from what you have seen in your experience of church life? How are they so?

2. Can you see such interactions happening in your congregation? Why or why not?

3. Was the outcome in each case story predictable? Why or why not?

4. What is difficult to understand about what happened?

5. What questions about Asian North American interpersonal style and congregational style and culture are raised for you by each case story?

Social and Cultural Analysis Questions

1. What do you see as the key cultural factors and dynamics operative in each story?

2. In each story, what is the pivotal moment or pivotal act that causes the end result (what happened)?

3. What causes this pivot or shift? How do the cultural factors and dynamics influence the outcome of each case?

As you read these stories, feel free to add your own questions.

Case Story 1: A Planning-Committee Decision

In planning an upcoming workshop for their church, the board members of a Chinese congregation ask their new pastor to ascertain the availability of guest speakers and to recommend someone at their next meeting. The young pastor agrees.

At the next meeting, following substantial research on speakers from different academic disciplines, the pastor reports with obvious delight that he has found someone of unquestioned competence: a Chinese person who not only had training and education in the theme and focus of the workshop, but who also was (a) an ordained minister who had been an assistant pastor in a Chinese congregation in another state in his younger years; (b) the holder of not one, but two doctoral degrees—one in counseling from an American seminary and one in social work from a university in the eastern United States; (c) currently a professor at a nearby university; and (d) a prolific writer who had published several articles and books before he was forty years old.

Hearing their pastor's report, the board members thank him for his work. However, he is surprised that instead of voting to select this obviously well-qualified speaker, they express the need for time to consider this recommendation. They decide to defer the decision for a week or two.

Disappointed, the young pastor spends a good part of the next few days wondering what he had done wrong. Had he misunderstood the board's request? Was there something negative about the guest speaker of which he was not aware? Given the status and impressive credentials of the professor, why wasn't the board ready to invite him?

Later that week, the pastor happens upon one of the church elders at the supermarket. "Don't worry, Reverend," she says. "We finally found someone we know in the professor's hometown. He says that the professor comes from a good family. He remembers that the professor was a good boy when he was growing up in that town. He should be OK for our workshop. I'm sure we won't have problems with inviting him to be our speaker."

Case Story 2: Intergenerational Communication in Public

Wanting to explore the theme "Improving Harmony and Communication in the Church," an Asian North American congregation invites a white counselor to be the keynote speaker for its annual All Members' Retreat. The speaker focuses one of the sessions on intergenerational communication.

To establish relevance for the congregation and to encourage openness in sharing, the speaker asks the youth present to identify issues about which they and their parents disagree. No youth responds. The speaker rearranges the audience, asking the adults to sit on one side of the room and the youth to sit on the other. She then rephrases the question to the youth, "Think about the last time you and your parents had an argument. What was it about?" Still no youth responds.

Desiring to be helpful, one of the adults new to the congregation suggests, "Hey, kids! Think of this as an opportunity for one of your 'rap sessions.' This is your chance to share how you *really* feel about the older generation. You get to talk about what you wish your parents would understand. Go ahead!" Still no response.

Trying once more, the adult member offers another suggestion, "Maybe the youth need more time to think up some things to say. Maybe they need anonymity! How about if we break up into two groups—one for the youth, one for the adults—for the next half hour so that each generation can come up with a list of what bugs them about the other generation. Each group could choose its own reporter so that we won't know who actually made the complaint in the first place." The retreat leader agrees with the suggestion. The members divide into the two groups and meet.

As the groups return to the plenary room, the youth are given the opportunity to report first. Their designated reporter approaches the lectern with a small piece of paper. She reads from it, "As the youth generation of this church, we appreciate the opportunity to share our opinions at this retreat. However, what our parents and we disagree about— well, we don't feel it's right to bring that up in public. We love our parents. What we argue about is between us. Thank you." She looks to the other youth. They nod in agreement. She returns to her seat.

Case Story 3: A Meeting to Address a Conflict

In a Japanese American congregation, a lay leader is aware of a conflict among some of the members and is unsure about how to respond. She consults a member of her denomination's regional staff, who offers to visit the church and to engage the members of the different sides in some conflict-resolution exercises.

In his meeting with the congregation, the denominational

executive calls for "openness in communication," encouraging members to come forward so that, face-to-face, they might "openly confront" their problems. In the daylong open meeting, the members are asked to practice conflict-resolution techniques "effective in other churches that have experienced conflict." Members present their side of the issue, answer his questions about background history, and engage in some exercises in developing open communication. The members cooperate with the executive, engaging in all the exercises and activities he asks of them.

At the end of this process, he presents to the congregation his findings, his analysis of the conflict based upon these findings, and his recommendations for what the congregation needs to do. One of the findings is the revelation that there is more than one conflict in the congregation, that some members reported disagreements with other members that have existed for over two decades, disagreements "allowed" to remain unresolved.

Included in this report is his "power analysis" of the congregation, revealing his perceptions of how power and authority have been skewed in favor of the older generation of the church for over two decades and how dysfunctional it would be for the congregation not to change such a situation. The executive then presents a series of changes that need to be made in order for the members to resolve their conflicts and to move forward together. He concludes his report by noting the positive results of confronting conflict and the importance of continuing such a face-to-face process. He thanks the congregation for its cooperation and indicates that he looks forward to hearing how they are doing in the future. The members thank the executive for his time and efforts and close with prayers for him and the church.

The day after this meeting, citing the statements made in public the day before, many of the members declare their decision to leave the congregation.

Case Story 4: A Workshop on Conflict Management in the Church

In a workshop for pastors and lay leaders on detecting, diagnosing, and responding to conflict in the congregation, the trainer presents the concept of conflict "levels" (Leas 1985:19-22), describing how conflicts begin and escalate and identifying the five stages of conflict intensity. "In order to know what must be done to manage a conflict," he says, "you must first watch and listen—watch the behavior of those involved in a disagreement and listen to the verbal interactions between them. The language they use to talk about and talk to each other will tell you where the conflict is—from lower levels involving only differences of opinion to higher, more explosive levels of fighting between individuals or groups."

As the trainer proceeds from one level to the next, describing the characteristic verbal interactions in each, a Korean pastor raises his hand. Rising to emphasize his frustration, he exclaims, "This system does not apply to Korean churches. We do not begin with low-level differences of opinion and then build up to more intense disagreement. There are none of these so-called 'early warning signs' for us! We *start* with emotional and explosive communications. Korean conflict *begins* with open fighting!"

The trainer thanks the pastor for his comment, then asks, "Are you saying that Koreans do not engage in disagreements in other than high-level conflict? Or are you saying that low-level conflict in Korean congregations occurs in ways that are not visible or detectable?"

Case Story 5: Involving a Former Pastor in a Church Conflict

A former pastor of an Asian North American congregation, still remembered with affection by the members, has been invited to return to the community for a special event. At the celebration, one of the lay leaders shares with his former pastor the desire to solicit his wisdom on a conflict emerging between some members of the church and the current pastor. Citing seminary training and denominational policy discouraging former pastors from involving themselves in the ministry of their successors, the former pastor gently but firmly declines the request. He adds that the congregation and the current pastor "will surely work things out."

Some weeks later, at a national conference on ministry in Asian North American churches, the current pastor of the congregation happens upon the former pastor. He approaches his predecessor, asking if he has time "to share a few insights about his former congregation and some of the members." Again citing denominational discouragement of continued involvement in the life and ministry of previous congregations, the latter declines.

A year later, a denominational executive is asked to intervene in the now open and seemingly unresolvable conflict between the current pastor and a substantial part of the congregation. This staff person telephones the former pastor and asks him for advice on how to handle the conflict in his former church.

Analysis: Decision Making and Conflict Management in Light of Asian North American Cultural Postures toward Power and Authority in Relationships

Each of the case stories you have just read is true. Each occurred in an Asian North American church or in gatherings of persons from Asian North American congregations. While not all persons of Asian descent will interact with one another in the ways presented in these stories, those Asian North Americans who choose to belong to and actively participate in an Asian North American congregation will probably conduct their relationships in highly similar ways. Researcher Kaoru Oguri Kendis helps us understand why in her work *A Matter of Comfort: Ethnic Maintenance and Ethnic Style among Third-Generation Japanese Americans.*

In studying types of ethnic identification and degrees of commitment to an ethnic identity among third- and fourth-generation Japanese Americans, Kendis distinguished between "low ethnic" and "high ethnic" persons. "Low ethnics" displayed a smaller degree of identification with other Japanese Americans and were more concerned with assimilation into mainstream society. "High ethnics" exhibited "a stronger psychological identification as Japanese Americans and were more likely to see more differences between themselves as Japanese Americans and the rest of American society. They took part in more activities that brought them into contact mainly with Japanese Americans while limiting the presence of non-Japanese Americans and preferred to keep the noninstrumental parts of their lives separated from the non-Japanese American community."

Such preferences involved not only one's self-identification, but also one's style in interpersonal relations. Such preferences also persisted across generations. Kendis found that while "high ethnics" are willing to adapt their behavior to meet their political and economic needs and, in fact, in these areas want to be a part of the larger society, they also want to keep an area of their lives separate in which they can "be themselves" with other Japanese Americans (1989:174–176).

Extending Kendis's findings among Japanese Americans to other Asian North American people and churches, we approach this discussion of decision making and conflict management with the assumption that Asian North Americans who actively participate in Asian North American congregations are "high ethnics" who intentionally affiliate with other Asian North American and who conduct their relationships with other Asian North American in ways consistent with such ethnic self-identification. While not all Asian North Americans may interact in the ways illustrated in these case studies, Asian North Americans who are intentionally involved in Asian North American churches ("high ethnic" Asian North American) probably do.

Kendis's finding that differences in ethnic style between "high ethnic" Japanese Americans and non-Japanese Americans were particularly apparent with respect to the area of interpersonal relations also provides a helpful frame of reference for examining the decision-making and conflict interactions in these stories. According to Kendis, "high ethnic" *Sansei* feel that they are less aggressive or assertive in their interpersonal interactions than non-Japanese Americans, with greater sensitivity to the thoughts and feelings of others. Concerned with saving face, they tended to avoid dealing openly with problems in relationships, seeking instead indirect methods and structuring interaction patterns in potential disagreement situations "so as to leave acceptable and graceful ways out" (Kendis 1989:177-179).

Studies of Asians and Asian North Americans by other researchers also lead us to such a frame. In his essay on the interpersonal behavior of the Chinese in China as well as "overseas" Chinese persons (living outside of mainland China), sociologist Ambrose Yeo-chi King noted that Chinese society is not individual based nor society based but relationship based. According to King, this focus upon relationships is rooted in Confucian social theory, in which human beings are understood as "relational beings." As such, persons need to develop themselves as "relation-oriented" ("*guanxi*-oriented") individuals (King 1991:64-68).

In light of such Confucian roots, attempts to understand Chinese social structure need to focus upon three sociological concepts that are essential parts of the "stock knowledge" of Chinese adults in their management of everyday life:

- *guanxi* (關係), or personal relationship, personal network, particularistic tie;
- *mianzi* (面子), or face; and
- *rénquing* (人情), or human obligation.

These three concepts still play significant roles in shaping and influencing the interpersonal interactions of modern-day Chinese persons inside and outside China, in rural as well as urban living situations. This is particularly true of *guanxi* (King 1991:63, 68).

The focus on relationships and the obligations that accompany relationships is also noted by Japanese American sociologist S. Frank Miyamoto. In his study of *Nisei* (second-generation Japanese Americans) difficulties in relating to members of the majority society in America, Miyamoto critiqued the work of non-Asian American behavioral scientists who seek the cause of such difficulties in the Japanese American personality. He argued for an alternative approach that instead focuses upon Japanese American culturally based styles and patterns of interpersonal interaction (Miyamoto 1986). Such styles and patterns are characterized by:

- communicative behavior distinctively Japanese in its complex rules about courtesy and strict formalizations of politeness in both verbal and nonverbal interaction;
- understandings that obligations between persons must be fulfilled, lest reneging on any obligations—explicit as well as not-so-explicit—undermines one's social status;
- decisions about individual behavior based not solely or even primarily upon one's own feelings, interests, and motivations but rather upon the others with whom one interacts and desires consensus.

Such styles and patterns are cultural in origin. *Issei* (first-generation Japanese Americans) cultivate such interpersonal style in their daughters and sons. In the relatively controlled medium for such cultivation—that is, the Japanese American family living within a Japanese American community in which the majority of interpersonal interactions are with other Japanese Americans—such style is normative. Such style is functional. It is not aberrant behavior indicative of dysfunctional personality.

However, it is dysfunctional, *Nisei* have often found, in their interactions with the majority society of non-Japanese Americans. For Miyamoto, the difference between the functional and the dysfunctional for *Nisei* lies not in their personality but in the difference between the Japanese American predisposition toward others and the majority American predisposition toward self. The predisposition cultivated in *Nisei* by their *Issei* parents requires a posture of continual interpersonal sensitivity, continual attention to other persons and the perceptions and feelings of those persons about them. The predisposition in the majority American society, while not ignorant of nor even insensitive toward others, emphasizes more attention to one's own feelings and motives.

As with the behavioral orientation of the Chinese described by King, the posture of the *Nisei* described by Miyamoto is relational. This predisposition is not limited to only second-generation Japanese Americans, though. The previously cited work of Kendis with *Sansei*, Dennis Ogawa's study of *Sansei* in Hawaii (1979), and Ronald Tanaka's research on *Sansei* in California (1988) all indicate similar orientations in younger generations.

Kendis echoes Miyamoto's emphasis on a cultural rather than psychological basis for understanding ethnic preference in Japanese American relationships:

> The question is why, given their situation, are (some members of the third and fourth generations) still ethnic? . . . (I)n the case of the third-generation Japanese Americans . . . , the major reason here seems to be one of *comfort*—comfort in knowing the rules of the game and the style in which it is carried out (Kendis 1989:69).

> The answer to *why* ethnicity endures among (third- and fourth-generation Japanese Americans) lies, ultimately, in cultural differences. Despite their high level of acculturation and the intermeshing of most aspects of their lives into American society, high ethnic Japanese Americans find significant differences between their own ways of interaction and those of the larger society. These differences are not the readily observable cultural elements of language, food, or dress but the more subtle and deeply rooted values, attitudes, and behavior patterns (that) result in particular forms of interpersonal relations.

These differences manifest themselves in *a sense of comfort*, which high ethnic Japanese Americans feel when interacting with others like themselves, deriving from a shared style of interaction distinctive from those found in the larger outside society.

To the outsider, these differences may seem insignificant, but they constitute *the* primary reason high ethnic Japanese Americans have for partitioning the social segment of their lives and limiting access to it almost solely to other Japanese Americans. The instrumental aspects of their lives—making a living, getting an education, taking part in the political system—are intermeshed with mainstream society. They choose, however, to act out the more personally meaningful and satisfying noninstrumental portions of their lives with other Japanese Americans (Kendis 1989:6).

The power of the cultural medium is further demonstrated in Ogawa's study of the communications characteristics of Japanese Americans in contemporary Hawaii (1979). Ogawa expected to confirm the assumption that the "Oriental attributes" of filial piety, family honor, shame, and saving face would be continually de-emphasized with each succeeding American-born generation. These attributes evolved from Chinese Confucian concepts that were transplanted into the Japanese social context. They took root in the Japanese conceptualization of *"ie"* ("house" or "household," signifying a large social network comprising one's family of procreation as well as other members associated by kinship or affiliation) and the concomitant concept of *"on"* (obligation to family, community, teacher, emperor). Since *"ie"* and *"on"* were operative in ancient rural Japan, Ogawa wondered if modernized and urbanized younger generations of Japanese Americans would find such behavioral predispositions irrelevant if not dysfunctional today.

Ogawa's findings contradicted these assumptions. While he did find that the *Sansei*'s ties to the larger Japanese American community were not as strong as their parents', this waning was overshadowed by their increasing familial identification. Ogawa concluded that the "kinship solidarity" he found indicated that familial values, behavioral influence, and structural relationships were becoming more, rather than less, prominent as a source for identification and communication for the *Sansei* generation (1979:331).

In studying the behavior of *Sansei* in management-level positions in state government, private industry, and the military, Tanaka sought to test the assumption that Japanese American managers, especially those of the third generation in America, do not function significantly differently from their white counterparts. This assumption was based upon reasons such as the Westernization of Japanese Americans (education in Western or American universities, training in Western business and management practices) and the lack of business-type background in the heritage of American-born Japanese (since their grandparents and great grandparents were not business executives in Japan, *Sansei* would not have learned the business concepts and practices now operative in Japan). Titling his study "The Hermeneutics of *Sansei* Management," Tanaka was conscious that he was a professor of English literature rather than a behavioral scientist. He therefore chose a hermeneutical, rather than experimental, approach. He conducted interviews in which *Sansei* managers described the perspectives and attitudes with which they approached their work. Tanaka then sought to interpret their comments, attentive to the cultural influences giving rise to such comments. He did so with the help of Asian American academic colleagues from other research disciplines (history, Asian American studies, business, economics, and religion).

One segment of his study involved the listing of maxims, the "words to live by" that, whether they believed in them or not, these *Sansei* managers knew and remembered from their childhood. Tanaka noted that "They weren't even written down anywhere. We just grew up with them. They were just 'understood.' And knowing them was part of what it meant to be Japanese, or at least a certain type of Japanese.

... Not all *Sansei* believed in these maxims. But all those to whom I have talked 'know what they mean' and to me that fact is much more significant than whether or not they agree" (1988:99).

A representative sample of the maxims compiled by Tanaka reflects congruence with the Confucian social postures of relationship, obligation, and face noted by the other Asian and Asian North American scholars previously mentioned:

- "Everyone is watching you because you are Japanese. If you bring shame upon yourself, you bring shame upon your family and all Japanese."
- "You are responsible for the well-being of all your workers—whether you like them or they like you."
- "Avoid confrontations at all costs. They always hurt both sides."
- "In any conflict, both sides are at fault. It is up to the side that is right to compromise if possible. Otherwise, the conflict may never be resolved" (Tanaka 1988:99-101).

Asian Canadian Roland Kawano echoes such observations in his article "Reflections on Asian Canadian Search for Identity":

> Western culture teaches me to make decisions as an individual, focusing on what would result in the best interests for me, the individual. Yet, through the years I have become aware of a secondary, underlying process that is also taking place. I have come to recognize that I intuitively check in with a network of internal images that represents parents, siblings, children, significant friends, etc. The decisions I make are made thus by checking in with this significant network of relationships (Kawano 1993:1).

Recent studies of Koreans in North America extend the Confucian connection to this Asian national ancestry group as well. In the "Psychiatric Care of Korean Americans," Luke Kim identified the following to be elements of the Korean ethos:

- *"Jeong"*—"a special interpersonal bond of trust and close-ness . . . (that) encompasses the meanings of a wide range of English terms—feeling, empathy, affinity, com-passion, pathos, sentiment, and love; an essential ele-ment in human life, promoting the depth and richness of personal relations"; and
- *"Che-myun"*—"face-saving . . . (which) is very important to Koreans in their public and social relationships. Maintaining *Che-myun* protects the dignity and self-respect of the individual as well as of his or her family. . . . "(H)onor is maintained by "*Che-myun*" (Kim 1992:349-350).

In a subsequent work, Grace Kim and Luke Kim compared the cultural values of Koreans/Asians and Euro-Americans. In highlighting differences in family relations, life philoso-phy, and communication style, this psychiatrist-educator team identified as key values for Koreans:

- respect for parents and elders, family loyalty, and filial piety (versus the Euro-American values of self-determi-nation and emphasis upon one's own happiness);
- duty, obedience, and acceptance (versus freedom of choice and independence);
- family and kinship bonds and collectivism (versus indi-vidualism);
- status consciousness and face-saving (versus "self-reali-zation" and "do your own thing");
- subtle, nonverbal language (versus emphasis on the verbal);
- control of feelings (versus free expression of feelings);
- flowery, indirect expression (versus direct and explicit language);
- no eye-to-eye contact (versus direct eye-to-eye contact); and
- honorific language (versus equality in language) (Kim and Kim 1994:14-17).

This brief sampling of recent research on Asian North Ameri-cans indicates that, for Chinese, Japanese, and Korean

Americans, relationship, face, obligation, familism, filial piety, propriety, and fidelity—social concepts and postures cultivated in the Asian North American cultural medium or context—abide in behavior-shaping forms. They are *predispositional* in nature, a sort of "cultural DNA" (to use a term spoken by Confucian scholar Tu Wei-Ming), not always consciously present but functionally operative in predisposing us to a distinctive way of engaging in interpersonal interactions. As such, they help create the posture with which Asian North Americans approach the interpersonal interactions of group decision making in the family, in community groups, and in the congregation.

With these understandings of the predispositions and postures influencing Asian North American interpersonal interactions, decisions, and approaches to conflict, let us return to the five cases reported earlier in this chapter. How do these understandings mesh with your reflections upon and analyses of these vignettes? Do the following questions help?

In case story 1, would the young Chinese American pastor have been surprised by the decision-making extension sought by his guest speaker selection committee if he had understood the Chinese orientation toward relationship (as presented by King) and Asian North American inclination for decision making based upon the feelings and interests of those with whom they sought consensus (Miyamoto 1986)? Further, would the pastor have used the same approach to providing his committee members with the information they needed to make their choice if he had realized the difference between *status* (position or rank in relation to others) and *esteem* (high regard ascribed by others) factors in Asian North American culture? In his report, the pastor emphasized status-related data (the guest speaker's degrees, achievements, publications). In their additional "research," the committee members sought esteem-related data (family roots, adherence to Asian North American values of filial piety, etc.).

In case story 2, would the white guest speaker and the

well-meaning adult have urged the youth to publicly disclose disagreements with parents if they had been familiar with the importance for Asians of relationship, face, and obligation (King 1991; Kim and Kim 1994)—even to the maintenance of filial piety and family honor among the third and fourth generations (Ogawa 1979; Kendis 1989; Tanaka 1988)?

In case story 3, would the denominational executive have engaged the Japanese American church members in such face-to-face confrontation of the conflicts had he been aware of the critical importance of face (Ogawa 1979), the difference between Western and Asian North American experiences of dysfunctional style in relationships (Miyamoto 1986), the disinclination toward direct expression of interpersonal problems (Kendis 1989), and the "maxims" for managing relationships imprinted on third-generation Japanese Americans (Tanaka 1988)?

In case story 4, would the Korean pastor have come to the same conclusion about the symptoms and stages of conflict in his congregation had he been more aware of the differences in values and characteristics between Korean and Western communication styles (Kim and Kim 1994)?

In case story 5, would the members, pastor, and denominational staff involved in responding to their congregation's conflict situation have been helped if denominational approaches to intervention were more sensitive to the Asian North American disinclination toward public addressing of conflict and predisposition toward indirect methods of addressing interpersonal problems that leave disputants with acceptable and graceful ways out of the conflict (Kendis 1989)?

Being on the Way: Findings and Observations about Asian North American Church Conflict

Observations like those presented in the preceding section are emerging from Asian North Americans seeking to identify and understand the dynamics influencing interpersonal interactions and the practice of community within Asian North American congregations. One such group of Asian North Americans is the Alban Institute Action Research Team on Conflict Management in Asian American Congregations. The insights arising from the team's activities are enlightening examples of being "on the way."

In 1988, aware that the approaches used by their conflict consultants were not effective with nonwhite congregations, Alban Institute leaders sought assistance from racial/ethnic pastors and denominational staff in developing strategies for managing conflicts involving such congregations. With a grant from the Hewlett Foundation, the institute established the Asian American Action Research Team as one response to this need in January 1990. The team initially focused its attention upon learning the Alban Institute approach to conflict intervention (as presented in Leas 1979, 1984, 1985; Synod of Lakes and Prairies 1988), analyzing the assumptions behind the goals and techniques in existing approaches, exploring ways to revise or replace elements in the Alban approach, and utilizing opportunities to test possible revised approaches in regional workshops, pastors' seminars, and local congregations.

The team also shifted the focus from the institute's initial interest in *intercultural* conflict (conflict between white and Asian North American congregations) to *intracultural* conflict (conflict *within* predominantly Asian North American congregations). Both the institute staff and the team members were aware of the increasing need to address tensions between Asian North American and white congregations in "nesting" situations (in which a white congregation makes its facilities available to a new or emerging Asian North American congregation on a long-term basis). However, team members felt that examination of such intercultural conflict needed to be deferred until after an understanding of the factors and dynamics *within* Asian North American congregations was developed.

The institute's desire for immediate development of culturally effective processes for conflict intervention, coupled with the team's hesitation due to the dearth of extant literature on Asian North American styles in conflict (much less church conflict), led to the adoption of a "being on the way" approach to the team's work.

Though analytical resources were limited, anecdotal resources were not. Persons from Asian North American congregations hearing of the project were eager to gather for workshops to share stories and observations about church conflict. Therefore, the team chose an "action research" posture, a "learning together on the way" approach characterized by the team's:

a. request for assistance in gathering insights on conflict in Asian North American congregations (experiences, learnings, and observations);

b. commitment to being especially attentive to the cultural lessons arising from such stories;

c. offer to share insights from other Asian North Americans, not as experts or trainers, but as colleagues and fellow learners in Asian North American ministry; and

d. promise to continue sharing insights as the team met with Asian North Americans from other parts of the church.

The team's research during its initial phase of work (1990-93) consequently involved a back-and-forth movement between the anecdotal and the analytical:

• team conversations in which conflict stories were shared, experiences reflected upon, and observations tentatively made;

• regional denominational and ecumenical consultations in which Asian North American church representatives provided additional stories and reflections, participated in testing team members' observations, and proposed responses helpful to their congregations; and

• team conversations and reflections upon data gathered from the most recent consultations and their implications for research findings.

Following this rhythm, the team offered workshops on conflict management at the annual meetings of the Japanese Presbyterian Conference (February 1989); Reformed Church in America Consultation on Pacific and Asian American Ministries (May 1989); National Conference of Chinese Churches (June 1989 and June 1992); and National Asian Presbyterian Council (June 1989, July 1991, and June 1992). Ecumenical Asian North American groups such as Pacific Asian American and Canadian Christian Education (PAACCE) also sponsored events (May and November 1991).

One of the processes used at such consultations is the following individual review and reflection exercise:

a. Think of a specific Asian American church conflict with which you are familiar (either in which you were involved or about which you have knowledge). In two or three sentences, describe the conflict (what it was about, who was involved, what happened).

b. How did the existence of the conflict come to be known in the congregation (by the pastor, by the lay people, etc.)? How early or late in the conflict did they make their discovery of the conflict? Why?

c. How, if at all, was the conflict dealt with?

d. What was the key factor, person(s), incident, or exercise in bringing this conflict to some conclusion (whether a positive or negative result)?

e. Was "outside help" (denominational staff or committee, outside consultant, etc.) involved? Was such "help" helpful in bringing about the results? Why or why not?

Reflections by Asian North Americans from Chinese, Japanese, Korean, Taiwanese, Thai, and Vietnamese congregations emerging from this and other processes have led to the following findings by the team "on the way":

• the power of the relational orientation;
• the predisposition toward preserving relationship;
• the problem of detecting nonverbal and nonconfrontational conflict;
• the perspective of the manager or intervenor;

- the pursuit of culturally relevant postures and processes; and
- the proposal for a paradigm shift.

The Power of the Relational Orientation

This finding confirms the applicability of previously cited research by King, Miyamoto, Kendis, Ogawa, and the Kims. Case story 1 (decision making regarding a guest speaker) and case story 2 (public sharing of intergenerational disagreements) are only two of the many stories confirming the team's suppositions about the function of the relational orientation in decision making. This predisposition was operative in situations ranging from "individual" decisions for all family members to receive baptism to group decisions deferred until members had time to consult elders and other members of the congregation.

The Predisposition toward Preserving Relationship

This relational orientation is more significant for understanding conflict dynamics. The team found that Asian North American workshop participants expressed a predisposition toward preserving their relationships with others involved in disagreements. Again confirming the previously mentioned Asian and Asian North American research on interpersonal styles, participants in all workshops noted the preference or tendency to *not* engage in face-to-face confrontation because of the possibility of "loss of face." In face-to-face interactions between Person A and Person B, there are four possible outcomes: A might lose face, B might lose face, both A and B might lose face, neither A nor B might lose face. Since three of the four possibilities result in loss of face, the odds for a face-saving outcome in any face-to-face interactions are not encouraging!

Consequently, as reflected in case story 3 (conflict-intervention session), differences and even disagreements may be allowed to remain unresolved over a long period of time in order to preserve (save) the face of others and therefore maintain (also save) some form of relationship. Asian North American church representatives in one workshop noted the existence of a "latent or tolerable" level of conflict, in which the persons involved do not feel the need to actively resolve their differences. In such situations, as reflected in case story 4 (conflict-management training event), conflict intensity is difficult to detect—and even more difficult to measure.

However, if a conflict involves a matter that cannot be tolerated or that reaches a point where it can no longer be tolerated—that is, if an issue supersedes even the predisposition to preserve relationships—then such a conflict will take on more visible and therefore detectable forms (more apparent interpersonal exchanges, clearer verbal and emotional indicators). In case story 3, the face-to-face interactions in the conflict-management process called for church members to publicly disclose long-standing differences and disagreements. The damage to the relationships among these members caused by this daylong loss-of-face experience may have led to the decision by many members the next day to leave the congregation.

The Problem of Detecting Nonverbal and Nonconfrontational Conflict

Asian North American face-preserving and relationship-maintaining predispositions that allow for latent or tolerable types of conflict limit (if not nullify) the usefulness of existing approaches to intervention and management such as those utilized by Alban Institute consultants. Since detection tends to occur only in situations or levels of visible or intolerable conflict, the problem may be more difficult to address by the time the dispute has escalated to that point.

In addition, participants in the team's workshops observed that such predispositions incline Asian North American persons in conflict to be neither verbal nor visible in their interactions with one another. The tendency is toward withdrawal rather than engagement, nonconfrontation rather than confrontation. Such reports support the previously cited research by Kendis that "high ethnic" Asian North Americans seek indirect (rather than open) methods of dealing with problems in relationships. With respect to detection and observation, Kendis noted that:

> None of the elements of this behavioral complex is immediately obvious to outsiders. Frequently, even *Sansei* are unable to articulate them, although they do recognize that they exist. These distinctive behavior patterns are normally learned first at home and reinforced and elaborated through interaction with other Japanese Americans. They are usually not consciously or deliberately taught and are so deep-rooted that they continue to be passed on despite the pervasive influence of the mainstream culture (Kendis 1989:177-178).

Thus, in case story 4, the pastor's assertion that the gradual "levels of intensity" model of conflict did not apply to Koreans because their conflicts *began* at the "open fighting" level was actually a complaint against the limitations of all approaches to conflict analysis that are based upon observation or monitoring of verbal interactions and exchanges. The problem with existing conflict-intervention approaches is the problem of detecting invisible and nonverbal interactions. Western tools are not useful. Clearly, alternative approaches are needed.

The Perspective of the Manager or Intervenor

This factor may seem to be outside the delineation of congregational conflict dynamics since it refers not to those in a conflict but instead to those seeking to provide assistance in such situations. However, the Asian American Action Research Team heard a number of workshop participants emphasize the need for awareness of the racism (in both individual and institutional forms) possibly operative in and affecting denominational staff and other white consultants' attitudes, assumptions, and approaches in conflict intervention and other work with Asian congregations. This concern about being aware of racism reminds those managing or intervening in conflicts that they themselves become factors affecting the outcome of the conflict.

The inclusion of "the perspective of the conflict manager or intervenor" in this list of key factors is based not upon the fear of the prejudice of racist intervenors but upon the more likely possibility of institutional racism practiced by individual intervenors ignorant of their own assumptions and insensitive to Asian North American values governing relationship.

The Pursuit of Culturally Relevant Postures and Processes

When consultation participants from Asian North American congregations turned their attention from understanding congregational decision-making factors and conflict dynamics to providing assistance in such situations, their comments centered on two key concerns:

1. Existing approaches used by most denominations (whether Alban Institute or other) are felt to be "too Western"—that is, not sensitive enough to the need to preserve face, too confrontational in posture.

2. The reliance of existing approaches upon intervention by "outsider third parties" (such as expert consultants in conflict or denominational executives with conflict skills) is not necessarily helpful; at best, outsiders are a mixed blessing.

In seeking more culturally relevant and potentially effective alternatives, representatives at the May 1991 consultation sponsored by Pacific Asian American and Canadian Christian Education Ministries in Oakland, California, capsulized their concerns, hopes, and visions in two intriguing images: "from surgery to acupuncture" and "from aspirin to ginseng."

As reported by Kendis and other researchers, the Asian North American predisposition toward addressing problems in interpersonal and intergroup relationships is one favoring indirect and subtle interactions. Approaches to conflict management in Asian North American congregations would need to be consonant with this predisposition. Current Alban Institute and other approaches are not. As reflected in case story 3, they involve Asian North Americans in direct, face-to-face interactions, personal disclosures in public settings, as well as provision of highly personal if not private information to outsiders or strangers. Like surgery, these approaches involve cutting the body open, exposing for examination (and therefore exposing to risk) delicate parts of the body, and sometimes even cutting and removing parts of the body. Such techniques are incising. Such techniques are invasive. They risk causing trauma— even death—to the body.

In contrast, acupuncture is less invasive, less incising, and less risky. Rather than presurgery X rays, probes, or the introduction of other foreign chemicals or instruments into the body, it involves noninvasive external observation of key points of the body. Rather than involving surgical incisions, this approach calls at worst only for the gentle insertion of small needles. Rather than identifying, examining, chemically treating, or cutting out parts of the body, acupuncture seeks to keep body parts in healthy relation to one another, working to free the flow of energy within the body and between its parts. An acupuncture-like approach is needed in Asian North American church conflicts.

Exploration of the acupuncture alternative led to consideration of the differences between treatment and prevention, relief and remedy, treatment of symptoms versus restoration of wholeness or balance in the body. From such distinctions emerged the image of a "ginseng tea" alternative to the "aspirin" approach. Representatives of Asian North American congregations expressed clear preference for resource persons skilled in training church members in maintaining balance and harmony in relationships so that intolerable conflict might be prevented. Such training was likened to drinking ginseng or taking other herbs that maintain balance and enable unobstructed energy flow in the body. Consultants or denominational staff members skilled in intervention, even experts in such work, were less preferred since they were perceived to enter a congregation's life *after* balance has been lost or energy blocked.

The acupuncture and ginseng images also led to a reexamination of intervention by third-party consultants in Asian North American settings. Team members were interested in probing the use of third parties other than professional consultants since reading a Mennonite study of the use of informal conflict mediators in villages in contemporary China (Kreider 1988).

As reflected in case story 5 (consulting a former pastor in addressing a conflict between the current pastor and the congregation), the Asian North American predisposition toward indirect interaction in times of interpersonal problems also inclines the disputants to seek the aid of third parties. However, not all third parties are acceptable—not even those deemed "expert" in conflict-management "process" because of their status as "professional" consultants. Asian North American participants in several of the Asian American Action Research Team's workshops expressed preference for third parties who, although they might be "outsiders" to the congregation in the formal sense, were actually "not-so-outsiders" because they were already familiar with the congregation as well as known and trusted by the members.

Such expressions reflected preferences for persons with esteem rather than persons with status regarding the granting or acceptance of authority in third parties. As reflected in case story 1, esteem-based authority is trust based upon relationship and upon demonstrated usefulness according to criteria valued by the community (the guest speaker came from a family that was known, a "good family"). Status-based authority is trust based upon claimed expertise or assumed usefulness according to criteria valued by those outside the community. Outsiders already enjoying the esteem of the congregation might be given more authority in an intervention situation than those who only have status (such as a denominational executive or committee representative). In fact, some Asian North American church representatives expressed preference for outsiders "with authority but not involved in the conflict or its outcome." Lay members did not perceive denominational staff or representatives as necessarily objective or neutral third parties in conflict intervention, especially in those involving the pastor.

Case story 5 provides a helpful example of the importance of "not-totally-outside" outsiders. Both church members and the current pastor sought assistance from the former pastor. He represented an avenue for indirect and nonconfrontational interaction. Yet seminary training, denominational policy, and existing Western human relations theory-based caveats concerning "maintenance of boundaries" and "avoidance of triangles" led the former pastor to decline. However, with the escalation of the conflict and the deterioration of the relationship between the current pastor and the congregation, even denominational staff sought out the former pastor's help.

A postscript to case story 5 may be helpful here: With the request of the denominational staff and the news that the conflict in his previous congregation had reached an almost unresolvable state, the former pastor relented and agreed to meet with the staff person. The information he provided—background on pivotal moments in the congregation's history, previous conflicts, key lay leaders (formal and informal) able to provide a moderating presence, anxieties and concerns of members and, most important, the "personality" and culture of the congregation—enabled the denominational staff and other representatives to assist the pastor and congregation in negotiating a resolution of their conflict. In such negotiations, there was no mention of the information or assistance provided by the previous pastor.

The elements and outcome of case story 5, coupled with the preference expressed at several workshops for "trusted" third parties, has raised:

a. the need to reexamine the validity of caveats against triangles in Asian North American conflict situations;
b. the possibility of a different kind of third-party involvement, in which the nature of such involvement is less invasive and interventionist since the third party is not a total outsider but one already related to the system of relationships of those involved in the conflict;
c. the possibility (in light of the above) of reconceiving the role of third-party mediators and even the process of mediation itself based upon the image of the go-between in indirect interaction and communication; and
d. the possibility of a new kind of consulting—"shadow" consulting—in which the third party, like the former pastor in case story 5, is never directly involved or present in the interactions of those in the conflict or those "official" or formal third parties seeking to assist in resolving the conflict but is active in providing advice and counsel (key background information, interpretations of "messages," etc.) to these persons as they interact with one another.

The Proposal for a Paradigm Shift

The Asian American Action Research Team's "being on the way" experience in understanding and addressing conflict in Asian North American congregations has included attention to the biblical and theological bases for current approaches as well. Team members have engaged Asian North American church representatives in sharing:

a. the biblical perspectives and theological understandings influencing their disposition toward conflict;
b. new insights from group study of biblical passages describing conflict in the early church; and
c. theological reflections upon the stories presented by workshop participants.

In several workshops, participants used the following questions for a fresh examination of the conflict between Paul and other apostles as described in Galatians 2:1-14:

1. What is the issue in this conflict?
2. What approach is used to resolve the conflict?
3. What decision(s) is (are) made?
4. What is the result of this decision?
5. How effective or lasting is this result?

Persons engaged in this study found their responses to these questions helpful in revising their understanding of church conflict. A key discovery emerged from a comparison of their answers to the first and third questions. The "decision" reported in this account did not fully address the issue originally necessitating the meeting between Paul's delegation and the other apostles—that is, the validity of Paul's (and the church's) mission to the Gentiles. The "agreement" that Paul and Barnabas should go to the Gentiles while James, Cephas, and John would go to the circumcised did not constitute a new commitment to a united mission direction, to an integrated mission, or even to joint mission activity. Instead, it was an allowance for *separate* mission directions and *separate* mission activities. There was agreement on united activity in only one demand: "They asked only one thing, that we remember the poor, which was actually what I was eager to do" (Galatians 2:10) and this unity of action was unrelated to the original issue of a mission to the Gentiles. Yet the decision still led to the disputants extending to one another "the right hand of fellowship."

For many of the participants in this Bible study, these discoveries about the conflict-resolution experience of their biblical predecessors at the Jerusalem Council became *pivotal* in their understanding of conflict resolution in the church by offering the possibility for a new theological foundation for this dimension of Christian community.

For these persons, the decision in the Galatians passage suggests that the concern for being in relationship (as reflected in the extension of the right hand of fellowship) outweighed the concern for a clear-cut, sharply defined decision (unified mission direction or joint mission activity). The decision focused on what the disputants could agree to and left "fuzzy" those things they could not agree to (possible integrated mission, support for one another's ministries).

Such a decision reflected for some participants the kind of predisposition based upon what Korean educator and theologian Yong-Bock Kim terms "the solidarity paradigm rather than the unity paradigm" for interpersonal interaction in the church. For Kim, the difference between the two paradigms is like the movement—the leap—from Newton to Einstein. A solidarity posture allows for diversity and difference more than a unity posture, for an emphasis or priority on unity tends to result in focusing upon how much (or how little) diversity is acceptable (Kim 1990).

Kim's insights are helpful for understanding Asian North American congregations like that presented in case story 3, in which a solidarity posture allowed for "tolerable" conflict to exist without the expressed need for resolution, even over two decades.

Attention to this solidarity posture as a factor in Asian North American conflict dynamics is also essential in light of research on Asian American institutions by Yen Le Espiritu. Her analysis of the ways anti-Asian violence has led to "protective ethnicity" and "reactive solidarity" among Asian Americans (Espiritu 1992:134-160) reinforces the Asian American Action Research Team's presuppositions about the relationship between experiences of racism and congregational solidarity in Asian North American churches.

The reexamination of theological resources for and influences upon Asian North American church conflict has been and continues to be an exciting part of being "on the way" for the team. Such reexamination has led to both new insights and new imperatives, as expressed by participants in one 1991 workshop who ended their day together with the declaration, "End of the unity paradigm—on to the solidarity paradigm!"

This proposal for a new paradigm represents an opportunity

for the wider church to be "on the way" as well. A solidarity rather than unity paradigm offers the possibility for reconceiving "basic" understandings of the nature of the church and Christian community. In such a paradigm, Christian community is a given rather than a vision or a possibility. The church therefore *begins* with the unity already given to it by the Christ common to all members of the church and *moves* to working on demonstrating solidarity with sisters and brothers united by and in this Christ. The task of the church is therefore not to work for unity (since it has already been *given* unity—one Lord, one faith, one baptism, one God and Creator of us all) but to work on solidarity. Understood in this way, the solidarity paradigm has implications for more than just the management of church conflict. (Recall that in chapter 2 "solidarity" is explained as a characteristic that binds Asian families together in a permanent fashion that cannot be broken.)

Implications for Asian North American Congregations and the Wider Church

When the Asian American Action Research Team began its work, the members accepted as their task the request of Alban Institute representatives to *adapt* current conflict-management approaches to Asian North American cultural contexts while suspecting that more than mere adaptation or refinement might be necessary. The findings reported above have confirmed these initial suspicions. Consequently, as the team continues being "on the way" with the institute and with Asian North American church representatives joining in their work at different points of the journey, the following represent signposts for the road ahead:

- exploring noninvasive responses to conflict using the insights of Takie Sugiyama Lebra's study of "nonconfrontational strategies" for management of interpersonal conflicts in Japan (1984);
- exploring parallels to the "ginseng tea" approach to

  maintaining balance using Robert Nye's identification of the three factors leading situations of difference to degenerate into situations of conflict—competition, domination, and provocation—and off-setting alternatives in the form of cooperation, equality, and civility (1973:81-91, 167-185);

- exploring ways to extend William Ouchi's description of "Theory Z" approaches to management to an Asian North American-relevant posture for pastoral leadership (1981:48-79);
- exploring the congruence between Barry Johnson's reconception of conflict resolution as "polarity management" (1992) and Yong-Bock Kim's "solidarity paradigm" for clues to a more acupuncture-like (as opposed to surgery-like) approach to conflict intervention; and
- exploring the utility of David Augsburger's proposal for a "medi-emic" (culturally unique) rather than "medi-etic" (universal) approach to conflict mediation involving different cultures (1992:35-40).

An "On the Way" Proposal for Responding to Asian North American Conflict

For persons seeking to utilize the insights and proposals emerging from this chapter in an Asian North American church conflict during this "in the meantime between paradigms" period, the following questions may be of help. They are offered not as the first questions developed for a new protocol to be followed for an Asian American conflict but as questions to be asked in an "on the way" spirit by those working with Asian American congregations.

Assessment of a Conflict Situation

  1. In what ways is ethnicity a factor in this congregation? Is the "high ethnic" or "low ethnic" distinction helpful in identifying cultural factors influencing the behavior of the

congregation? How has such ethnicity been a factor during times of previous conflict?

2. Which of the five key factors and dynamics affecting Asian North American conflict are present and operative in this congregation? To what degree are they present among the members? In what ways are they operative?

3. How does the culture of the congregation's members provide ways for persons in conflict to manage or resolve their differences? Which of those ways are operative in this congregation?

4. To what extent does the congregation already use third parties or go-betweens in interpersonal interactions, decision making, conflict? How have they been helpful in the past in this congregation?

Developing a Response to a Conflict Situation

5. What "ginseng-type" activities does the congregation engage in to maintain balanced relationships, energy flow, and so forth?

6. In a conflict situation, what might constitute an "acupuncture-like" approach to responding?

7. Given the "energy flow" image in the acupuncture metaphor, how is the energy flow of the congregation at this point? What keeps it flowing? Is there any blockage? What is needed to unblock the energy flow?

8. If go-betweens are used, are any available (willing) to assist in enabling nonconfrontational communication and interaction between the parties in the conflict?

9. Would a "shadow" consultant be helpful and acceptable?

An "On the Way" Conclusion

Jesus Christ brings us into relationship with God. In so doing, Jesus Christ also brings us into relationship with other believers who are in relationship with God. In this book, we have chosen to study Christian community through examining relationships between and among Christians within congregations, for it is through our participation in congregations that we experience what being in such community means.

While this is so for most Christians, it is so for Christians in Asian North American congregations in ways quite different from those in Euro-American congregations, ways distinctive to our cultural traditions. Asian North Americans bring to their experience and practice of Christian relationship and community deep, complex, and rich traditions with respect to interpersonal interaction—traditions shaping our predispositions and postures toward such relationships and community. Consequently, the question of "Christ, Culture, and Community" addressed in this book is essentially a question about the cultural influences upon the conduct of relationships between and among those Christians who belong to Asian North American congregations.

The cultural influences described in this chapter provide more than an understanding of the Asian North American part of the Christian family. They also provide the whole church with an opportunity to refresh its understanding of and living out of Christian community with some "gifts of faithful ethnicity" from Asian North American Christians. However, as these gifts are offered from Christians of an Asian North American cultural predisposition to Christians of other cultures, more than mere translation of words and phrases will be needed in order for such gifts to be appreciated and utilized.

Western doctors seeking to understand acupuncture needed first to realize that the energy grid in the human body used by acupuncturists did not coincide with nor correspond to any chart of the human anatomy or neurological system. In chapter 2 of this book, David Ng and Heup Young Kim remind us that there is no Chinese term for the English word "community." Yong-Bock Kim likens the shift in understanding from "Christian unity" to "Christian solidarity" to the leap from Newtonian physics to Einsteinian physics.

Such is the challenge and the task before us in this time of shifting paradigms. As we seek to be believers "on the way"

rather than persons standing in the way, may we find both
call and comfort in recalling the Easter experience of the two
disciples on the Emmaus road. Journeying together, reflecting together on their experiences with Jesus and sharing
bread together, their eyes were eventually opened to the
Christ in their midst. May God so bless us as we journey in
relationship and in solidarity with one another.

Questions for Discussion

1. Which of the Asian North American cultural traditions,
   factors, and dynamics described in this chapter are operative in your congregation? How are they helpful or not
   helpful in the decision-making life of the congregation?

2. How do you and your congregation see Christian community? Is community a given reality or a goal to be achieved?
   How is this understanding reflected in the ways your
   congregation practices life together with other Christians?

3. How do you see the difference between "unity" and "solidarity"? How helpful is the concept of "solidarity" presented in this chapter in understanding Christian
   community? How might "solidarity in diversity" be a helpful next step in the church's quest for "unity in diversity"?

4. What have been your congregation's experiences of church
   conflict? What lessons and insights have emerged from
   these experiences—especially about helpful versus un-
   helpful responses and approaches?

5. Which biblical passages—stories as well as sayings—guide
   your understanding of and response to church conflict?

6. How helpful is the concept of an "acupuncture" alternative
   to more "surgical" conflict management in the church—
   that is, seeking ways to unblock or release the congregation's creative energy rather focusing on exposing and
   removing the congregation's "problem"?

References

Augsburger, David. *Conflict Mediation across Cultures: Pathways and Patterns.* Louisville: Westminster/John Knox Press, 1992.

Choi, Chang Wook. "Managing Conflict in the Church." In *Korean American Ministry: A Resource Book.* Edited by Sang Hyun Lee and John V. Moore. Louisville: Presbyterian Church (USA), 1993, 88–100.

Choy, Virstan. "Ginseng Before Aspirin; Acupuncture Instead of Surgery: Insights from the PAACE West Event on Conflict Management in Asian-American Congregations." *PAACE Newsletter.* Vol. 7, no. 4, October, 1991, 1–2, 4–5.

Espiritu, Yen Le. *Asian American Panethnicity: Bridging Institutions and Identities.* Philadelphia: Temple University Press, 1992.

Johnson, Barry. "Polarity Management." In *Identifying and Managing Unsolvable Problems.* Amherst, Mass.: HRD Press, 1992.

Kendis, Kaoru Oguri. *A Matter of Comfort: Ethnic Maintenance and Ethnic Style among Third-Generation Japanese Americans.* New York: AMS Press, Inc., 1989.

Kawano, Roland. "Reflections on Asian Canadian Search for Identity." In *PAACCE Ministries.* Vol. 9, no. 2, August, 1993, 1–2.

Kim, Grace, and Luke Kim. *Korean American Immigrants and Their Children.* New Faces of Liberty, Zellerbach Family Fund Project. San Francisco: Many Cultures Publications, 1994.

Kim, Luke. "Psychiatric Care of Korean Americans." In *Culture, Ethnicity, and Mental Illness.* Edited by Albert C. Gaw. Washington, D.C.: American Psychiatric Press, 1992, 347–375.

Kim, Yong-Bock. "The Mission of God in the Context of the Suffering and Struggling Peoples of Asia." In *Peoples of Asia, People of God: A Report of the Asia Mission Conference,* 1989. Christian Conference of Asia, 1990.

King, Ambrose Yeo-chi. "Kuan-Hsi and Network Building: A Sociological Interpretation." In "The Living Tree: The Changing Meaning of Being Chinese Today." *Daedalus.* Vol. 120, no. 2, spring, 1991, 63–84.

Kreider, Robert. "The Chinese Resolve Conflicts." *Mennonite Life.* Vol. 43, no. 1, March, 1988, 19–20.

Leas, Speed B. *A Layperson's Guide to Conflict Management.* Washington, D.C.: Alban Institute, 1979.

———. *Discover Your Conflict Management Style.* Washington, D.C.: Alban Institute, 1984.

————. *Moving Your Church through Conflict.* Washington, D.C.: Alban Institute, 1985.

Lebra, Takie Sugiyama. "Nonconfrontational Strategies for Management of Interpersonal Conflicts." In *Conflict in Japan.* Edited by E. S. Krauss, T. P. Rohlen, and P. G. Steinhoff. Honolulu: University of Hawaii Press, 1984, 41–60.

Miyamoto, S. Frank. "Problems of Interpersonal Style among the Nisei." *Amerasia Journal.* Vol. 13, no. 2, 1986\87, 29–45.

Nye, Robert D. *Conflict among Humans: Some Basic Psychological and Social-Psychological Considerations.* New York: Springer Publishing Co., 1973.

Ouchi, William G. *Theory Z.* New York: Avon Books, 1981.

Ogawa, Dennis M. "Communication Characteristics of Asian Americans in Urban Settings: The Case of Honolulu Japanese." In *Handbook of Intercultural Communication.* Edited by M. Asante, E. Newmark, and C. Blake. Beverly Hills: Sage Publications, 1979, 321–338.

Pai, Young, and Jonghan Yi. *Korean-American Ministry Survey: A Data Report.* Kansas City, Mo.: University of Missouri School of Education, 1990.

Synod of Lakes and Prairies. "Coping with Conflict" (two-part video series). Bloomington, Minn., 1988.

Tanaka, Ronald. "The Hermeneutics of Sansei Management: Some Conceptual Parameters." *Journal of Ethnic Studies.* Vol. 16, no. 1, spring, 1988, 85–105.

Suggested Resources

Augsburger, David. *Conflict Mediation across Cultures: Pathways and Patterns.* Louisville: Westminster/John Knox Press, 1992. A helpful comparison of the ways in which conflict is understood and addressed in different cultures. Proposes a "medi-emic" approach to mediating conflict within a cultural group, which is sensitive and attentive to that culture.

Johnson, Barry. *Polarity Management: Identifying and Managing Unsolvable Problems.* Amherst, Mass.: HRD Press, 1992. An intriguing proposal for reconceiving some conflicts as "polarities to manage" rather than "problems to solve." Introduces an approach to identifying the disputants in a polarity as "crusaders" and "tradition bearers," diagnosing the positive and negative aspects of each position, and prescribing actions that enable them to "live within the tension" of the polarity.

Kendis, Kaoru Oguri. *A Matter of Comfort: Ethnic Maintenance and Ethnic Style among Third-Generation Japanese Americans.*

New York: AMS Press, Inc., 1989. A revealing study of the *Sansei* and of the importance of ethnic identity and ethnic institutions for this generation.

Kim, Luke. "Psychiatric Care of Korean Americans." In *Culture, Ethnicity, and Mental Illness*. Edited by Albert C. Gaw. Washington, D.C.: American Psychiatric Press, 1992, 347-375. A helpful presentation of key elements of the Korean American ethos.

King, Ambrose Yeo-chi. "Kuan-Hsi and Network Building: A Sociological Interpretation." In "The Living Tree: The Changing Meaning of Being Chinese Today." *Daedalus*. Vol. 120, no. 2, Spring, 1991, 63-84. An introduction to the foundational social concepts of relationship, face, and obligation for Chinese and Chinese Americans.

CHAPTER 13

Varieties of Congregations for Varieties of People

By David Ng

Introduction

Chapter 13 continues the practical path taken in this final cluster of chapters. However, in dealing with the types of congregations common to Asian North American Christians, the author, David Ng, a professor at San Francisco Theological Seminary and director of the Christ, Culture, and Community Project, does not follow the path of statistics or structures. Rather, this chapter elicits the reader's imagination to consider the"types" of Asian North Americans who are potential or actual churchgoers. Given certain characteristics of age, generation, language, national background, culture, and so forth, what types of congregations are likely to attract and serve the needs of the varieties of people who are called "Asian North American"? Do existing types of congregations need to adapt? Will new types need to be created? These are real questions in need of real solutions. This chapter calls upon Asian North Americans to join together on the way to effective ministries and relevant congregations.

Where Shall We Go for Worship Tomorrow?

Scene: Saturday evening, in a student apartment near the campus of a metropolitan university. Four students are conversing following an informal meal. Ben is fourth-generation Japanese American; Lisa is second-generation Chinese American; Jung is a recent arrival from Korea; and Chong

Hee is "1.5," coming from Korea as a young child fourteen years ago.

Ben: Well, folks, welcome to the student apartments, to Jefferson U., and to Valley City! Hope we all have a good school year.

Jung: Will any of you be going to church tomorrow? I'd like to find a good church to go to.

Chong Hee: Me too. Maybe we can go together and start the year off on a good note.

Lisa: Sounds good. Not so easy to do, though. I've been here three years and tried a bunch of places. But if we go together, maybe we'll find a church we like.

Chong Hee: I tried the Korean United Methodist Church. They meet in the building of Wesley United Methodist, on Statler and Main. Trouble is, they're a "nesting church" that just rents the building, so their services are at one o'clock. Guess none of their members watch football on TV. Besides, I hear they might move—been having problems with the landlord. The white folks don't like the noise and the strange odors coming from the kitchen.

Ben: Ha! They won't have to move out. If I know Asians, they can buy the church and the other folks will have to move out! No offense, Jung and Chong Hee—just a little ethnic humor. There's this Canaan Bible Fellowship that meets on campus each week. Bible study on Fridays, worship on Sundays. But I'd rather not go. They have some rather limited views of the Bible. And of life.

Jung: Then there's the Pan Asian New Church Development out in Henley Groves, near the industrial park. Yeah, it's an hour away. I went to it. It's supposed to be Pan Asian—you know, all Asian nationalities. It was pretty good, but they also meet in a nest situation, and worship is at noon. Everything is in English. But it's mostly Chinese American engineer types, and they're mostly young families. I don't mind the Chinese American thing, but those engineers! And there are no folks our age.

Lisa: Hey, I'm Chinese American! But I know what you

mean, that church is still working on being Pan Asian. We could make it Pan Asian just by showing up! But have you all heard about Stewart Memorial Church? You know, the one in the downtown district that's supposed to be multicultural? It was an old, mostly white church, but now it's a mixture of Anglos, Hispanics, African Americans, and some Asians.

Chong Hee: An interesting church. I went a couple of times. Interesting mix of people. That's where my car got broken into twice. Now you know why I don't have a radio in my car. But I'd be willing to go back if you all go with me—and if we only go in the daytime!

Ben: Chong Hee, didn't you used to go to Daesung Korean Church?

Chong Hee: A nice church. Big—maybe five hundred or so. Lots of programs. I liked it and didn't like it for the same reasons! There's a big push in that church to be Korean and to use the Korean language. It's good to maintain the culture. But, hey, I was only five when I left Korea. I lost most of my language, and I couldn't follow what was going on in the service. The people there are OK, a bit intense. They seem to look back to Korea more than they look forward to being in North America. I'd go to the church and see a lot of the teenagers on the sidelines, like they didn't want to go in. That church needs a second-generation ministry—in English!

Jung: Hey, let's go there! And I'll volunteer *you*, Chong Hee, to work with the kids! But Ben, didn't you come from the Santiago Japanese Church? How's that church?

Ben: Right—it's on Santiago Street, and that's why it's called "Santiago Japanese Church."

And it isn't all-Japanese anymore. A lot of other Asians, most third-generation, also go there. We still have an *Issei* service early on Sundays in Japanese, but most of the programs and the eleven o'clock service are in English. Have to be—most of the members are third-, fourth-, or fifth-generation. If you go, I can show you around and have you meet the pastor, Chuck Yamauchi. He's young and has a lot of ideas about recovering our Asian culture, like using Asian art and music in the service. And he's very strong on combatting racism.

Jung: It sounds like we all want to go to church. Now to decide which church . . .

Varieties of Congregations

Anyone who is interested in attending a worship service in a metropolitan area is faced with numerous choices. Is the church nearby? of one's denomination? large, small, or medium sized? focused on worship or on programs? people centered? middle class or not? Does it have good preaching and/or good teaching? certain theological perspectives?

These choices and many others confront Asian North Americans. The scene above dealt with some of those choices, reflecting the complexities of the Asian North American context.

A. There is the issue of *acceptance.* This should not be an issue in any church for anyone. But the reality is that especially for Asian North Americans, who are a numerical minority, acceptance is a question in one's mind as one considers attending a church for the first time. Some Asian North Americans find, upon growing up and moving away from home and home church, that they feel a degree of self-consciousness attending a church that is almost all Caucasian. They may actually be warmly received, and yet there is a small but persistent feeling that "I'm a stranger here; something isn't quite meshing." It may be the well-intentioned but jarring question "How long have you been in this country?" Or it may be a deeper realization that they are the only ones interested in cultural background and its appreciation; it seems the others don't even know there is such a thing as ethnic or cultural heritage. Acceptance is usually available, and yet some Asian North Americans wonder if in order to be accepted, they have to work at it. (But the *other* folks—the "majority folks"—don't have to work at it. They don't have to explain themselves to anyone.)

In an Asian North American church, Asian North Americans don't have to explain themselves. Being in such a church is quite natural.

B. The possibilities for *personal relationships* are often a concern for those seeking a church or, to use a common term, seeking a "church home." This issue is present for almost anyone in any kind of church. For Asian North Americans, a range of concerns are present. A woman recently arriving from Korea or Taiwan, for example, may want a congregation and church members who relate to her in her own native language, since English is not a comfortable language or is not spoken at all. This newcomer may want to be accepted and supported in ways that will help her adjust to a new land and culture. If the church has classes for learning English or in some way provides help in obtaining civil and community services, then the newcomer may find the church to be a "church home." To have someone in the church explain how to obtain medical care and how the system works is a real, practical blessing! When the newcomer can come to a church meeting and be able to understand what is said and be understood, that is quite a comfort. To be able to relate to others who share experiences of leaving the homeland and having to start a new life in a strange setting, that, too, is quite a comfort.

For those who are not necessarily newcomers to the land, such as second-generation young persons, the desire for personal relationships within a congregation takes a different path. The factors for nurturing personal relationships may be harder to find. Usually the language of choice is English and the interests, concerns, and issues relate more to the dominant Western culture rather than the culture of origin in Asia. Some Asian North American churches are doing a good job of being a "church home" for second and succeeding generations. This is so in many Japanese congregations. They have been in existence for several generations and the people in charge of planning and conducting programs are bicultural. For Taiwanese, Korean, and other recently established churches, the idea of a ministry to the second generation is a new phenomenon. Culture and language are barriers to communication and to the forming of close relationships between old and young. An encouraging development is the formation of education and support groups in several denominations, such as the Coalition of Second Generation Ministry of the Presbyterian Church (U.S.A.). These organizations bring church educators and pastors together, usually on an annual basis, for training, inspiration, and support. These leaders get help in ministering to second-generation parishioners. Most of the trainees are young—recent graduates from seminary and with few years of pastoral experience. Bringing them together is itself an opportunity for sharing about the difficulties of serving in congregations often ruled by hierarchial styles in which the senior pastor is treated by the Asian North American parishioners like a patriarch and the younger assistant to the pastor has very little authority. The coalitions of second-generation ministry serve an important pioneering function of seeking relevant forms of ministry to the growing numbers of members who are not fully served by a congregation that focuses on pastoral ministry to immigrant people in a native language.

An interesting phenomenon of second-generation ministries is the development of indigenous leadership. Often young persons in their twenties and thirties find they have to "do their own programming." There is not much help from the senior pastor, whose own background and world-view are Asian rather than Asian North American. These young adults form their own study groups and pastoral-care networks and find their own forms of mission and outreach. They are relating with each other. The results are not always refined and smooth, and their theology is not always traditional or well informed. But there often is a spirit of community and an amount of experimentation that bodes well for the Asian North American churches. Also, as more second-generation persons attend seminary and as seminaries offer more relevant courses to prepare people for racial/ethnic ministries, the churches may become more hospitable to the younger generation.

C. Many Asian North American persons seek a congregation that offers *racial / ethnic / cultural affirmation*. This era is a time of transition. (It seems every era of modern times is a time of transition!) Fifty years ago one ideal that was lifted up was that of an integrated church—every congregation being a unity of people without regard for race, class, or national origin. In recent years this ideal has been modified by the desire for racially, ethnically, or culturally specific congregations that cater to persons of similar national origin, race, language, or culture. Even in so-called "multicultural congregations" it is recognized that some sort of unity can be sought that allows for diversity so that one's racial, ethnic, or cultural heritage is honored rather than diminished and one's heritage is a gift to be brought to the Lord's Table, where all kinds of people are gathered. As Asian North Americans realize they can affirm their particular ethnic and cultural heritage within Canadian and U.S. communities, they also are realizing that their churches can be places for affirming who they are and what their heritage is. Now the ideal is for a church unity that allows for diversity within the unity.

As in the first Christian Pentecost experience, people are realizing they can hear the gospel and understand it *in their own tongue*. To paraphrase, crudely, the claim in Paul's Letter to the Galatians, even as the Greek Galatians didn't have to practice Jewish rituals to be Christians, Asian North Americans don't have to be "white" to be Christians. As advocated throughout this book, Asian North Americans have ethnic and cultural treasures that enrich their Christian life and practice. In such a milieu (perhaps a more appropriate phrase is "on such a path or such a *tao*") it is not only all right but it is encouraged of Asian North Americans that their ethnic and cultural identity and heritage be honored, studied, and expressed. Churches finding ways for this to happen may be just the type of congregation that is needed today.

In reality, Asian North American Christians do not auto-

matically support a congregation's efforts to honor culture
and heritage. Some were brought into the Christian faith
with the understanding that becoming Christian was a total
commitment requiring the giving up of "pagan" ways. Buddhist, Taoist, Confucian, shamanist, and other religious
forms and practices had to be given up. So for some Asian
North American Christians, syncretism—mixing into the
Christian faith some elements of other faiths—is not right.
Asian cultural practices also had to be given up. Other
chapters in this book, especially chapters 2, 4, and 7, address
this conflict. At issue is which religious and cultural ideas
and practices enrich the Christian faith and life and which
dilute it and take away commitment and loyalty to the one
God. Many Asian North Americans are personally wrestling
with the issue of how one's ethnic heritage can be brought
into dialogue with one's life in a non-Asian society. While the
church may not have come to a complete resolution of this
matter, it may be an encouraging signal that the church also
is wrestling with such issues. It seems that a congregation
that is working on racial, ethnic, and cultural issues is one
that meets many people at an important place in their lives.

D. Another area of concern for churches has to do with
generations. The needs of immigrant persons, especially
those who came to North America within the last five years
or so, are pressing realities. It takes much gathering of
information to know how to be a legal resident or to move
toward citizenship in a new country. Getting started in work,
business, or school is daunting. Learning how to raise children in a second culture is perplexing and oftentimes frus-
trating, especially when the children exhibit a preference for
the second culture and disdain for the original language,
customs, and courtesies. Sooner or later the tension between
generations emerges in every Asian North American congregation. Some, such as many Japanese and Chinese churches,
faced these tensions some time ago and have some accumu-
lated experience, if not wisdom, in these matters. Others,
such as Taiwanese and Korean congregations, being of recent

arrival in North America, are baffled by the chasm between generations.

There is some help coming from groups that are trying to find ways to minister with second-generation people. Creative pioneering is being tried in education, worship, and leadership. Young people need understandable Christian education that equips them for life as bicultural persons. Parents, usually immigrants, need sympathetic support in coping with situations that question the old authority, value system, and customs that were assumed to be basic in the Old Country. Asian North American congregations find themselves having to decide which languages to use, and how much translating is needed, in each worship service and what resources can be used to be both Asian and Christian. Chapter 7 in this book raised concerns about how worship might satisfy both generations and be faithful both to Christian tradition and cultural ways. Once again, the congregation and the church leaders who are willing to wrestle with these issues may not find immediate, complete solutions but will signal to church attenders that their congregation is trying to be relevant to their spiritual and personal needs.

Leadership in the congregation has generational implications. Immigrant membership usually implies pastoral and elected lay leadership that comes from the first generation. Asian perspectives on relationships and leadership prevail. But as the church continues, younger generations come along with their different needs and often very different attitudes about leadership styles. Where the pastor is personally secure and open to a diversity of perspectives, there often are workable accommodations. Leadership is conducted in nonauthoritarian ways and a generally democratic form of community decision making is practiced. But many of us know of Asian North American congregations where this is not the case. There are congregations where the people, holding traditional views of authority, want the pastor to be like a wise teacher and firm father to the "church family." And there are any number of pastors (almost always men) who are quite willing to assume such a pastoral role. No matter what the denominational polity, such congregations practice an authoritarian mode of governance. Or there are congregations where one family or a small cluster of families hold on to the prerogatives of being founding members. They control everything: where and when to meet, who is to lead, and who is invited to participate. Needless to say, the younger generation finds churches with traditional pastoral leadership or single-family leadership to be unattractive.

Given the complexities of Asian understandings of relationships and the traditions of male-dominant, elder/father hierarchies, there will be years of struggle and change before acceptable styles of leadership evolve that will satisfy young and old in Asian North American congregations. Some leadership problems may be resolved as young, second- or later-generation leaders enter the ministry or are allowed to hold elected office in congregations.

How to provide *intergenerational* relationships is a challenge for any church. Even in Asian North American congregations, which supposedly reflect an Asian or Confucian heritage of honoring family and extended family or communal interlocking relationships, intergenerational activities are difficult to design and implement. The complexities of generational differences, languages, and social customs pose challenges. Just as one example, it is still typical in some congregations that in the half hour or so before a churchwide potluck supper, the children are running around the dining room, the young people are clustered in niches and on benches outside the building, the men are seated and talking with each other in one corner of the dining room, and the women are terribly busy in the kitchen or doing all the work of setting up the tables! Throughout the activity, continued separation of ages and groups is manifest. The grace before the meal is in a native language that the young barely understand if at all. The young people may be asked to lead in some singing, but their guitar-based music makes no sense to the older folks. The program, if there is one, will be understood by the native speakers or by the English speakers, but not by both. And during that time, the children are shunted to a basement room to watch cartoons on videotape. Asian North American congregations need help in becoming genuinely intergenerational.

E. Closely related to the issue of generations is the *availability of age-group and other specific-group programs* in Asian North American congregations. Especially in small-membership churches, the opportunities for people to meet with others in their own age group and stage of development are few. Often there is a lack of leadership or the leaders are limited by lack of training or of appropriate resources. But change is in the wind. Ten years ago we would have seen more instances of "programming by desperation." For example, to keep the young people coming and occupied, some Asian North American churches would hire a Caucasian youth worker. If the youth worker was skilled and theologically well grounded, the youth program might be quite effective. Indeed there were instances when such a youth worker became a catalyst for the Asian North American young people to learn their own heritage and cultural identity. But such use of outside leaders belied the lack of trained leaders within the congregation. A major problem was that many otherwise qualified adult leaders for children or youth could not relate to them because they could not communicate in English. Their world-view was Asian, whereas the children and youth were struggling with assimilation into a Western society.

Some denominations are trying to help. Especially for the large numbers of Korean North Americans, there are curricular resources and leadership training materials in Korean and English. As time moves on, leadership is developing for age-group programs.

Denominational Christian educators and seminary professors need to teach Asian North American teachers how to teach relevantly. One immediate need is for assistance, from the outside, in curriculum selection and adaptation.

The potential is there for age-group programs to be an

effective means of helping Asian North Americans and for reaching out to those who are not in the church. Consider the potential for reaching young adults if a church were to have programs that helped them deal with issues of vocation, career, family, social justice, media and values, and spirituality. A growing store of novels and films created by Asian North American novelists and movie directors is available. Some very stimulating programs on ethnic identity could revolve around reading novels such as *The Joy Luck Club* by Amy Tan or *Bone* by Faye Myenne Ng or *China Boy* by Gus Lee. An exciting series could revolve around films such as *The Joy Luck Club; Chan Is Missing; Dim Sum; The Wedding Banquet; Eat, Drink, Man, Woman;* and numerous others.

Educational leaders and pastors in congregations need to be informed of the creative and relevant ways the various age groups can be reached. Such groups include older persons, who have their specific interests; it is not only children and youth who are to be served through educational programs. One interdenominational organization that has been training leaders and creating resources for nearly two decades is Pacific Asian American and Canadian Christian Education (PAACCE). This group, many of whose members hold significant positions in denominational educational agencies or theological seminaries, offers workshops and useful resources on youth ministry, worship, church school teaching, multicultural education, women's issues, and so forth—the things that will support a congregation wishing to do a good job in age-group ministries.

F. As can be seen by the frequent mention of it throughout this chapter, *language* is a pervasive concern in Asian North American congregations. Many churches have double or parallel programs in which a worship service is offered in the native language and then one in English. Corresponding ministerial services of pastoral care and educational programs are offered too. Other congregations have one service, with either the native or English language predominant. There may be translating of the sermon, announcements, or other parts of the service. The bulletin may be tightly filled with information in two languages. Few congregations will claim they have found "*the* solution" to the language problem. Some solutions double the amount of work and tend to separate groups of people. Other solutions compromise the needs or abilities of one language group for another.

At this time perhaps all that can be said is that each congregation must find its own best solution and review it from time to time. As members change, so will the ways in which language is used change. It may be disingenuous to suggest that, lacking an easy resolution to the language problem, a church can at least show that it is concerned, is trying, and is willing to make changes. The congregation will need to show that it is trying to communicate with everyone and not let one language group be favored over another. The church needs to emphasize its sense of community. The members' commitment to each other is the basis for each person's attempt to understand and communicate with one another—commitment, community, and then communication!

G. The *role of women* in Asian North American congregations is a major concern. On the surface there are many questions each congregation must consider relative to whether or not women are in leadership equally with men, whether or not there are programs and services that address the needs of women, and so forth. Deeper issues are present in Asian North American churches, as can be seen in most of the chapters of this book. The Confucian and Asian heritage has, over the years, evolved into a social system that has not valued women. It should be of great importance to men and women in the Christian church that the Christian faith accepts women as equals, honors them as persons, and criticizes the social injustices of any system that oppresses women. But thousands of years of teaching, ritual, and practice will not change overnight. If there is change in favor of understanding women to be equal to men, such change can happen in the church. Some change already is occurring. The

Asian North American church does have some women in leadership. Some churches are trying to teach that "there is no longer male and female; all of you are one in Christ Jesus" (Galatians 3:28). This is the right path, but there is a long way to go on this path. (For a detailed consideration of the role of women in the church, see chapters 4 and 5.)

H. *Pastoral leadership* has been mentioned in many of the topics above. Asian perspectives can inform the church of the role of the pastor as one who is concerned about the welfare of everyone in the "church family." The pastor is like a loving and wise parent, like a teacher, and like a priest who offers spiritual direction. Like a shaman, or *mudang,* the pastor tries to dispel evil and bring healing to the people.

Asian North American pastors are only now getting to these roots of Asian understandings of religious leadership— pastoral leadership. It may be possible that as these roots inform how pastors relate with the people, some deep intuitions may resonate to bond pastor and people. Some Asian pastoral roles and styles are implied in the previous chapter on how conflicts are dealt with in Asian North American settings. Pastors may find some "feeder roots" as they "dig into" and experiment with Asian forms of leadership.

Pastors and their congregations also need to come under the judgment of the gospel. The gospel does not support forms of pastoral leadership that assume clerical privilege. Nor does the church as formed by the ministry of Jesus Christ support the ascension of one person as a ruler (or patriarch) over others. The wisdom of one person is not hierarchically superior, as may have been the practice in Asian cultures.

In the current situation, Asian North American pastors will be helpful and effective leaders if their ministry is characterized by humility, sincerity, mutuality, reciprocity, benevolence, and love. Those who are familiar with classic Confucian teachings recognize these character traits. Like bamboo, pastors will be strong and flexible. As companions on the way, pastors will walk with the people and share stories. As one Korean American student said just prior to his graduation from seminary, "When I become a pastor, I will be a story-listening pastor, and a storytelling pastor."

I. To list *location, parking, and facilities* as an issue Asian North American congregations must consider is to move from the sublime to the mundane, perhaps. Congregations, especially those that are getting started, need to be accessible to their constituents. Often beginnings are modest—perhaps even in someone's living room or garage. Then there is the renting of space in an existing congregation or a community room. Then there is the purchase of a church building. The new church development process is hit-or-miss. Some buildings are "just right," with adequate space, a good worship area, and a building in good condition. Sometimes church facilities reflect previous glory and previous neighborhood viability; such facilities may be in changing neighborhoods fraught with problems of safety, transportation, parking, and usefulness. Much of the financial resources then are spent on renovation, repairs, and security.

Congregations catering to Asian North American constituents usually are not neighborhood churches in the classic sense. The membership is drawn from ethnic or cultural groups and from national-origin groups. Thus to come to the church, the members drive long distances or require public transportation or church vans. With their work schedules and driving distances, the schedule and program offerings of the church are restricted.

Most of these matters are mundane and only need logical minds and practical inclinations to be resolved effectively. But Asian North American congregations usually have complexities! One complexity involves the renting of space in a "nesting" arrangement. Some are strictly business arrangements in which one congregation rents space to another without any attempts to relate programmatically. Such an arrangement is fairly simple to administer. But often the nesting arrangement includes intentions for some degree of sharing of Christian relationships and religious activities. The potential for cross-cultural sharing is great. So are the

costs. The potential is great for misunderstandings, condescension, or cultural imperialism. If sharing of programs,
staff members, resources, or anything else is a part of the
arrangement, then both parties must recognize that significant amounts of time and effort must be spent to make the
nesting arrangement work. Cross-cultural sharing is considered in chapter 11 of this book.

Who we are as a congregation, how we worship, and how
we teach each other are theologically based questions that
eventually are answered in practical ways. Thus location,
parking, and facilities are theological issues too. In one ironic
instance a rapidly growing Korean American congregation
dealt with its identity, program, and mission by locating in
an old warehouse. By doing so the members were able to
obtain a very large facility that could be made into worship
and educational rooms relatively inexpensively. The results
of the remodeling do not give the people who attend any
feeling of being in a secondhand, run-down Gothic-style
church that has seen better days. And they've got enough
parking space to see them into the next century. People enjoy
being in this church. This facility has become their place,
their sacred space. Locating in an old warehouse was a
theologically sound decision.

J. *Mission* is a vital issue for Asian North American congregations. Mission has been basic to the nature of the church
since its founding. Asian North American congregations need
to review and restate their mission frequently. The .original
intent to be evangelistic can be reaffirmed in the light of
demographic shifts. Who can be served by the church? At first
it may have been recent arrivals from Asia. In some metropolitan areas there is at this time a steady stream of new
immigrants. As families develop, new constituents may ap-
pear: young persons, young adults, second-generation people.
The mission of outreach is always present, but the "audience"
for this outreach and the forms of evangelism need frequent
adjustments and renewal. The constituents of the church
also influence the types of services it will offer. First, second,

and succeeding generations each have unique interests and needs. The first generation may need help and support with adjustments to new cultural settings and demands. The second generation may need the gospel presented in fresh ways that do not assume that being born into a Christian family automatically makes one a Christian. Issues of identity, cultural affirmation, and help with bicultural life are subjects for the church to deal with as it seeks to serve second-generation people.

Mission also involves people and activities beyond the congregation. Most Asian North American congregations gladly concern themselves with matters of global outreach, especially in support of proclaiming the gospel in Asia. Fewer congregations support the work of the larger church in social service and social justice. Few Asian North American congregations have any ministry with the neighborhood at their doorstep. Being immersed in local concerns about survival as immigrants or persons struggling with assimilation into a larger and different culture requires so much energy that little is left for dealing with the social problems that seem unrelated or far away. But some of these social issues are not really far away at all.

Racism is one social issue that is close. Every Asian North American person, family, and institution knows the pain and oppression of life in a racist society. An Asian North American church may be a haven from racism, but this tactic is like building a little fort that temporarily staves off the hordes of attackers. Fortress life is limited. Every Asian North American congregation, and Asian North American people as a whole, must aggressively deal with racism. Much needs to be done within the congregation to help heal hurts and to prepare people to affirm their worth as people of a certain ethnic or cultural heritage. Christian nurture and education of church members affirm God's call for minority persons to enter into the loving, accepting community of faith.

God's call into community includes a call to mission. Being of minority status places on Asian North American Christians the call to combat racism by reaching out to other people to confront their racist attitudes and to help them to change their ways. Some strategies for such a witness to the inclusiveness of the church are presented in chapter 11. Here in this chapter the emphasis is that if Asian North American churches are to be relevant to their members, they must actively engage in mission, including a mission of replacing racism with the inclusiveness of the gospel.

K. *"Viability"* is used here to gather all the issues listed above that Asian North American churches must deal with in order to attract people to the church and to serve their needs. Congregations that are doing *something* about most of these issues will impress people as being "viable churches." There is life and vitality, even if not all issues are resolved and not all questions are answered completely. Such churches, in their many efforts, have not "arrived" but are "on the way"; they are viable. For Asian North Americans, that is all they ask—to be on the way together.

Questions for Reflection

1. How would you state the theological and missionary rationale for the Asian North American congregation in which you participate?

2. What types of Asian North American congregations have you come across? What are the strengths of each type? the weaknesses?

3. How can congregations minister to people who are not yet fluent in English? How can congregations minister to Asian North Americans who are fluent only in English?

4. What can be done to develop effective leadership for Asian North American congregations?

5. What do you think is the future for Asian North American congregations? What new forms of congregations might be needed?

6. How can Asian North American Christians and congregations help each other?

Suggested References

Fong, Kenneth Uyeda. *Insights for Growing Asian-American Ministries: How to Reach the Increasing Numbers of Americanized Asian Americans for Christ*. Rosemead, Calif.: EverGrowing Publications, 1990. (Available from EverGrowing Publications, 1255 San Gabriel Blvd., Rosemead, CA 91770, U.S.A.) Evangelism among English-speaking second-generation Asian North Americans, especially young adults.

Friendship Press series on multicultural issues in the church. Forthcoming in 1996. This series includes a chapter by David Ng on biblical rationales for a multicultural church and how to educate for multiculturalism.

González, Justo L. *Out of Every Tribe and Nation: Christian Theology at the Ethnic Roundtable*. Nashville: Abingdon Press, 1992. A stimulating summary of the conversations of seventy church leaders about cultural and multicultural issues facing the Christian church.

Kim, Grace Choong, ed. *Ways to Be a Good Teacher: A Manual for Korean American Church School Teacher Training*. Louisville: Presbyterian Publishing House, 1993. Korean and English. Workshop designs and chapters on aspects of leadership and teaching in Korean American congregations. Adaptable to most ethnic settings.

Kawano, Roland. *The Global City: Multicultural Ministry in Urban Canada*. Oakville, Ontario: Wood Lake Books, 1992. Social and theological rationales for multicultural churches, with suggestions for action from the author's experiences.

Kim, Young-Il, ed. *Knowledge, Attitude, and Experience: Ministry in the Cross-Cultural Setting*. Nashville: Abingdon Press, 1992. Essays on cultural and cross-cultural ministry.

Law, Eric H. F. *The Wolf Shall Dwell with the Lamb: A Spirituality for Leadership in a Multicultural Community*. St. Louis: Chalice Press, 1992. Theological and cultural anthropological perspectives on why cultures in power marginalize other cultures. Suggestions for both the "wolves" and the "lambs."

Lee, Sang Hyun, ed. *Korean American Ministry*. New York: The Program Agency, Presbyterian Church (U.S.A.), 1987. Korean and English. Biblical and sociological interpretations of the pilgrim or sojourner experience of Korean American immigrants, with suggestions for ministry.

Matsuoka, Fumitaka. *Out of Silence: Emerging Themes in Asian*

American Churches. Cleveland: United Church Press, 1995. A force-ful statement of the issues Asian North Americans must confront and what they can contribute to the whole church.

Ng, David. *A Colorful Community: Ministry with Racial/Ethnic Minority Youth.* Network paper no. 41. New Rochelle, N.Y.: Don Bosco Multimedia, 1991. (475 North Avenue, New Rochelle, NY 10802, U.S.A.) An essay on ministry with minority persons, with emphasis on young people.

Ng, Donald, ed. *Asian Pacific American Youth Ministry: Planning Helps and Programs.* Valley Forge, Pa.: Judson Press, 1988. Out of print but available in seminary libraries and some congregations. A pioneering work that offers theological, historical, sociological, and developmental perspectives on ministry with Asian North Americans. Combines theory and practice and serves as a model for doing educational ministry.

Pacific Asian American and Canadian Christian Education (PA-ACCE). *Mobile Resource Case.* Available on loan by writing to Rev. David Chai, Asian American Leader Development, Presbyterian Church (U.S.A.), 100 Witherspoon Street, Louisville, KY 40202-1396, U.S.A. A portable case with about two hundred resources for Asian North American congregations. Users pay a small fee and shipping. (Note: In the next few years PAACCE will publish several new guides for Christian education and youth ministry in Asian North American congregations.)

Rogers, Donald B., ed. *Urban Church Education.* Birmingham, Ala.: Religious Education Press, 1989. Aspects of programs and education in urban settings, with practical models.